BLACK STUDIES
Threat — or — Challenge ?

KENNIKAT PRESS

NATIONAL UNIVERSITY PUBLICATIONS

SERIES IN AMERICAN STUDIES

General Editor

JAMES P. SHENTON

Professor of History, Columbia University

Nick Aaron Ford

BLACK STUDIES
Threat-or-Challenge

National University Publications
KENNIKAT PRESS
Port Washington. N.Y. —London—1973

Copyright © 1973 by Nick Aaron Ford. All Rights Reserved.
No part of this publication may be reproduced, stored in a retrieval
system, or transmitted, in any form or by any means,
electronic, mechanical, photocopying, recording, or otherwise,
without the prior written permission of the publisher.

Library of Congress Catalog Card No: 72 - 91171
ISBN: 0 - 8046 - 9034 - 0

Manufactured in the United States of America

Published by
Kennikat Press, Inc.
Port Washington, N.Y./London

Preface

This book is a labor of love and anguish and hope. It is a report of one man's two-year search to understand and to derive a meaning from the sudden upsurge of Black Studies, a revolutionary development in American education with as great a potential for change in priorities as had the Declaration of Independence and the Emancipation Proclamation. My interest was electrified because since 1936 I had sought to promote such a development by personal and professional means in the area of literature. To me, this burgeoning movement toward fitting recognition of the "black experience" as a legitimate concern of formal education is a dream come true, but a dream with nightmarish as well as satisfying possibilities.

Impelled by the desire to learn as much as I could of the strengths and weaknesses of the objectives, operational techniques, personal commitments of teachers, directors, and college administrators, and the apparent impact of such programs upon the campuses which inaugurated them, I sought and was granted a sabbatical leave from my teaching duties at Morgan State College, where for twenty-three years I had served as chairman of the Department of English. A grant from the National Endowment for the Humanities enabled me to visit whichever campuses I chose in pursuit of my goal. At the end of the first year I found that I needed more time to complete the study, and with the cooperation of Morgan State College and a renewal of the grant I was able to complete the project.

I recently read a letter from a white woman which included the following comment: "The name 'Black Studies' on first impression sounds exclusive—for blacks only, as catechism is for Catholics only.

BLACK STUDIES: THREAT OR CHALLENGE

One realizes this is not the intent of purpose *if* one gives it thought—But how many give this a second thought? . . . To one who is uninformed, unaware and unconcerned, how does he find the answers unless he is stimulated to think about Black Studies, the need for them, what they help achieve?"

I think this woman, as well as many other concerned citizens, white and black, who perhaps harbor similar unasked questions, should be "stimulated to think" about this problem in the manner the writer has suggested. Therefore, I have accepted the challenge.

The aim of this book is to present in language which a layman can understand a professional evaluation of the past history, present practices, and future possibilities of Black Studies (sometimes referred to as Afro-American, African, and Negro) in the officially recognized educational programs of American colleges and universities. Although the approach is humanistic rather than scientific, the evaluation is based on personal visits to more than 100 representative campuses for interviews with appropriate administrators, teachers, and students; the study of brochures, catalogs, and other program descriptions; analyses of questionnaires completed by concerned officials in selected institutions. To insure the national representativeness of the study, I divided the 48 mainland states into nine regions on the basis of the optimum degree of homogeneity in racial attitudes and educational philosophy: Northeast (Maine, New Hampshire, Massachusetts, Connecticut, Vermont, Rhode Island), Mid-Atlantic (New York, New Jersey, Pennsylvania), Border (Delaware, Maryland, District of Columbia, Virginia, West Virginia, Missouri, Oklahoma, Kentucky), Southeast (North Carolina, South Carolina, Georgia, Florida), Southcentral (Alabama, Mississippi, Tennessee, Arkansas, Louisiana), Southwest (Texas, Colorado, Arizona, New Mexico), Midwest (Kansas, Indiana, Ohio, Illinois, Iowa, Minnesota, Wisconsin, Michigan), Northwest (Nebraska, Wyoming, South Dakota, North Dakota, Utah, Nevada, Idaho, Montana), and Far West (Washington, Oregon, California). In each region I selected a reasonable number of the most representative institutions, with a balance between private and public, small and large, and in the southern and border regions between predominantly white and predominantly black.

Although this study is concerned primarily with Black Studies in colleges and universities, it reflects indirectly, and to a lesser degree, attitudes and practices in elementary and secondary schools, since administrators and teachers are trained in these higher·institutions for leadership in the lower schools. It can be fairly assumed that interest in and concern for Black Studies on the elementary and secondary level can be no greater than, and in all probability not as great as, such manifestations at the higher levels.

It is the author's hope that this evaluative study will serve to point out to professional educators, teachers, parents, and concerned citizens the basic reasons for including Black Studies in the required curricula of all schools, colleges, and universities in order to insure an adequate, realistic, relevant education for all Americans; to reveal the wide variety of organized and unorganized programs, good and bad, now being conducted at colleges and universities, so that no one need be guilty of praising or condemning Black Studies in general because he knows only what is being done in a few such programs; to focus on the desirable and undesirable tendencies in current programs in the hope of encouraging the positive trends and eliminating the negative; to begin to plan new creative directions which will make Black Studies a part of the mainstream of American education and which will provide opportunities for specialized courses in black culture of the same recognized intellectual value as that of other ethnic studies which are already a part of academic programs in reputable American institutions of higher learning.

Nick Aaron Ford

Baltimore, 1973

Acknowledgments

For Financial Assistance

The National Endowment for the Humanities for grants to defray partially travel expenses and other supporting activities connected with this study during 1970-72.

Morgan State College for sabbatical leave from all teaching duties for 1970-71 and partial teaching duties for 1971-72.

For Personal Assistance in Gathering Information and Materials

John Blassingame, Acting Director of Afro-American Studies, Yale University; Robert A. Cotner, Department of English, Montgomery College; John F. Cross, Chairman, Social Science Division, College of the Virgin Isles; Harold Cruse, Director of Afro-American Studies, University of Michigan; Michael Fabre, Professor of American Literature at the University of Paris and Secretary of the French Association of American Studies; Walter Fisher, Director of Library, Morgan State College; Leonard Jeffries, Director of Afro-American Studies, San Jose State College; Richard A. Long, Director of the Center for African and Afro-American Studies, Atlanta University; Thomas Matthews, Director of the Institute of Caribbean Studies; Ernest R. McKinney, Assistant to the Executive Director, A. Philip Randolph Educational Fund; Charles E. Mosley, Director of Black Studies, Chicago State University; Lonnie Peek, Director of Black Studies, Wayne County Community College; Margaret Walker, Director of Institute for the Study of History, Life and Culture of Black People, Jackson State College.

For Editorial Assistance

My wife Ola M. Ford, Assistant Professor of English, Morgan State

College; Frances L. Easterling, Instructor of English, Morgan State College; Doris Oakcrum, Morgan State College student; Michelle A. Ford, secretarial assistant.

For Special Permission to Quote

King V. Cheek, Jr. "Black Students, Black Studies, Black Colleges." Reprinted from *Chronicle of Higher Education*, November, 1971; "Black Nonsense." Editorial reprinted from *The Crisis*, Volume 78, No. 3, p. 78; S.I. Hayakawa. "The Meaning of Black Studies." Copyright 1970, The Register and Tribune Syndicate; Maurice Jackson. "Toward a Sociology of Black Studies." Reprinted from *Journal of Black Studies*, Volume I, Number 2 (December, 1970) pp. 132, 135, 136, by permission of the publisher, Sage Publications, Inc.; Russel Kirk. "Black Studies Ebb, Giving New Student Perspectives." Copyright, General Features Corporation. Reprinted with permission; New Jersey Department of Education. "Questions and Answers on Teaching Black History." Prepared and published by the New Jersey Urban Education Corps, Division of Curriculum and Instruction; Boniface I. Obichere. "Challenge of Afro-American Studies." Reprinted from *Journal of Black Studies*, Volume I, No. 2 (December, 1970), pp. 169-170, by permission of the publisher, Sage Publications, Inc., Bayard Rustin. *Black Studies: Myths and Realities.* New York: A. Philip Randolph Educational Fund, 1969; Shelia Walker. "Black English: Expression of the Afro-American Experience." *Black World*, Volume XX, No. 8. Reprinted by permission of *Black World*;

Contents

BLACK STUDIES
Threat — or — Challenge ?

I

INTRODUCTION

1
Preliminary Considerations

Meaning and Scope of Black Studies

The phrase *Black Studies* has become an acceptable designation for all studies primarily concerned with the experience of people of African origin residing in any part of the world. Its use here is most appropriate, for it includes the experiences of Africans, Afro-Americans, Afro-Asians, Afro-Europeans, and African descendants of the Caribbean and other island territories. In addition, it has taken on a new meaning of pride rather than shame, thus indicating a state of mind rather than simply of color. It has brought about the enhancement of pride of heritage in those whose origin had been despised by themselves and denigrated by others for so long.

Bayard Rustin, black executive secretary of the A. Philip Randolph Educational Fund, in the introduction to a pamphlet entitled *Black Studies: Myths and Realities*, asks:

Is Black Studies an educational program or a forum for ideological indoctrination? Is it designed to train qualified scholars in a significant field of intellectual inquiry, or is it hoped that its graduates will form political cadres prepared to organize the impoverished residents of the black ghetto? Is it a means to achieve psychological identity and strength, or is it intended to provide a false and sheltered sense of security, the fragility of which would be revealed by even the slightest exposure to reality? And finally, does it offer the possibility for better racial understanding, or is it a regression to racial separatism? The power — and also the danger — of "Black Studies" as a slogan is that it can mean any or all of these things to different people.[1]

Rustin's conclusion is irrefutable. The alternate focus of each of his questions defines the general nature and scope of the current field of Black Studies. No program now in existence can truthfully swear that all of its participants are wholly committed to one or the other

3

of these focuses. The quality and genuine worth of each program depends upon the degree to which it subscribes to the "right" alternative. But, of course, it is contrary to human nature (as well as to the nature of freedom of thought and individual judgment) to assume or insist that "right" is the same for all intelligent people of good will. Consequently, the meaning and scope of Black Studies are diverse and broad.

Arthur L. Smith, director of Afro-American Studies Center at UCLA and editor of *Journal of Black Studies,* suggests:

> Seldom in the history of academic disciplines has an area of study been born with so much pain and anguish as Black Studies, also called Afro-American Studies. Discussions initiated, for the most part by university students, produced significant reevaluations of curricula, research, and pedagogy. But the sustained intellectual development of this area, as in all areas, cannot be based on awakening rhetoric; it is time that we be about the work of Alain Locke, Carter G. Woodson, W. E. B. DuBois, Melville Herskovits, and a host of others who have labored to tell the truth about people of African descent.[2]

Smith, unlike some of the younger black students and teachers now engaged in the organization and promotion of Black Studies, recognizes that studies about the heritage of black people in literature, the arts, politics, and other phases of the history of civilization are not new but have recently demanded a new and more insistent urgency. Black scholars in black colleges and historical and cultural independent organizations have been engaged in Black Studies for more than a half-century. Such distinguished scholars as W. E. B. DuBois, Carter G. Woodson, Alain Locke, and Benjamin G. Brawley (who will be discussed later in this volume) have made significant contributions to these studies. More than a hundred black colleges and numerous black secondary schools in the South, public and private, have also aided in enlightening their students concerning the black heritage.

However, the nonblack schools and institutions of higher learning have deliberately ignored the validity or educational value of black culture as a worthy subject for study, except in a context of debasement and racial denigration. Though the quaint folk humor of "Uncle Remus" as interpreted by white Joel Chandler Harris and the artificial dialect of Topsy created by white Harriet Beecher Stowe could be occasionally used in the classroom as a left-handed acknowledgment of the existence of a black culture, neither the competent fiction of black Charles Chestnutt, nor the deeply moving autobiography of black Frederick Douglass, nor the black historical studies of Harvard-trained W. E. B. DuBois, were considered worthy of study. Not until the early 1960's when militant black high school students demanded classroom consideration for African studies including Swahili, and later that decade militant black college students challenged college and university administrators with uncompromising demands for a new deal, did the study of black culture really begin in the schools. Thus Vincent Harding, director of the Institute of the Black World, Atlanta, could truthfully say of the black student revolution of 1968:

> So they are not impressed by the black and white (but mostly white) academicians who ask them to respect the great traditions of the university, to do things in its honored style, to submit their Black Studies programs to the wisdom of the faculties. They know that these are the same faculties who had never heard of Horace Mann Bond, Charles W. Chestnutt, Martin Delany, or Charlie Parker five years ago, who never thought the black experience was worth one course three years ago . . . This is part of the meaning of the struggle for autonomous Black Studies programs.[3]

The author wishes to emphasize that the citation of the above quotation must not be taken as evidence that he is in favor of "autonomous Black Studies programs," but it is only cited to help the reader to understand why students were willing and ready to defy the authority of respected administrators at distinguished universities.

Maurice Jackson, of the Department of Sociology, University of California at Riverside, has defined the meaning and scope of Black Studies as follows:

> Black Studies, simply put, is the systematic study of black people. In this sense Black Studies differs from academic disciplines which stress white experience by being based on black experiences. Black Studies is an examination of the deeper truths of black life. It treats the black experience both as it has unfolded over time and as it is currently manifested. These studies will examine the valid part that black people have played in man's development in society. In so doing, Black Studies will concentrate on both the distinctiveness of black people from, and their interdependence with, other people. To develop this kind of knowledge, Black Studies must extend beyond the limits prejudice has placed on knowledge of black people . . .[4]

> Black Studies, then, is not the study of black ethnic minority, however valuable that may be. An ethnic minority, by virtue of being a minority, is by definition in a disadvantaged position which facilitates the characterization of black people as problems, as being essentially inferior, and so on. Black Studies, in contrast, is the study of black people with a history and a current position with many strong points, with both a rich heritage and a rich com-

plexity, which can be sources of pride. It is the study of people who have done much more than survive under the more difficult and trying circumstances, in and out of slavery, in and out of the ghettos. Without assuming that achievement is the mark of a man, it can be said that some of the greatest achievements in this society have been those of black men like Frederick Douglass who moved from slave to diplomat and Presidential advisor, or the host of black men who stood for freedom in unfree circumstances.

The study of black people as an ethnic minority has forced comparisons between them and other ethnic minorities, so defined. One of many comparisons is that between black people and Jewish people which generally fails to recognize the Constitutional provision for the independent existence of religious groups but not racial groups. In many ways the differences between ethnic minorities are such that intensive independent study of each is warranted. For instance, black people constitute the largest minority in the country; they are distributed throughout the nation; they are the only group in the country to undergo slavery; they are the only group under jurisdiction of the Jim Crow laws, and so on. Furthermore, they have developed distinctive music, literature, and art forms. Finally, with the exception of black people, the unique features of other groups in our country refer to the lands of their ancestors — which is to say that many things black developed in this country.[5]

Many critics of Black Studies, black as well as white, refuse to discuss the subject except in terms of its most vulnerable manifestations. They never admit that fairness demands that an idea or a practice should be judged in terms of its highest potential for good rather than its inherent susceptibility to abuse. Thus their arguments are studded with examples of absurdities. The syndicated columnist Russell Kirk succumbs to such sophistry in his column of July 5, 1971, when he declares, "Nowadays the tide of Black Studies at colleges and universities appears to ebb. One trouble has been lack of enrollment in such curricula, perhaps because the only prospect of employment from pursuit of such studies is appointment as a professor of Black Studies somewhere else." Suggesting that a further explanation of this decline in the appeal of Black Studies may be the result of the reassertion of a sense of humor among black and white collegians, he reproduces an amusing spoof sent to him by a correspondent from a white college. The spoof consists of a detailed absurd proposal for a collegiate program in Studies in the Nature of Poor White Experience in Society (SNOPES). It includes lectures on such absurd subjects as "Gas Station Graffiti: the Phallic Symbol," "Bowling: Recreation or Ritual Dance," "Demonstrations and Para-Violent Confrontation," and finally, the Presidential Address by L. C. Q. Le Mieux, Ph.D.: "Achieving Professional Status for Redneck Studies." Kirk explains, "Actually, this prospectus is *no* burlesque of Black Studies seminars held on many a campus; it is merely an inversion of roles. Such novelties pall, and it is *no* more reasonable to expect Negro students to sustain interest in Black Studies than it would be for red-headed students to endure four years of a curriculum in Titian-Tress Studies . . . There is such a thing as African culture, and such a thing as European culture; but these were not created by complexions. Chinese or Oriental studies are very serious indeed; *yellow* studies would *not be* . . . One of the advantages of a collegiate education is that it lifts the student out of his sub-culture, rather than immersing him in trivialities."

Because Kirk's faulty thinking about Black Studies is typical of many who ordinarily are less guilty of unfounded generalizations when dealing with noncontroversial subjects, let us try to understand the bases for his errors. His willingness to accept unfounded rumor concerning a subject about which he has a negative attitude is only partly responsible for his errors. The major fault lies in his lack of knowledge of the meaning and scope of the subject he so nonchalantly attempts to discuss. It is true that very few black students are now majoring in Black Studies, but no fewer than in former years. However, only a small number of colleges and universities offer a true major in the area. Generally a "major" in Black Studies means a "concentration" of from twenty-four to thirty hours of required work in the field with a major in an established discipline such as history, English, psychology, art, etc. The prospect of employment, therefore, is not decreased but actually enhanced. Since the graduate is required to have a "first major" or major in an established discipline as well as a concentration in Black Studies, he is not dependent upon "appointment as a professor of Black Studies somewhere else."

Furthermore, Kirk is evidently not aware that hundreds of colleges and universities which do not offer a major concentration in Black Studies do offer individual courses in the field which are anchored in established departments. Consequently, black and white students who do not want a concentration take individual courses of their choice in the area of Black Studies. Contrary to Kirk's belief, enrollment in these individual courses in most colleges and universities is increasing so rapidly that there is unprecedented demand for qualified instructors to teach such courses, whereas for almost all other courses, teacher availability is in excess of the need.

Another dimension of Black Studies at most colleges and

universities is the intimate relationship between course work and community involvement. Nathan Hare, former director of Black Studies at San Francisco State College, says, " . . . to be most effective this instruction [academic] must involve or integrate the student into his community, augmenting his function in the community, and indirectly, in society and the world at large. The fostering of identity with the black community, the development of community consciousness, black consciousness (including black America, Africa and black spectrum around the world) would, other things being equal, commit the black student more to the task of helping build the black community, when once his studies are done, in contrast to the currently induced frenzy (within the educational institution and elsewhere) to escape the black community."[6] Although the average black student may admit that one of his major goals is to flee the ghetto, he will insist that another goal of equal importance is his everlasting commitment to the improvement of the ghetto for the benefit of those who cannot or do not wish to leave.

Compelling Reasons for Black Studies
in American Education

The need to make education completely honest, representative of all aspects of American culture, and relevant to the realities of modern life demands that Black Studies become an intricate part of the curriculum at all levels. A national educational program which allows a student to pass through kindergarten, elementary school, high school, and university without learning a single noteworthy fact about the culture and individual achievements of black Americans, who comprise the largest minority in the nation, is indefensible. Yet that has been a fact of American life since the founding of the nation.

Joe R. Feagin, associate professor at the University of Texas, in discussing the findings of a recent study he made of white attitudes toward black Americans, says that the whites who indicated a positive attitude toward black contributions cited "such things as the role of slave labor in building up Southern agriculture, important Negro inventors and educators (particularly Carver, Washington, Bunche, and King), sports, the Negro role in American wars and in the military, music, dance, religion, and the current civil rights struggle. Those who were negative in their general evaluation of

Negro contributions typically noted their personal lack of knowledge of important Negroes in politics, business, or science, Negro lack of ambition, Negro lack of opportunity, ghetto riots, or lack of intelligence on the part of Negroes themselves."[7] He indicates in his conclusion that the exposure to Black Studies could greatly improve the appreciation by whites of the contributions of blacks to American culture.

He explains:

> Yet to this observer these exploratory data suggest some additional lessons for educators. First, the limited understanding of the Negro role in history even among those whites who consider that role to have been important, reflected in an emphasis on such things as sports, dance, religion, slavery, and one or two notable Negro leaders, indicates the need for Black Studies programs for whites, courses of study emphasizing the many accomplishments of black Americans as portrayed in the now burgeoning scholarly literature. New courses of study provide one answer to this problem; accentuating the role of Negro Americans in existing courses of study provides another.[8]

Kurt Schmoke, a black senior history major at Yale University and one of 32 senior college students in the United States selected as Rhodes Scholars to study at Oxford University during 1971-72, recently expressed his reasons for believing that Black Studies are valuable and valid contributions to the curricula of institutions of higher learning:

> First of all, it is a program which helps young blacks gain a sense of pride in their race. The importance of this should be evident to all who have any knowledge of the history of the struggles of black Americans.
>
> Secondly, the black American experience is an area of our cultural heritage which has been neglected by most colleges and universities but which demands attention, for the study of a country cannot be complete if the history and achievements of 15 percent of its population are ignored.
>
> Finally, the programs have as their end not merely learning facts but also gaining understanding. And if the U.S. racial problems are to be solved, mutual understanding cannot be attained if schools teach only one side of the story. Although many wrinkles remain to be ironed out in these programs, I believe that the incorporation of Black Studies in the college curriculum is an important step on the road which leads to the solution of the American racial dilemma.[9]

Congresswoman Shirley Chisholm, the first black woman to be elected to the United States Congress, and an experienced school-teacher, believes that true education consists of a full and free inquiry into all phases and segments of human existence. Without a fuller exploration of the black experience than has been the rule in

American educational institutions, she sees no hope of acquainting the American electorate with the nature and extent of the most pressing problems facing our society. "Perhaps the most optimistic measure of the nation's worth," she explains, "would be the courage and tenacity of her citizens in analyzing the problems, being unafraid of their solutions even though these break with some of America's most widespread assumptions and traditions; to utilize fully another American tradition – that of profound enquiry. This purpose would be major affirmation of America's capacity for self-renewal."

In an article entitled "The Meaning of Black Studies," S. I. Hayakawa, president of San Francisco State College which initiated the first organized Black Studies program in a predominantly white institution, stated:

> Black Studies, first of all, is the study of American Negroes – their art and music and literature, their sociology, their special problems, their place in the history and culture of America. Surely the story of 22 million of our fellow citizens in the U.S. should be studied, not only by blacks but by everybody!
>
> But that story has never been properly or fully written. For almost a century after Emancipation, America's solution to the race problem was not to think about it. The state of scholarship about Negro history and culture reflects the public's long-standing lack of interest in the subject. Even liberal historians like Charles A. Beard and Vernon Parrington, writing in the decades before the 1954 Supreme Court decision on school desegregation, never discussed the Negro. An enormous amount of research needs to be undertaken in this neglected area.
>
> Black Studies that serve to round out our knowledge of America by studying the Negro's contribution are, then, a legitimate and necessary intellectual enterprise.
>
> A second goal sought under the title of "Black Studies" is the strengthening of the Negro's self-concept – the first step of the process being to abandon the term "Negro" in favor of "black."
>
> The self-concept of a Chinese, like that of most people coming from intact cultures, can be bruised, but cannot easily be crushed. The situation of the American black youth, however, is different. Cut off from the history and culture of his ancestors, deprived of a sense of his own worth by the heritage of slavery, many blacks (by no means a majority) have been brainwashed into believing in their own inferiority . . . The basic goal of "Black Studies," so conceived, is therapeutic.[10]

It is interesting to know that Nathan Hare, the first coordinator of the Black Studies program at San Francisco State College, and whose violent disagreements with President Hayakawa led to his dismissal, also considers the therapeutic value for blacks as one of the important reasons for the promotion of such studies. He says, "In the embryonic stage black studies basically have two functions. On the one hand they are therapeutic. They help build ethnic confidence, a sense of ethnic confidence, a sense of ethnic destiny which will serve as a springboard toward acquiring a new future not only for the black race but for human beings who happen not to be black. Principally courses in black history and black culture will serve this purpose."[11] He lists community involvement as the other significant function.

In an article entitled "Challenge of Afro-American Studies" Boniface I. Obichere, professor at the University of California (Los Angeles), presents several compelling reasons for the necessity of Black Studies:

> What is needed is the realization that the absence of systematic teaching and vigorous inquiry concerning the black experience constitutes a grievous and culpable shortcoming in any university. Black students contend that this neglect is not accidental, but rather the result of calculated anti-Negro policies adopted many years ago by most white universities and colleges. The short-run goal of the demand for black studies is the correction of this shortcoming on the part of the institutions of higher learning. The long-term goal of the implementation of Black Studies would be the creation of viable links between universities and the black community. These links could be similar to those that have been forged between the white community and the universities, but would take cognizance of the variables and peculiarities of the black community. The idea of the "black community" is a very strong cornerstone of the effervescence of the new black students of today. In over fifty position papers on Black Studies written by black students in various colleges and universities all over the United States, I have observed a strong sentiment of attachment to, and concern for, the black community. For example, the students who initiated the creation of the Afro-American Studies Program at UCLA defined this university-community relationship precisely. They declared in one position paper:

> We have begun to say that perhaps colleges and universities as they now exist are, at least, irrelevant, often even destructive to Black Students in terms of the recognition of new needs in the Black community . . . We are saying that in our own college experience that if a college's purpose is to make students productive members of society, then that purpose is for the *entire* society, including the Black community. This means that in some way the concept of education, its goals and methods, have to be re-examined and made relevant to a larger number of students than to whom it is now important. We are saying that the university must fulfill its duty to produce vanguard intellectuals and creative individuals. We are saying that the university must foster modernizing changes in society and sever the regressive umbilical cord of conservatism.

> Therefore, the establishment of Black Studies is not an end in itself but a means to a larger, more important end. The students are not asking for more

than a domestic Marshall Plan. Afro-American studies centers should play an important role in the pursuit of these lofty objectives. Others argue cogently that Black Studies centers "must become a dynamic force in the creation of an educational revolution."[12]

2
Definition of Terms with Contrasting Interpretations

In order to make this discussion as enlightening and as meaningful as possible, I shall not only offer objective definitions of the most controversial terms used in such discussion but shall present, whenever possible, the most significant contrasting interpretations which represent the thinking and attitudes of a variety of individuals and groups concerned with the subject. The selected terms are *racism, the black experience, soul, integration, black nationalism, black liberation,* and *black English.*

Racism

The *American College Dictionary* defines racism as follows:

1. a belief that human races have distinctive make-ups that determine their respective cultures, usually involving the idea that one's own race is superior and has the right to rule others
2. a policy of supporting such asserted right
3. a system of government and society based upon it

My own definition is: racism is the belief that race is the measure of the man, that some races are innately inferior, that no amount of talent, learning, or experience can erase that taint of inferiority from an individual belonging to such a race, and that organized society is obligated, overtly or covertly, to maintain fitting barriers of separation between the so-called inferior and superior races. My definition applies to both the white and the black variety, the latter being of comparatively recent origin, generated by the excesses of the former. According to the report of the President's National Advisory Committee on Civil Disorders, white racism is responsible for the current black revolution and the terrifying riots that marked its beginning.

Strangely enough, black and white racism advocate many of the same goals, but for different reasons. Black racism is simply a counter-reaction to white racism. By fighting savagely for more than fifteen years against every effort to make integration a fact as well as a legal statute, white racists convinced blacks that they would never be accepted on equal terms by white society. Consequently, many blacks decided to no longer beg the whites to let them share equally a culture that has been developed by the contributions of both. These blacks rejected every aspect of so-called white middle-class culture and began to glorify everything that distinguishes black from white — the black skin, the bushy, kinky hair, and the exaggerated dialectal jargon invented especially to confuse and exasperate whites. This pride of race and glorification of color are not ordinarily a manifestation of black racism, but when the Black Muslims add to it their doctrine that all white people are human beasts — serpents, dragons, and devils (a doctrine that Malcolm X publicly repudiated when he returned from Mecca) — the result is black racism.

Chester Pierce, black member of the Faculty of Education and of Medicine at Harvard University and chairman of the American Psychiatric Association's Committee on Academic Education, describes American racism thus:

> Racism in the United States is a public health and mental health illness. It is a mental disease because it is delusional. That is, it is a false belief, born of morbidity, refractory to change when contrary evidence is presented concerning the innate inferiority of any person with dark skin color. Thus everyone in this country is inculcated with a barrage of sanctions which permit and encourage any white to have attitudes and behavior indicative of superiority over any black. Since everyone is involved in this delusion, then by definition it is a public health problem. The extent of the public health involvement is judged in terms of other definitions of a public health illness. In the classical mode of such illnesses, racism, besides affecting masses of population, also defies therapy on a one-to-one basis, produces chronic, sustained disability, and will cost large sums of money to eradicate. . . .
>
> Yet another medical relationship of racism is the fact that it is a perceptual illness. In almost any black-white negotiation each participant views things differently, depending on whether he is white (the offender) or black (the offended). For instance, the psychological hallmark of racism is the altogether too well-known tendency for whites to congratulate themselves, before a black, concerning what marvelous "progress" is being made. To the perception of the white offender, this is true and reasonable. From the vantage point of the black offended, however, this is both untrue and

unreasonable. If the black offended then indicates in any manner whatsoever that he is not convinced that congratulations are in order, he is gruffly perceived as at best an ingrate or at worst an ignoramus who refuses to comply to the rules set up by his oppressor. This sparks white animosity and hostility. In turn the poorly understood black is goaded to counter-hostility. It is in this way that the micro-aggressions of offensive maneuvers can accumulate and build to explosive white violence and retaliative black counter violence.[13]

Margaret Walker, professor of English at Jackson State College and author of the award-winning volume of poems *For My People* and the Houghton Mifflin Award novel *Jubilee*, charges that because of white racism black children in America have been taught to hate themselves and to imitate people whom they have been taught to believe are superior.

The white child has been taught to value Race more than humanity. He has been taught to overestimate his intelligence and human worth because of race, and at the same time to under-estimate the human worth and intelligence of anyone who is not of his race. The white American is therefore basically ignorant of the cultures of other people, and has no appreciation for any other language, art, religion, history, or ethical system save his own. He is in no way prepared to live in a multi-racial society without hostility, bigotry, and intolerance. He believes that he must convert all people to his way of thinking because he cannot possibly conceive that his way of thinking may not always be right for everyone else. Everyone must dress, think, pray, and amuse himself as he does. Every socio-economic and political system must emphasize or epitomize the values of his mechanistic and materialistic society. He falsely assumes that his values are idealistic and altruistic, that he is democratic and Christian while all others are totalitarian and pagan, yet in all his actions he contradicts his preaching. His every waking hour is spent getting and spending for himself, while denying his brothers any and all of the same rights he claims for himself. Self-righteous and self-centered, he thanks God daily that he is not as other men (meaning other races) are.[14]

The Black Experience

As a part of my data-collecting process for this study, I sent out questionnaires to the chairmen of 200 English departments in representative colleges and universities. One question was: "Does your department offer any course which has the avowed aim of integrating as fully as possible 'the black experience' into the normal 'mainstream' subject matter?" At least six of those who completed the questionnaire refused to answer this question because, they said, they did not know the meaning of "the black experience." Three requested an explanation of the phrase. One asked if there is also a "white experience" and a "red experience."

The *American College Dictionary* suggests, "experience implies being affected by what one meets with (pleasant or unpleasant), so that to a greater or less degree one suffers a change." If one adds the adjective black he has an objective definition of the term *the black experience*. A practical illustration could be Richard Wright's experience in a segregated train coach en route from Atlanta to New York in 1940 after his authorship of *Uncle Tom's Children* and *Native Son*. Noticing a typewriter in the seat beside Wright, the conductor wanted to know why he was traveling with this unnecessary baggage. When Wright explained that he was a writer, the conductor was incredulous. He was certain Wright was lying. (Perhaps he thought he had discovered a thief, transporting stolen goods). He could believe a black man might be a teacher or a preacher, but his white experience had not prepared him to accept the possibility of a black writer, especially one who could use a typewriter. The significance of this simple encounter, as reported by Wright, had to be fundamentally different from a report of the same incident by the conductor because the personal attitudes, past experiences, and racial memories of each were fundamentally different. Therein lies the meaning of "the black experience."

W.E.B. DuBois, in his famous book of essays, *The Souls of Black Folk* (1903), defines the black experience poetically as the experience of a people who are doomed to conceive of the world through a veil, a veil that requires the black person to see himself through the revelation of others. "It is a peculiar sensation, this double-consciousness, this sense of always looking at one's self through the eyes of others . . . One ever feels his two-ness, – an American, a Negro; two souls, two thoughts, two unreconciled strivings; two warring ideals in one dark body, whose dogged strength alone keeps it from being torn asunder."

But when DuBois died in 1963, the black liberation movement was about to begin, a movement which has now destroyed the concept of the black experience as DuBois and his generation lived it and were forced to tell it. Now blacks are no longer forced to feel a "two-ness." They are now seeing themselves through their own black eyes and are telling the world exactly how they feel down in the very depths of their own personal computers. And what is even more significant, they are reassessing and reinterpreting their past experiences in the light of their new independence. All of this is what is meant now by "the black experience."

Ralph Ellison, author of *Invisible Man*, one of the most distinguished novels of the twentieth century, intimates in *Shadow and Act* that through their interpretation of the black experience black thinkers and writers are answering for themselves and all who will listen such fundamental questions as: "Who am I? What am I? How did I come to be? What shall I make of the life around me, what celebrate, what reject, how confront the snarl of good and evil which is inevitable? What does American society *mean* when regarded out of my *own* eyes, when informed by my *own* sense of the world, how express my vision of the human predicament, without reducing it to a point which would render it sterile before that necessary and tragic – though enhancing – reduction which must occur before the fictive vision can come alive?"[15]

Charles V. Hamilton, professor of political science at Columbia University, illustrates by comments on "Just How Unstable Is the Black Family?" not only the differences between the black and white experiences in the United States, but also how the same black experience interpreted by black and white observers, equally qualified by academic training and scientific competence, differs in educational and social meaning.

Last week, a set of figures on American blacks was released – a special study by the Federal Government entitled "The Social Economic Status of Negroes in the United States, 1970." As expected, it painted a somber portrait. But by a coincidence most unexpected, the issuance of the study coincided exactly with the release of another report, this one set forth by the National Urban League at its annual convention in Detroit. And though both studies were based on the same statistics, conclusions drawn by many social scientists and those drawn by the league were worlds apart.

Thus, for example, the Government study shows that 28.9 per cent of black families are headed by females, an increase from 22.4 per cent in 1960. The familiar sociological analysis: A significant indication of continuing social deterioration and family instability. The view of the league: The assumption of instability in "matriarchal" households ignores the extended-family adaptation common in the black community – the strong kinship bonds between aunts, uncles and grandparents and the family's children. Some black sociologists go further; they argue that, in fact, roughly 70 per cent of these families actually do have a father present.

Another example: The Government study showed that, in order to obtain and maintain a median family income comparable to that of whites, both the black husband and his wife must – and often do – work. Conventional wisdom holds that this is a negative fact, since it is claimed that such families tend to be less stable than those in which the father is the sole breadwinner. But many black social scientists deny the claim, citing the prevalence of the extended-family adaptation – and they see the fact not as an indication of family deterioration but as proof of an attitude of cooperativeness and a strong work orientation in these families.

Sometimes the different approaches to statistics partake of a sparring match. Thus, one social sceintist may point to figures that clearly show that, in 1970, black persons 14 to 19 years of age were more likely to be high school drop-outs than were white persons in that age group. But another sociologist will counter with data showing that, since 1964, the number of blacks going to college has more than doubled, from 234,000 to 522,000. And he might add that these new students are mostly the first generation of their families to attend college, indicating a strong and increasing orientation toward achievement.

On the face of it, these arguments among social scientists over statistics that, by and large, both sides accept may seem to be nothing more than an exercise in academic semantics. But for the Urban League leadership, and for many black sociologists, the issue has far greater importance.

The manner in which these figures are interpreted, they feel, serves to delineate and identify the black community – in the eyes of whites and blacks alike. Statistics, heedlessly broadcast, are dangerous. And the customary negative interpretations reinforce negative generalizations, ignoring the actual and potential strengths of the black community.[16]

Soul

The most appropriate dictionary definition of soul as used in such expressions as "soul-brother" or "soul-singer" is "the emotional part of man's nature, or the seat of the feelings or sentiments." The reaction of black slaves to disappointment, overbearing sorrow, and physical cruelty inflicted by unfeeling masters was usually emotional, since sullenness and brooding were regarded by masters as signs of a rebellious spirit that might lead to revolt. The test of the depth of religion as practiced by black slaves was measured in terms of the power and strength of emotional response. Thus chants of "Amen!" and "Hallelujah!" were signs of "soul." James Weldon Johnson describes religious services in black churches which he visited in preparation for the writing of his volume of poems *God's Trombones* as electrifying. The preacher "strode the pulpit up and down in what was actually a very rhythmic dance, and he brought into play the full gamut of his wonderful voice, a voice – what shall I say?–not of an organ or a trumpet, but rather of a trombone . . . He intoned, he moaned, he pleaded, he blared, he crashed, he thundered."[17] Both the preacher and the shouting congregation were expressing soul. Soul has now come to mean the investing of all the energy one can muster in whatever endeavor, religious or secular, one is committed to.

Margaret Walker defines soul as the expression of the essence of the black experience compounded of heroic and redemptive suffering and of a recognition that the true spirit of life does not reside in physical possessions, such as property, money, and all the trappings of affluent society.

Stephen E. Henderson, co-author with Mercer Cook of *The Militant Black Writer* and professor of English at Howard University, says:

> Soul, then, is all of the unconscious energy of the Black Experience. It is primal spiritual energy. One frequently hears it expressed in terms like: "Soul is putting everything you have into it." "He sure got a whole lot of Soul in it." "Soul is deep down feeling . . ." And one recalls the early appearances of James Brown on the *Ed Sullivan Show*. For about five minutes on one occasion Brown sings, dances, preaches, croons, seduces, wails, makes love, and almost drops from sheer exhaustion. The stunned white audience responds with a polite patter of applause, unable to handle all of that energy, all that love — survival motion set to music. It overloaded their circuits, burnt them out!
>
> I have called this energy spiritual, but really such a designation is false, for it is physical as well, in fact, physical and spiritual at the same time, the expression of a powerful total personality, drawing its reserve from centuries of suffering and joy compressed in the music of the black Baptist church, lashing out in the dozens, flashing out in the black lightning of the blues. Nor is the effect of this expression altogether pleasant by Western standards, for the rasp of the breath, the hoarseness of James Brown's voice, somehow hurts our own throats, and despite the incredible gracefulness of the intricate dances, we are painfully aware of the sheer physical drive involved in their execution. And when James Brown is through with us, we feel curiously exalted.[18]

Lerone Bennett, Jr., black historian and senior editor of *Ebony* magazine, explains soul as follows:

> The whole corpus of the tradition, in fact, is compressed into the folk myth of *Soul,* the American counterpart of the *African Negritude,* a distinct quality of Negro-ness growing out of the Negro's experience and not his genes. *Soul* is a metaphorical evocation of Negro being as expressed in the Negro tradition. It is the feeling with which an artist invests his creation, the style with which a man lives his life. It is, above all, the spirit rather than the letter: a certain way of expressing oneself, a certain way of being. To paraphrase Sartre, Soul is the Negro's antithesis (black) to America's thesis (white), a confrontation of spirits that could and should lead to a higher synthesis of the two.[19]

Integration

The dictionary defines integration as "the act or process or an instance of integrating: as a: incorporation as equals into society or an organization of individuals of different groups (as races)."

Although *racial integration* is often used as a synonym for desegregation, in reality the two concepts differ significantly. The latter has a negative connotation: it simply means the removal of barriers of separation. Thus Funk and Wagnalls' *Standard Dictionary* defines desegregation as the "act of ending segregation of races, as of Negroes and whites, in schools and public facilities." On the other hand, all reputable dictionaries stress in their definitions of integration the positive factor of *bringing together* parts into a whole, or *incorporating* differing individuals and groups into a working relationship. It in no way implies that any part of the integrated whole must surrender its distinguishing characteristics or become absorbed or assimilated into any or all of the other parts. Consequently, the authors of *Ebony* magazine's special issue "Which Way Black America?" could understandably assert, "Genuine 'integration' is a reciprocal process in which blacks and whites gravitate toward each other, sharing decision-making control over institutions and communities and melting their ethical and esthetic values."[20]

Harold Cruse, author of *The Crisis of the Negro Intellectual*, argues that true integration is not attainable in the United States because it is a nation dominated by the social power of groups, classes, in-groups and cliques, both ethnic and religious. "Although the three main power groups — Protestants, Catholics, and Jews — neither want nor need to become integrated with each other, the existence of a great body of homogenized, inter-assimilated white Americans is the premise of racial integration. Thus the Negro integrationist runs afoul of reality in the pursuit of illusion, the 'open society' — a false front that hides several doors to several different worlds of hyphenated Americans. Which group or subgroup leaves its door wide open for the outsider? None, really."[21]

Roy Wilkins, executive secretary of the NAACP, disagrees with Cruse's interpretation. Although he admits that the goal has not yet been achieved, he still believes it is the best option available to blacks:

> The word "integration" as used here is not employed as a synonym for "assimilation." The policy of integration does not mean, as so many

opponents seem to contend, a melting into other peoples, the loss of color, identity and the racial heritage that 350 years of life as Americans have built into the Negro population.

Despite the clamor of a minority of the minority, despite penetration of its spokesmen and ideological followers into key spots in electronic communications, the daily press, the magazine and book-publishing industry . . . , the overwhelming majority of the Negro American population, ranging as high as 95 per cent and as low as 78 per cent, choose integration.[22]

Black Nationalism

Nationalism is defined by the dictionary as "the policy of asserting the interest of a nation, viewed as separate from the interests of other nations or the common interests of all nations." *Nation* is defined as "an aggregation of persons of the same ethnic family, speaking the same language or cognate languages; also a body of people associated with a particular territory who are sufficiently conscious of their unity to seek or to possess a government peculiarly their own." If we substitute race for nation and modify race with the adjective black, we have an objective definition of *black nationalism*.

James Turner, associate professor and director of the Africana Studies and Research Center at Cornell University, suggests:

> Unlike the civil rights movement, which focused on the struggle for legal equality and integration, Black Nationalism addresses itself to the cultural and psychological malaise of the oppression Blacks have had to endure. Nationalism has taken many forms among Africans in America. Some of the most recent varieties are Religio-Nationalism, represented by the Nation of Islam [Black Muslims] ; Cultural Nationalism of Ron Karenga and Amiri Baraka [LeRoi Jones] ; Marxist Revolutionary Nationalism of the Black Panther Party; Economic Nationalism of the Black Capitalism Advocates; Political Nationalism of the Republic of New Africa; and Pan-African Nationalism of Brother Malcolm X. [In a footnote Turner adds that these varieties are not mutually exclusive and that any individual or organization usually assumes any number of combinations of these varieties]. As a political orientation the basic proposition shared by all variants of Black Nationalism (though advocating different social blue-prints at times) is that all things created and occupied by Blacks should be controlled by Black people, and that the purpose of every effort should be toward achieving self-determination (variously defined) and a relatively self-sufficient Black community.[23]

Black writer James Cunningham finds nationalism incompatible with individuality and personal freedom. He complains: "Nationalism, be it black or white, must by its very nature conceive of revolution as a public rather than a personal event. As a result, individualism is one of its primary objects of attack, and diversity, one of its first casualties. This initial attack is prompted by a sincere desire for unity. And reasonably enough public minded movements have never been content to pursue unity without seeking to control the people they would unify."[24]

Ron Karenga, head of the Organization for Black American Culture, admits Cunningham's charge but defends the practice specifically as it applies to cultural nationalism. He says, "A [black] artist may have any freedom to do what he wishes as long as it does not take the freedom from the people to be protected from those images, words and sounds that are negative to their life and development. The people give us the freedom from isolation and alienation and random searching for subject matter, and artists, in view of this fact, must not ask for freedom to deny this, but on the contrary must praise the people for this."[25]

A current example of black political nationalism in the United States is Soul City, North Carolina, conceived and first announced by Floyd McKissick in January, 1969, with 2,000 acres of land already purchased for its use and another 2,800 acres now in the process of being acquired. Asked recently if he would like to see whites become inhabitants of his new black city, he is reported to have replied, "If you are asking me, do I want to live side by side with white people all my life, I don't. I want to live with my people."[26]

Historically, the concept of black nationalism originated more than a century and a half ago. Its major goal was the establishment of a black nation outside the borders of the United States. Its proponents "reasoned that uplift of the black race, whether in Canada, the Caribbean, Central America, or Africa would have a 'reflex influence' on the plight of those still held in bondage and on those only partly removed from its curse in America. A black nation would in time accomplish the goals which an oppressed people could not accomplish for themselves . . . Of such conviction were Martin R. Delany and Robert Campbell, two black Americans who penetrated into the Egba and Yoruba areas of what is now western Nigeria [in 1859-60] in the search for a place where, in Biblical language so meaningful to Americans of the mid-nineteenth century, 'Ethiopia might stretch forth her hand'."[27]

Black Liberation

Liberation is defined as "the act of liberating or the state of being liberated"; and liberate is "to set free, as from bondage."

When blacks speak of black liberation they may mean one or more of the following interpretations:

(1) Complete freedom to choose the life-style that one wishes to follow, without restraint or harassment from whites or fellow blacks, provided that it does not violate the canons of civilized conduct. Thus one would be free to choose as a way of life *integration, assimilation,* or *separation* without unfavorable repercussions from whites or blacks.

(2) Freedom to reject white standards or judgment and behavior in social and economic life, in morals, in educational content and methods, in literature and the arts, and in language usage.

(3) Freedom to censure and harass other blacks for failure to follow self-appointed black leaders who demand allegiance and conformity of all blacks to a militancy which insists that failure to surrender one's individuality for the "good" of the cause is treason to the race. The rationality for this point of view is that since blacks are oppressed as a group they must react to oppression as a group; consequently, to indulge oneself in the luxury of individuality is to endanger the very existence of the group with which one is inseparably identified.

(4) Freedom to condemn all whites as racists who can never shed their racism and, consequently, cannot be trusted to collaborate in any honest manner on an equal basis with blacks.

(5) Freedom to see and believe that all white values are hypocritical, decadent, and unfit for black consideration, and that only black values are pure, honest, and wholesome, thus capable of saving the human race.

Black English

The *American College Dictionary* defines English as "the Germanic language of the British Isles, widespread and standard also in the U.S. and most of the British Empire, historically termed Old English or Anglo-Saxon (to 1150), Middle English (to 1450), and Modern English." American English is, of course, the variety used in the United States. There are numerous dialects (defined as provincial or rural sub-standard forms of the basic language) of American English characteristic of communities of various sizes and types. According to the dictionary, language is applied to the general pattern of a people or a race: the English language; dialect is applied to certain forms or varieties of a language, often those which provincial communities or special groups retain (or develop) even after a standard has been established: Scottish dialect. Dictionaries further explain that a vernacular is the authentic natural pattern of speech, now usually on the colloquial level, used by persons indigenous to a certain community, large or small: to speak in a vernacular. On the basis of the preceding widely accepted information, it is difficult to find justification for the classification of the language of black Americans as black English. The most justifiable descriptions are dialect and vernacular. As a rule, black Americans tend to use the basic dialect of their native regions. Thus Juanita Williamson, professor of English at Lemoyne College and one of the most reputable black linguists, insists there is no such thing as a black language or black English in the United States. In her research studies of southern regional dialects she has documented evidence to prove that differences between black and white varieties are infinitesimal. There are some linguists, however, black and white, who insist that the nonstandard usage of American English by blacks varies widely enough from standard usage to be considered a separate language.

Ralph Ellison, the most distinguished living black novelist, says, "In my own case, having inherited the language of Shakespeare and Melville, Mark Twain and Lincoln and no other, I try to do my part in keeping the language alive and rich by using in my work the music and idiom of American Negro speech, and by insisting that the words of that language correspond with the reality of American life as seen by my own people."[28]

According to Ishmael Reed, the black author of two revolutionary novels and editor of the anthology *19 Necromancers From Now*, ". . . it may turn out that the great restive underground language rising from the American slums and fringe communities is the real American poetry and prose, that can tell you the way things are happening now. If this is not the case, then it is mighty strange that a whole new generation exploits this language, in what White racist critics call 'folk rock lyrics.' "[29]

In a recent letter to *The New York Times*, under the caption "Just Black WASPS?" Dr. Harold Kirshner, assistant professor of

Communication Arts and Skills, New York City Community College, complains that black actors, reporters, and commentators who appear on television are cheating the public by not speaking their native black language. He says, "It is good to 'see' on TV a number of new voices that are Black and Puerto Rican . . . But aside from the question of quantity, there seems to be one of quality that needs attention . . . If you keep your eyes closed, what is the color and background of the speaker? . . . Why cannot an actor, a reporter, or a commentator speak like the Black man he is?" At least this professor of the Communication Arts and Skills is certain that there is a black language that is native to all black people.

On the other hand, Joe Black, black vice-president of the Greyhound Corporation, began a weekly article in an Afro-American newspaper in the following manner:

"Hey, Baby, let it all hang out!"
"Tell it like it is."
"Don't blow your cool."
"Heavy, Baby."
"Do your own thing, Dude."
"Crazy, Dad."

Two black cats rapping? Wrong. This conversation is from the Sunday comics. I reprint it here to prove a point: There is no Black language. There are the African languages, of course. But I'm referring to the communication tool of the Black people born in the United States.

The editors of *The Crisis,* official organ of the NAACP, present the prevailing point of view of middle-class blacks in the following excerpts from a recent editorial entitled "Black Nonsense":

The new cult of blackness has spawned many astounding vagaries, most of them harmless, some of them intriguing and others merely amusing. One which has recently gained a measure of academic and foundation recognition is not only sheer nonsense but also a cruel hoax which, if allowed to go unchallenged, can cripple generations of black youngsters in their preparation to compete in the open market with their non-Negro peers.

It appears that . . . [a black teacher at a distinguished college, with the aid of a $65,000 Ford Foundation grant] is trying to transform a vernacular which is more regional than racial, i.e., more southern than Negro, into a full-fledged distinct language which the college offers as a course. This language is merely the English of the undereducated with provincial variances in accent and structure from locale to locale throughout the English-speaking world. One might as well call the cockney of the London East Enders or the speech patterns of the Appalachian whites separate languages. The so-called black English is basically the same slovenly English spoken by the South's undereducated poor white population.

What our children need, and other disadvantaged American children as well — Indian, Spanish-speaking, Asian, Appalachian and Immigrant Caucasians — is training in basic English which today is as near an international language as any in the world. To attempt to lock them into a provincial patois is to limit their opportunities in the world at large. Black children can master Oxonian English as well as any WASP child of the English Midlands. But each has to be taught the language. No one is born speaking "black," cockney, pidgin, standard or "white" English. Children learn to speak what they hear and are taught. Let our children have the opportunity, and be encouraged, to learn the language which will best enable them to comprehend modern science and technology, equip them to communicate intelligently with other English-speaking peoples of all races, and to share in the exercise of national power.[30]

The prevailing point of view of many younger black writers is presented in the following excerpts from "Black English: Expression of the Afro-American Experience," by Shelia Walker, a young black Ph.D. candidate in anthropology at the University of Chicago:

My fundamental premise is that Black English, the particular idiom of Black Americans, is a "separate but equal" dialect of the English language. It is distinct from standard American English in the same way that the latter differs from the brand of English spoken in England (which also has its own distinct dialects). Just as American English is as serviceable and respectable as British English, Black English must be accorded the same status with respect to standard American English. . . .

The version of English developed by the slaves became the language of Blacks in America. The slaves lost their original languages and this Black version of English became their mother tongue. It became the mode of linguistic expression of a group which was sharing common experiences and developing a total cultural system. These Blacks were neither physiologically nor intellectually incapable of learning the standard dialect. They never had the opportunity to do so because of their limited verbal contact with whites. Once they had developed their own language they had no need to try to learn the white dialect. The patterns they developed have managed to remain so unchanged because Black people have continued to communicate mainly with other Black people, reinforcing the original patterns. . . .

Since standard English is the vehicle of communication of mainstream America, anyone who wants to participate fully in the society must have full command of it. Black people who do not know standard English have one more strike against them in dealing with the white American system. This is especially true in the areas of the total society which most affect Black lives — employment and education. A person who does not know standard English is limited in his employment possibilities to jobs where skilled verbal communication in the standard dialect is not essential. This eliminates many desirable job possibilities and provides potential employers with one additional excuse for not hiring Black people. . . .

Unless American society undergoes some radical changes, standard English will retain its dominance. Anyone who wants to make it in the system must be able to read, write, speak and understand it well, which is not presently true of many members of the Black community. This situation can only be remedied in the educational process. Black people need to learn standard English not because of any inherent value it possesses, but as a means of what America has to offer. Many Black people are already bi-dialectal, that is, they are fluent in both the Black idiom and standard English, and are able to use either in the appropriate context. . . .

Thus the approach advocated here with respect to language is commensurate with the core concerns of the Black Revolution. This is a good example of the relation between linguistics and social and cultural realities. If we look at language as a tool for dealing with the world, being bi-dialectal seems to be the most realistic linguistic response that Black people can make to our current position in America. We must turn to our own language as a symbol, expression, and artifact of our cultural and social unity as proud, conscious Black people. Yet we must also learn the language of white America so as to deal with it as effectively as possible for the benefit of our race. We must know, love, and keep what we have while acquiring the tools to get more.[31]

W. Edward Farrison, a linguistic scholar and author of *William Wells Brown: Author and Reformer* (first black American to publish a novel), argues against the misconception supporting the idea of the existence of black English or black dialect spoken exclusively by black people. He explains:

Basic among these misconceptions is the notion that there is such an entity as Negro dialect; that is, a group of speech habits which are the result of Negroness rather than the product of regional and class influences, which in fact they are. It was this notion which led Richard Wright to assume that a voice he heard over a telephone one day in 1942 was, says one of his biographers, "that of a Negro or a Southern male"; and it still leads many into snap judgments that somebody talks or does not talk "like a Negro." As dialectologists know, there is no such entity as Negro dialect nor a racial dialect of any other kind. If there were, one might well expect to find a Jewish German dialect in Germany, a Jewish French dialect in France, a Jewish Spanish dialect in Spain, a Jewish British dialect in Great Britain, and a Jewish American dialect as well as a Negro dialect in America, for Jews have been in all of these countries for centuries — certainly long enough for linguistic adaptations to occur.

. . .If Negro dialect is a function of Negroness, how much of a Negro need one be for it to be endemic to him? Is it fully characteristic of only full-blooded Negroes, fifty percent characteristic of mulattoes, twenty-five percent characteristic of quadroons, and so on? Or should Negroness be considered an immeasurable sociological quality, which is basically a matter of class, and which, therefore, leads back to the consideration of the speech habits in question as the product of regional and class influences, without regard to the imponderable called race?[32]

II

THE PAST
Before 1967

To assert there was no significant activity in the area of Negro studies (now referred to as Black Studies) before 1967 is to deny facts; but to say that such activity was woefully inadequate is to express a regrettable truth. There is no intention here to explore the argument in depth, but it is desirable to comment briefly on two important types of activity: research by black and white scholars, and the multiple role of the black college in the promotion of an understanding and appreciation of black history and culture at a time when white society scorned the very idea of such a consideration.

3
Research Studies
on Black Subjects

Black Scholars

Passing over early writers before 1860 who sought to discover and record historical facts about their race, we shall briefly review the records of a few black scholars whose achievements during the first half of the twentieth century have been noteworthy.

Foremost among this group is *W. E. B. DuBois,* whose productive career extended from 1896 to 1963. Born in Great Barrington, Massachusetts, February 23, 1868, he earned B.A. degrees at black Fisk University in 1888 and Harvard University in 1890, an M.A. from Harvard in 1892, and a Ph.D. from Harvard in 1896 after study at the University of Berlin from 1892 to 1894. His dissertation, *Suppression of the African Slave Trade to the United States of America, 1638-1870,* was one of the first publications in the *Harvard Historical Series,* 1896. In his *Autobiography* DuBois explains his precarious situation as follows: "I knew by this time that practically my sole chance of earning a living combined with study was to teach, and after my work with [Professor Albert Bushnell] Hart in United States History, I conceived the idea of applying philosophy to an historical interpretation of race relations. In other words, I was trying to take my first steps toward sociology as the science of human action. It goes without saying that no such field was then recognized at Harvard or came to be recognized for twenty years after. But I began with some research in Negro history and finally at the suggestion of Hart, I chose the suppression of the African slave trade to America as my doctor's thesis." [1]

31

His *Philadelphia Negro: A Social Study* was published by the University of Pennsylvania Press, 1899, two years after he had resigned as assistant professor at the University of Pennsylvania to become professor of economics and history at black Atlanta University in Georgia. Then followed important literary productions in the forms of essays, short stories, sketches, novels and a biography of John Brown. His major research continued to be published: *The Negro* (1915); *The Gift of Black Folk: Negroes in the Making of America* (1924); *Africa: Its Geography, People and Products* (1930); *Africa: Its Place in History* (1930); *Black Reconstruction in America, 1860-1880* (1935); *Black Folk, Then and Now: An Essay in the History and Sociology of the Negro Race* (1939); *Encyclopedia of the Negro* (with a white sociologist Guy B. Johnson, 1945); *Color and Democracy: Colonies and Peace* (1945); *The World and Africa: An Inquiry into the Part Which Africa Has Played in World History* (1947). During the fifty years between his graduation from Harvard and his eightieth birthday he produced eleven major volumes of research, collaborated in and edited fifteen additional volumes, and, according to evidence compiled by Herbert Aptheker, contributed approximately ninety shorter articles, essays, and pamphlets to research studies concerning the history, culture, and activities of black people throughout the world.

In 1961 at the age of ninety-three DuBois was invited by President Nkruma of Ghana to accept the directorship of the *Encyclopedia Africana* project, a task which the aged scholar had once hoped to be able to undertake at the age of forty-one. However, at the age of sixty-six he had begun a similar project, entitled *Encyclopedia of the Negro,* under the sponsorship of the Phelps-Stokes Fund, but the necessary financing could not be arranged and he was forced to abandon the project after the publication of a preparatory volume. After two years of work as director of *Encyclopedia Africana* in Ghana, he died on August 27, 1963, and was buried in Accra.

Carter G. Woodson was the second most distinguished black research scholar of the early twentieth century to make important contributions to the study of Negro life and culture. Born in Buckingham County, Virginia, December 19, 1875, he did not enter high school until the age of twenty, having worked as a miner for six years in Fayette County, West Virginia, where his family had moved. He earned B.A. and M.A. degrees at the University of Chicago and a Ph.D. at Harvard, using as subject for his doctoral dissertation *The Disruption of Virginia.*

He started his professional career as a high school teacher, later being promoted to a principalship. In 1919 he became dean of the School of Liberal Arts at Howard University, from which he resigned the following year. After serving two years as dean of the West Virginia Collegiate Institute (now West Virginia State College), he decided that his greatest interest was in research rather than teaching or educational administration. Consequently, on September 9, 1915, he, with five other associates, organized the Association for the Study of Negro Life and History. The following month the Association was incorporated under the laws of the District of Columbia with the avowed purpose of preserving and publishing the records of the race. In 1916 he initiated *The Journal of Negro History,* a quarterly publication, which is still devoted to the encouragement and publication of significant research studies of the history of black people throughout the world. Today, it is one of the most reputable historical journals, recognized by scholars and historians everywhere.

Recognizing the difficulty of finding commercial publishers willing to publish books by Negroes dealing with racial studies, he organized Associated Publishers in 1921 to fill this gap. Among such studies published by Associated Publishers are Woodson's own *The Education of the Negro Prior to 1861* (1915); *A Century of Negro Migration* (1918); *History of the Negro Church* (1921); *The Negro in our History* (1922); *Negro Orators and Their Orations* (1925); *Free Negro Heads of Families in the U.S. in 1830* (1925); *The Mind of the Negro as Reflected in Letters during the Crisis, 1800-1860* (1925); *Negro Makers of History* (1928); *African Myths* (1928); *The Rural Negro* (1930); *The Story of the Negro Retold* (1935); *The African Background Outlined* (1936); *African Heroes and Heroines* (1939).

Woodson died in Washington, D.C., on April 3, 1950.

Charles S. Johnson was born in Bristol, Virginia, July 24, 1893. He was educated at black Virginia Union University in Richmond, Virginia, where he received a B.A. degree in 1917. The following year he earned a Ph.B. at the University of Chicago. While there he was greatly influenced by Robert E. Park, then called "the father of American sociology." During the Chicago riot of 1919, Johnson received a gunshot wound. He was appointed aide to the Governor's Committee to investigate the riot and became co-author of the committee's report, *The Negro in Chicago,*(1922).He attributed the riot to the vast migration of Negroes from the South to Chicago which, he said, was not "unlike that of the Jews out of Egypt."

In 1921 he was appointed director of research for the National Urban League with headquarters in New York City. His first assignment was to make surveys of race relations in Baltimore and six other cities including Los Angeles. Two years later he founded and became the first editor of the official organ of the League, *Opportunity: A Journal of Negro Life,* which published not only significant research on Negro problems but literary writings by a talented group of young black poets, playwrights, and fiction writers. Thus Johnson has been often called, along with Alain Locke, a nursemaid of the Harlem Renaissance.

He left the Urban League in 1928 to accept the position as director of the Department of Social Science at Fisk University. He also served as director of the Institute of Race Relations held annually at Swarthmore College from 1933 to 1938. He became the first black president of Fisk University in 1946 and remained in the position until his death. Among his significant publications are *The Negro in Chicago* (1922); *Ebony and Topaz* (1927); *The Negro in American Civilization* (1930); Report to the International Commission on Slavery and Forced Labor in Liberia (1931); *Negro Housing* (1932); *Economic Status of Negroes* (1933); *Shadow of the Plantation* (1934); *Race Relations* (1934); *The Collapse of Cotton Tenancy* (1934); *A Preface to Racial Understanding* (1936); *The Negro College Graduate* (1938); *Growing Up in the Black Belt* (1941); *Patterns of Negro Segregation* (1943); *To Stem This Tide* (1943); *Culture and the Educational Process* (1943); and *Into the Mainstream* (1947).

E. Franklin Frazier, author, scholar, and outstanding sociologist, was born September 24, 1894, in Baltimore where he is reported as a youth to have spat upon a building of the Johns Hopkins University because he knew he could not attend there. He obtained his first degree with honors at Howard University in 1916 and his M.A. degree in sociology at Clark University in Worcester, Massachusetts, in 1920. He became research fellow at the New York School of Social Work in 1920 and from 1927 to 1929 was research assistant in the Department of Sociology at the University of Chicago where he received his Ph.D. in 1931. He was granted a Guggenheim Fellowship in 1940, and in 1949 completed an independent research project on race and culture contacts in the West Indies. He was for twenty-five years chairman of the Department of Sociology at Howard University and served one term as president of the American Sociological Association and of the International Society for the Scientific Study of Race Relations. In 1949 he was named chairman of UNESCO's committee of experts on race. Later, he served as chief of UNESCO's Applied Science Division in Paris. Among his major publications are *Negro Youth at the Crossroads* (1940); *The Negro in the United States* (1949); and *Black Bourgeoisie, The Rise of a New Middle Class* (1957).

In the controversial *Black Bourgeoisie* Frazier maintained that the Negro middle class had isolated itself from the problems of marginal or poverty-stricken Negroes and furthered its own frustrations by "creating a world of make-believe centered around the myths of Negro business and Negro society." He received the coveted MacIver Award of the American Sociological Association for this work. He died in Washington, D.C., in 1962.

John Hope Franklin, historian and educator, was born January 2, 1915, in Rentiesville, Oklahoma. He studied at Fisk University where he received a B.A. degree in 1935. The following year he received his M.A. at Harvard and a Ph.D. in 1941. For four years, beginning in 1939, as professor at black St. Augustine's College, Raleigh, N.C., he carried on research on the legal status and economic position of the Negro in North Carolina before the Civil War. He published his findings in several articles including "The Free Negro in the Economic Life of North Carolina" (1942) and "Slaves Virtually Free in Ante-Bellum North Carolina" (1943), and in his book *The Free Negro in North Carolina 1790-1860* (1943). In the preface to his *From Slavery to Freedom: A History of American Negroes* (1947), which became a leading college textbook, Franklin explained that his effort to consider the forces affecting the development of the Negro in America "involved a continuous recognition of the mainstream of American history and the relationship of the Negro to it." His other important studies include *The Diary of James T. Ayers, Civil War Recruiter* (1947); *The Militant South* (1956); *Reconstruction: After the Civil War* (1961); *The Emancipation Proclamation* (1963); *Color and Race* (1968); and *George Washington Williams and Africa* (1971).

Benjamin Quarles has won wide recognition as a college teacher as well as an outstanding historian whose research and writings have contributed greatly to a re-appraisal of many aspects of earlier versions of Negro history. Born in Boston, Massachusetts, he, like W. E. B. DuBois, journeyed south for his undergraduate education. At black Shaw University in Raleigh, North Carolina, he distinguished himself as a scholar and went on to the University of

Wisconsin for his M.A. and Ph.D. degrees, where he was awarded the President Adams Fellowship in Modern History. While serving on the faculties of such predominantly black institutions as Shaw University, Dillard University, and Morgan State College, he not only encouraged and inspired hundreds of black students to seek and find new meanings in and more enlightened interpretations of their racial heritage, but he also published the following volumes of research: *Frederick Douglass* (1948); *The Negro in the Civil War* (1953); *The Negro in the American Revolution* (1961); *Lincoln and the Negro* (1962); *The Negro in the Making of America* (1964); *Black Abolitionists* (1969); *The Black American: A Documentary History* (with co-author Leslie H. Fishel, Jr., 1970).

In addition, he has published more than thirty important articles dealing with black history in national periodicals, including "What the Historian Owes the Negro," in which he declares:

> It is no longer somewhat unsettling to come across a book that credits the Negro with enlarging the meaning of freedom in America, giving it new expression. In today's schools, a youngster would react more receptively than ever to finding out, for example, that the first non-Indian to explore portions of Arizona and New Mexico was a Negro; that a Negro was the first to die at the Boston Massacre; that a Negro wrote the second book of verse published by any woman in colonial America; that a Negro was the first Chicagoan; that a Negro was one of the three commissioners who laid out the city of Washington; that a Negro preached the first Protestant sermon heard west of the Mississippi; that a Negro invented a vacuum cap that revolutionized the sugar industry; that another Negro invented the shoe-lasting machine that had a similar effect on industry; that a Negro accompanied Perry at the discovery of the North Pole; and that the first American fatality in World War II was a Negro.[2]

Many signal honors have been accorded Quarles for his preeminence among the interpreters of black history. Three times he has been selected as Fellow of the Social Science Research Council and twice as Fellow of the Carnegie Corporation for the Advancement of Teaching. He has also been granted fellowships for research by the Rosenwald and the Guggenheim Foundations. In 1969 he was chosen to head the Maryland Commission on Negro History and Culture, which was created by the General Assembly to consider the establishment of a state-financed museum of black culture.

Benjamin Brawley was born in Columbia, South Carolina, in 1882. His father, a graduate of Bucknell University in Pennsylvania, was a descendant of a black family whose members had been free as far back as they could remember. At an early age Benjamin became interested in Latin and Greek and was somewhat proficient in both by the age of fourteen. He received an A.B. degree at Morehouse College, Atlanta, at the age of nineteen. Five years later he earned a second A.B. degree at the University of Chicago and went on to Harvard University where after two years of study he was awarded an M.A. degree. In 1912 he returned to Morehouse College as professor of English and the institution's first dean. In 1920 he left Morehouse to go to Africa to make an educational survey of the Republic of Liberia. Upon his return to the United States he accepted a position as professor of English at Shaw University, which he resigned eight years later to accept a similar position at Howard University.

Of the twenty-six publications attributed to Brawley in the catalog of the Library of Congress, the most important ones based on research in the history and culture of black Americans are *The Negro in Literature and Art in the United States* (1929); *Your Negro Neighbor* (1918); *A Short History of the American Negro* (1921); *A Social History of the American Negro* (1921); *Early Negro American Writers* (1935); *Negro Builders and Heroes* (1935); *Paul Laurence Dunbar: Poet of His People* (1936); *The Negro Genius* (1937); and *The Best Short Stories of Paul Laurence Dunbar* (1938). He refused, however, to limit his scholarship to research in Negro life and culture. He believed that black Americans could best achieve proper recognition by demonstrating excellence in broad activities and surpassing the white scholar in his own areas of strongest competence. He set an example in this respect by the publication of his popular *A Short History of the English Drama* which was used as a text in many well-known white universities even in the South. He died in Washington, D.C. at the age of fifty-six.

Alain Locke, literary and art critic and interpreter of the Negro's contributions to American culture, was born in Philadelphia, September 13, 1886. He attended Harvard University where he completed work for both B.A. and Ph.D. degrees. As a Rhodes Scholar from Pennsylvania, he did graduate work at Oxford University in England from 1907 to 1910. He also studied at the University of Berlin from 1910 to 1911. He was professor of philosophy at Howard from 1912 until his retirement in 1953.

His major contributions to research and scholarship are in the areas of literature, art, and music. His first publication, *The New Negro: An Interpretation* (1925), broke new ground in the appreciation and recognition of Negro literature and art on a national basis. His efforts stimulated the Harlem Renaissance and opened new opportunities for young black creative writers, artists, and performers. In addition to *The New Negro*, his most influential publications were *The Negro in America* (1935); *The Negro and His Music* (1936); *Negro Art—Past and Present* (1937); *The Negro in Art* (1941); *Plays of Negro Life* (1927); *Race and Culture Contacts* (co-author, 1941); and the Bronze Booklet Series issued by Associates in Negro Folk Education (1937), studies in Negro music and art. At the time of his death in 1954 he was in the process of writing, with the aid of a grant from the Rockefeller Foundation, *The Negro in American Culture*, which was completed by Margaret Just Butcher and published in 1956.

Sterling Brown was born May 1, 1901, in Washington, D.C. He was educated at Williams College, Williamstown, Massachusetts, where he received a B.A. degree with honors in 1925. In 1930 he was awarded an M.A. degree from Harvard. Except for brief periods during which he served as visiting lecturer at the New School for Social Research, Vassar, and the University of Minnesota, he has spent his entire teaching career since 1929 as professor at Howard University. He was awarded a Guggenheim Fellowship for creative writing in 1937 and later the same year published two research studies: *The Negro in American Fiction* (1937), and *Negro Poetry and Drama* (1937). He was editor on *Negro Affairs, Federal Writers Project* from 1936 to 1939. He also served as staff member of Gunnar Myrdal's research team which conducted the monumental study of the Negro in American life first published in 1944 under the title of *The American Dilemma.*

In addition to his own published studies, as chief librarian of Fisk University, Nashville, Tennessee, for more than twenty years, *Arna Bontemps* has made a significant contribution to the encouragement and promotion of research dealing with black life and culture. He was born in Alexandria, Louisiana, in 1902, and educated largely in California where he received an A.B. degree from Pacific Union College in 1923. After further study at the University of Chicago and Columbia University he began his tenure as librarian at Fisk University and continued until 1968. Later he served two years as professor of English at the University of Illinois (Chicago). In 1970 he accepted the position as curator of the James Weldon Johnson Collection, Yale University Library.

His major research studies include the historical novels *Black Thunder* (1936), a vivid re-creation of the famous slave revolt led by Gabriel Prosser in 1800, and *Drums at Dusk* (1939), a fictional presentation of the Haitian struggle for liberation under the leadership of such black military heroes as Dessalines and Toussaint L'Ouverture; *The Poetry of the Negro* (with Langston Hughes, 1949); *Book of Negro Folklore* (with Langston Hughes, 1958); *Story of the Negro* (1958); *100 Years of Negro Freedom* (1961); *American Negro Poetry* (1963); and *Great Slave Narratives* (1969).

White Scholars

Some white American scholars during the first half of the twentieth century undertook significant research pertaining to black life and culture which broke the stereotyped patterns and emphasized new points of view previously ignored by the white world.

Born in Luzerne County, Pennsylvania, February 14, 1864, *Robert Ezra Park* studied at the University of Michigan. Upon graduation in 1887, he worked for newspapers in Minneapolis, Detroit, and Chicago for more than ten years. He entered Harvard's Graduate School and received an M.A. in 1899. Five years later he earned a Ph.D. at the University of Heidelberg, Germany. Returning to the U.S., he sought active participation in the study of human behavior with special emphasis on race relations, which he considered the most pressing problem in America during that period. From 1905 to 1914 he worked in the South, much of the time with Booker T. Washington in an informal capacity of secretary and research associate. Having accepted an invitation to become secretary of the Congo Reform Association to help advertise the atrocities occurring there, Park became genuinely interested in the problems and conditions plaguing the Congo. He had become interested enough to go to Africa to study the situation first hand when Booker T. Washington invited him to visit Tuskegee and start his studies of Africa in the southern states. In Park's own words, "I learned more about human nature and society, in the South under Booker T. Washington than I had learned elsewhere in all my previous studies." After Washington's death he accepted a professorship in the Department of Sociology at the University of Chicago, where he remained until his retirement. In 1936 he became visiting professor of sociology at Fisk University in Nashville, Tennessee, and worked as a research associate with the black sociologist Charles S. Johnson, president of Fisk. His research and keen insight opened new vistas for research in the field of race relations.

The second white scholar to make a significant contribution to the study of Negro life and culture in the United States was *Edward Byron Reuter* who was born on a farm near Holden, Missouri, in 1880. After serving as instructor for four years at the Reform School in Booneville, Missouri, he entered the University of Missouri in 1906 as a major in sociology and remained there until he earned an M.A. degree five years later. After three years as a high school principal in California he enrolled at the University of Chicago, where he was awarded a Ph.D. degree, *magna cum laude,* at the age of 40. The next three years he taught consecutively at the University of Illinois, Goucher Collge, and Tulane University. In 1921 he began his long tenure at the University of Iowa, where he was chairman of the Sociology Division of the Department of Economics and Sociology for more than twenty years. When he resigned from the staff of the University of Iowa in the summer of 1944, he accepted the position of professor of sociology at Fisk University, succeeding the late Robert E. Park, and remained there until his death in 1946.

His most consuming interest during his mature years was race relations and the social problems of black Americans. One of his former students who edited the revised edition of *The American Race Problem* confides that "Reuter often began his class, as he does also in *The American Race Problem,* with popular views of Negro problems, and he was quick to show how certain views had no legs to stand on save that of individual prejudice."[3] Like Robert E. Park, one of his favorite professors at the University of Chicago, the major themes of his research were concerned with such questions as "What is race? What is the nature of race prejudice? What are the relations between prejudice and discrimination?"

His major published research dealing with Negro Americans includes *The Mulatto in the United States* (1918); *The American Race Problem* (1927); *Race Mixture: Studies in Intermarriage and Miscegenation* (1931); and *Race and Culture Contacts* (1934).

Herbert Aptheker was born in Brooklyn, New York, July 31, 1915. He was educated in New York where he received B.S., M.A., and Ph.D. degrees from Columbia University. In the preface to his book *To Be Free: Studies in American Negro History* (1948, rev. ed.) Aptheker says, "Tremendous progress has been achieved in the past generation in the Negro Liberation movement . . . Part of the effort to cleanse the U.S. of racism is to cleanse its educational system of that blight." Toward that end Aptheker has played a substantial role in demolishing the "racist mythology" which denies that Afro-Americans have had as significant a history as any other people and the specific denial that Afro-Americans have played central roles in the entire past of the United States. He is also author of the following books: *The Negro in the Civil War* (1938); *Negro Slave Revolts in the United States* (1939); *Documentary History of the Negro People in the United States* (2 vols., 1951); *The Labor Movement in the South during Slavery* (1954); *The World of C. Wright Mills* (1960); *Soul of the Republic* (1964); *One Continual Cry* (1965); *Nat Turner's Slave Rebellion* (1966); *The Nature of Democracy, Freedom, Revolution* (1967); and editor of *The Autobiography of W. E. B. DuBois* (1968).

4
The Black College:
Background, Problems,
and Achievements

Background

The predominantly black colleges in the United States had their origin in the enactment of legislation creating a "Bureau of Refugees, Freedmen, and Abandoned Lands" and signed into law by President Abraham Lincoln on March 3, 1865. But in the beginning there were no provisions concerning education, and General O. O. Howard, who was appointed first commissioner of the Bureau (later known simply as the Freedmen's Bureau) by President Andrew Johnson on May 12, 1865, found it necessary to request an amendment including such a provision. Satisfactory bills including the necessary amendment were passed by both houses of Congress on two occasions and vetoed by President Johnson. However, the second bill was passed over the veto of the President and became law July 16, 1866.

Dwight Holmes, in his *The Evolution of the Negro College,* recounts how opposition in the South expressed itself against the Bureau's efforts to encourage the establishment of elementary and secondary schools for blacks.[4] White and black teachers from the North were assaulted by the Ku Klux Klan and driven out of community after community while many school buildings were burned. Nevertheless, the General Superintendent of Education for the Bureau reported in June, 1866, "the eagerness of freedmen for knowledge and their willingness to sacrifice for its attainment, calling attention to figures which indicated that in the District of Columbia seventy-five per cent of the Negro children attended school as against forty-one per cent of the white children; while in Memphis,

42

Tennessee, 72 per cent of the Negro children attended school as against 41 per cent of the white children; in Alabama 79 per cent, and in Virginia 82 per cent. . . . One school, where three hundred pupils were taught entirely by cultured colored men, could be favorably compared with any ordinary school in the North."[5]

Out of the pressing need to train black teachers in sufficient supply to staff these newly established schools grew the insistent demand for the creation of black colleges in every state in the South. In 1866 it was estimated that 20,000 teachers were needed immediately for the million or more Negro children ready and eager to attend school. Thus black colleges began to appear in areas where the need was greatest with little or no prior preparation, often in abandoned or make-shift buildings. In Tennessee the now famous Fisk University, one of the four black colleges with chapters of Phi Beta Kappa, was opened in an old military hospital. In the nation's capital, Howard University, now the largest and most prestigious of all predominantly black universities, began classes in a rented frame building previously used as a German dance hall and saloon.

Except for Howard University, which began as an independent institution aided greatly by the Freedmen's Bureau but which very early in its history became the only civilian institution for higher learning to be entirely supported by the government of the United States, all but one of the black colleges and universities[6] that were founded during the first decade after the close of the Civil War were established by religious denominations, including Congregationalists, Baptists, Methodists, and Presbyterians, or the interdenominational American Missionary Association. Later the Protestant Episcopal Church and the Roman Catholic Church expanded their educational programs to include four-year colleges. Although there has been some criticism of the failure of these religious Boards of Education headed by northern white sympathizers to adapt their curricula to the practical needs of newly emancipated black students, W. E. B. DuBois praised these leaders for their efforts. In his famous essay "The Talented Tenth" he says:

> Out of the colleges of the North came, after the blood of war, Ware, Cravath, Chase, Andrews, Bumstead and Spence to build the foundations of knowledge and civilization in the black South. Where ought they have begun to build? At the bottom, of course, quibbles the mole with his eyes in the earth. Aye! truly at the bottom, at the very bottom; at the bottom of knowledge there where the roots of justice strike into the lowest soil of Truth. And so they did begin; they founded colleges, and up from the

colleges shot normal schools, and out from the normal schools went teachers, and around the normal teachers clustered other teachers to teach the public teachers; the colleges trained in Greek and Latin and mathematics, 2,000 men; and these men trained fully 50,000 others in morals and manners, and they in turn taught thrift and the alphabet to nine millions of men, who today hold $300,000,000 of property. It was a miracle—the most wonderful peace-battle of the 19th century, and yet today men smile at it, and in fine superiority tell us that it was all a strange mistake . . .[7]

Today there are approximately 111 predominantly black colleges and universities, of which thirty-nine are public. According to Stephen J. Wright, former president of the United Negro College Fund, in an article published July 20, 1968, approximately sixty-eight percent of these institutions are fully accredited by the appropriate regional agencies. Although in 1968 it was estimated that more than fifty percent of all black students were then enrolled in these 111 colleges, the percentage in 1970 was less than forty per cent. In 1968 Wright stated that enrollments in black colleges had been increasing, in recent years, at approximately the same rate as all institutions of higher learning, but a report released August 28, 1971, by the Office of Civil Rights, Department of Health, Education, and Welfare, stated that the total black student enrollment rose from 303,397 in 1968 to 379,138 in the fall of 1970, an increase of 24 percent, while the percent of increase over that of 1968 for the white student population rose only 5.7 percent. Although the rate of increase in the population of the black colleges was not as high as the rate for black students in predominantly white institutions, the rate was higher than the overall average for the white colleges.

Wright, who previously served as president of Fisk University for nine years, suggests:

It is clear, then, that Negro colleges and universities comprise a significant part of the nation's higher education establishment—a part that is serving the changing needs of both the Negro community and the nation. It is true, too, that they are held in high regard in the Negro community—which explains, in part, the continuing increase in their enrollments. But although these institutions do not differ from others in higher education in either kind or degree, they do have some special problems—and some special opportunities —that stem from their history, from the deep-seated racial attitudes that dominate American life.[8]

Problems

The special problems to which Wright alludes in the preceding quotation include the inadequate preparatory training of the majority of the students enrolled, the lack of sufficient financial resources for the employment of an adequate faculty and the construction of necessary buildings and other facilities, and the inability to offer their students (many of whom are from impoverished families) sufficient loans and scholarship aid to pay for their education. Asserting that the educational task confronting black institutions is the most formidable in the whole realm of higher education, Wright discloses that "we spend $1,025 less today to educate a student in a predominantly Negro college than we do in a comparable so-called white college. Yet the Negro students' need for special courses and guidance is still the greater . . . at least 40 percent of the Negro families in the United States live in or near poverty by federal definition. Last year, for example, the thirty-six private colleges of the United Negro College Fund (UNCF) provided more than $17,000,000 in loans, scholarships, grants-in-aid, and work opportunities."[9]

The problem of recruiting and retaining a competent faculty is now and has always been acute. Prior to 1960 the black college and university offered practically the only opportunities for black teachers to find employment in institutions of higher learning. Consequently, difficulty in staffing did not result from competition of more affluent white institutions, but from the scarcity of black applicants with sufficient advanced academic training. For example, while I was chairman of the forty-five-member English department at a prestigious black college for twenty-three years, at no time did the number of professors with Ph.D. degrees represent more than twenty percent of the total (despite desperate efforts and extraordinary inducements to attract a larger percentage). During that period there were many other departments that I knew with fewer than ten percent of their members possessing a doctorate. One of the major reasons for this predicament was the inability of even the best black colleges to pay their top professors salaries sufficient to sustain life at the minimum level of comfort. It was, therefore, much more profitable for black men with M.A. and even Ph.D. degrees to accept such menial jobs as redcaps at New York's Grand Central and Pennsylvania Railroad Stations and as Pullman porters and dining car workers than as college teachers. Incidentally, since 1967 when the black college has been able to offer its teachers at least a minimum living wage its inability to attract black faculty results from the competition of white institutions which are now offering black recruits higher salaries than white applicants with the same training and experience. Ironically, black colleges are now flooded with applications for employment from highly trained, experienced whites who are willing to accept lower salaries than blacks of similar training and experience. So the basic problem remains.

The problem of inadequate budget has been always the most crucial for the black college. Organized philanthropy has greatly aided state-supported as well as private colleges by offering funds for current expenses as well as for the construction of new buildings on a matching basis. The largest contributions to black institutions of higher learning have come over the years from the Julius Rosenwald Fund, the General Education Board, and the Ford Foundation. These organizations, as well as a number of others, have also contributed to the increase in the supply of black teachers by offering fellowships for advanced study to faculty members upon recommendation of college administrative officials. The annual report of the General Education Board for 1928-29 contains the following data: ". . . the Board made appropriations to a number of state-supported institutions with a view especially to increasing their capacity for training teachers. Among the larger appropriations may be mentioned the following: To the Prairie View State Normal and Industrial College, $75,000 toward $305,500 for permanent improvements; to the State Agricultural and Mechanical Institute, Normal, Alabama, $100,000 toward $300,000 for permanent improvements; to the State Normal School at Fayetteville, North Carolina, $35,000 toward $70,000 for the construction and equipment of a practice school; to the North Carolina College for Negroes, Durham, $45,000 for furniture and equipment for a classroom and administration building . . ." [10]

Finally, the problem of taking poorly prepared high school graduates and giving them the necessary compensatory aid to enable them to master college courses on every level of experience without engendering in them a feeling of inferiority and resentment is a formidable task. And to do this without reducing the quality of the experience below the level of collegiate acceptability is an art as well as a science. But this is a requirement for the effective black college, for the overwhelming majority of its students is "prepared" in the poorest, most overcrowded, most understaffed, and most under-equipped schools in the nation.

Achievements

The more formidable the problem, the more satisfying are the solutions when they occur. Thus the black college can boast of some undeniable achievements that deserve reiteration. Dr. Wright declares:

> The stronger predominantly Negro colleges are not on trial as American institutions of higher learning. They have produced the great majority of Negro leaders at all levels, perhaps 85 per cent of the physicians and dentists, the great majority of the teachers, lawyers, ministers, and trained businessmen. Such leaders as Justice Thurgood Marshall, Senator Edward Brooke, Congressmen William L. Dawson and Charles C. Diggs, Whitney M. Young, Jr., the late Martin Luther King, Jr., and at least four federal judges are the proud products of Negro higher education. Writers such as Frank Yerby, Ralph Ellison, and John Killens were educated in Negro colleges; singers such as Mattiwilda Dobbs and Leontyne Price, and social psychologist Dr. Kenneth B. Clark are prominent alumni. Of equal importance are the literally thousands of physicians, lawyers, professors, librarians, social workers, and enlightened ministers who are the leaders and movers of their communities. These institutions can, without doubt, continue to develop such people—and they are the ultimate test of relevance and quality.[11]

One striking example of the extraordinary achievements of the black college is the success of its graduates who enter the most prestigious white universities and receive advanced degrees with no more difficulty than the average white graduate student encounters, although when they entered the black college as freshmen their scores on the entrance examinations were considerably lower than the minimum for admission to the predominantly white college. Of course, the difference between success and failure does not result from the sheer magic of a black campus, but from formal and informal compensatory programs administered on a crash basis and dedicated to overcoming within a four-year period the inadequacies of twelve years of precollege training.

Furthermore, statistics show that a larger percentage of the graduates of black colleges rise to places of leadership in the larger community than black graduates of predominantly white colleges. The basis for this phenomenon is probably the close relationship between the black college and the black community. Not only is the student of the black college acutely aware of the problems of the surrounding black community, but the activities of the college, curricular and extracurricular, constantly alert the student to the relationship. In learning situations even in mathematics and the sciences supplementary illustrations are often drawn from the most immediate surroundings, which are obviously the black community. Visiting lecturers, artists, and performers are usually black, thus reminding the student not only of his racial heritage, but also that he too has a chance to achieve recognition on a national level.

Above all, the graduate of a black college is less likely to suffer from the so-called identity crisis. Until militant black students angrily confronted white administrators in 1967 demanding that the "black experience" be officially acknowledged as a legitimate and necessary part of the college and university curriculum, a student could earn elementary, high school, college, and university diplomas with highest honors without having been exposed to a single worthy fact about black people in America or the world. Although black colleges aped white institutions in many respects and even failed to devote sufficient time in a formal manner to the many aspects of the black experience in America and the world, a student could not graduate from a black college without knowing some worthy facts about his black heritage. Moreover, many black colleges have had formal courses in what can be rightly called Black Studies for approximately fifty years.

Fisk University, Nashville, Tennessee, founded in 1865, is one of the four oldest black institutions of higher learning (preceded only by Lincoln University and Cheney State College of Pennsylvania, and Atlanta University) in the United States. In order that I might ascertain to what extent Fisk has made Black Studies an integral part of its curriculum during the past fifty years, a study was made of each of its catalogs from 1921-22 to 1970-71 and the results tabulated below with an indication of the year each course was first introduced.

1921—22

| Music 113 | The Study of Negro Music and Composition |
| Sociology 124 | Problems of Negro Life Social Service Training Course (classwork and field work) |

1925—26

| English 123 | A Study of Negro Literature |

History 106	The Negro in American History

1927–28

Anthropology 103	Aboriginal Africa
Religion 138	The Negro Church

1930–31

Anthropology 101	Elementary Ethnology of Africa

1934–35

English 238	The Negro in American Literature
Anthropology 350	Ethnography of Africa
Anthropology 360	Social Integration

1936–37

Anthropology 391–92	Research Work in African Linguistics
Sociology 396–397	Race and Culture
Sociology 304	Race Differences
Psychology 212	Race Psychology

1937–38

Sociology 386	Field Course in Negro Rural Communities

1940–41

Music 314	Origins of the Negro Spiritual

1942–43

Education 384	Socio-Economic Backgrounds of Education in the South
Education 385	Problems of the Negro Youth: Educational Implications
Religion 325	The History and Development of the Negro Church

1943–44

Education 205	Education of the Negro in the U.S.

1944–45

Education 265	Indigenous African Education
Anthropology 205	Introduction to African Studies
Anthropology 207–208	African Cultures and Institutions
Anthropology 235–236	Study of an African Vernacular

1945–46

Education 302	Education in the Rural South

Religion 239   Christian Social Action in Negro-
                             White Adjustment
Sociology 327–330   The Natural History of Race
                             Relations (four semesters)
Anthropology 210   Native Peoples and Cultures of
                             Africa
Economics 262   The Economics of Caribbean
                             Countries

1946–47
Anthropology 212   European Contacts and Culture in
                             Africa

1948–49
English 123   The Negro's Contribution to the
                             Literature of America
Sociology 258   American Minority Groups

1956–57
Psychology 280   Differential Psychology

1966–67
Art 297   African and Afro-American Arts
Education 252   Growing Up in the Inner City
Education 275   Education in the South
Political Science 211   Politics of Minority Groups

1968–69
Art 297   Seminar in Negro Art
Education 285H   Education of the Negro
Political Science 224   African Political Systems

1969–70
English 281–282   African Literature
Education 390   Studies of Negro Intelligence and
                             Achievement
Education 395   Research on the Education of the
                             Negro
French 215   Black French Poets
French 217   Black French Literature
Music 208   Cross Currents in Afro-American
                             Music
Music 225   Fisk Jubilee Singers
Economics 267   Economic Development of Africa
                             and the Caribbean

Political Science 225	Africa and International Politics
Anthropology 224	Cultures and Institutions of Under-developed Areas
Sociology 257 or 303	The Negro in America
Sociology 260 or 304	Social Adjustments of Negro Americans
AFCA 101–102	African Civilizations
AFCA 103	Africa Since 1800
AFCA 201	History of West Africa
AFCA 202	History of Central and South Africa
AFCA 203	History of East Africa
AFCA 204	History of North Africa
AFCA 205	The Black Man in America in the Twentieth Century

1970–71

Art 99–100	Experimental Forms in Afro-American Art
Art 251–52	Image of the Black Man in American Films
Art 295	Afro-American Art
Art 296	Seminar in African Art
Art 297	African and Afro-American Arts
English 18 or 118	Introduction to African and Afro-American Literature
English 206	The Oral Tradition in Black Literature
English 280–81	Negro Literature
English 282–83	Survey of African Literature
English 291–92	Seminar
Education 252	Growing Up in the Inner City
Political Science 201	Political and Social Change in the Black Community
Anthropology 208	Cultures and Institutions of Africa
Anthropology 210	Seminar in Social Anthropology
Sociology 209	The Afro-American Family
Sociology 257	The Afro-American Experience in the U.S.
Sociology 258	Racial and Cultural Minority Groups
Sociology 282	Contributions of Afro-American Sociologists

It is a remarkable fact that Fisk University has offered a total of eighty-five different courses in Black Studies during the past fifty years, three having been offered as early as 1921, and forty-two before the black student revolution of 1967. Despite its past history of emphasis on Black Studies, it acknowledged a still greater need for additional emphasis by adding forty-three new courses between 1967 and 1971.

A similar study of fifteen other black colleges and universities, selected with concern for their representativeness, reveals the following pattern:

Courses Primarily Concerned with the Black Experience

	Year Founded	1921–22 Courses	1931–32 Courses	1941–42 Courses	1951–52 Courses	1961–62 Courses	1971–72 Courses
Lincoln University, Pennsylvania	1854	none	1	2	4	5	44
Atlanta University, Georgia	1860	none	1*	8	7	5	20
Lincoln University, Missouri	1866	3	3	5	7	7	13
Howard University	1867	3	12	11	13	25	82
Talladega College, Alabama	1867	none	none	1	1	1	5
Morehouse College, Georgia	1867	none	3*	1	2	3	18
Hampton Institute, Virginia	1868	1	3	10	4	3	22
Benedict College, South Carolina	1870	none	2	2	3	1	17
Tuskegee Institute, Alabama	1881	1	8	5	4	5	14
Virginia State College	1883	1	1	5	3	3	8
West Virginia State College	1891	3	5	6	6	12	6
South Carolina State College	1895	1	1	1	2	2	4
Kentucky State College	1896	2	1	2	2	1	10
Southern University, Louisiana	1914	none	2	2	1	4	16
North Carolina Central University	1925	N.A.	none	4	5	7	24

*Four additional courses available through cooperative arrangements with Morehouse and Spelman Colleges whose campuses adjoin. The arrangement is still in effect (with the addition of Morris Brown and Clark Colleges in 1956), which increases the number of available courses beyond the catalog offerings of each institution.

III

THE PRESENT
1968-1973

I have defined the *Present* as the five-year period between 1968, when the first Black Studies program at a predominantly white institution of higher learning was officially established at San Francisco State College, and 1973. During this period the battle for acceptance of the idea of the validity of Black Studies as an intellectual discipline was fought and won. Although there are some institutions and individual teachers who are still unconvinced of the viability of the concept, the major problems now are the shortage of qualified teachers to carry out the programs already established and in the process of being established, the selection of the most effective administrative pattern or organization for the particular institution, and the necessary commitment for adequate funds to support such programs

5
Objectives of
Black Studies Programs

For the 200 programs upon which this study is based, approximately 200 objectives are listed with enough variation in wording to be considered different. However, I have selected for presentation here seventy of the most representative and have grouped them into seven major categories.

The first category, the one that includes the basic idea underlying the initial confrontation between black students and the administrators of white colleges and universities, is concerned with the need for the educational experience *to provide for black students a feeling of personal identity, personal pride, and personal worth.* Although the goal has now become multidimensional, the original purpose of the confrontation is still high among the priorities. The questions "Who am I?" "What is my origin?" "What am I worth?" especially disturbed black students who were born and/or reared outside the South, where they could progress through kindergarten, elementary school, high school, college, and university to the very highest academic degree possible without ever having been exposed by the educational establishment to any information about worthy achievements of black people or a single living example of such achievements. Despite the commitment in the South to rigid segregation and grossly inferior schools and colleges for blacks, black children in those schools did see living examples of teachers with whom they could identify and of black school principals with some administrative authority. These schools annually celebrated Negro History Week with programs featuring information about black history, black literature, black music and art, and black personalities

55

who had achieved some degree of success in various occupations and professions. Thus the average black youth of the South was not as distressed about the identity crisis as his northern counterpart.

The objectives that follow are taken verbatim from brochures or college catalogs describing Black Studies programs now in operation:

> To provide the major with a more informed—and hopefully more positive—basis than is available for developing his own identity, his own evaluation of his self-worth, and his system of values.

> To provide the black student an opportunity to confront the dualism of being black and being an American and to understand the possibilities of cultural pluralism.

> To provide an opportunity for all students to understand and appreciate the striving of individuals of all races for recognition and ethnic pride.

> To offer education that will promote the liberation of the individual and his community . . . . The thrust of this perspective is to resist any simple accounts of what a person "really" is or intends to become, and allows for distinction between one's real self and one's apparent self. The real self is . . . dynamic and expanding and defies prima facie, or merely quantitative, assessment. Individuality pre-supposes a social context and, yet, underscores the uniqueness of each person in that context.

> Black educational programming must operate on the premise that the life-styles of black people in America are basically African in nature despite 400 years of forced separation from the mother continent and *not* the result of a condition of poverty.

The second category is based on the assumption that a study of black history and culture will aid blacks in understanding the basis for an identity that is satisfying and fulfilling. Although the more militant black is no longer concerned about the attitudes of whites concerning his personal identity, many black students are still anxious for whites to know enough about black history and culture to gain a fairer and more realistic knowledge and appreciation of the racial heritage. The major emphasis, however, is upon the enhancement of black pride. The following specific objectives suggest various meaningful shades and nuances involved in the achievement of the general goal:

> This major is designed for students who desire a comprehensive appreciation of the special heritage, life, culture, problems, and prospects unique to Americans of African descent.

> To provide for nonmajors service courses that will at the very least introduce them to the most salient features of Afro-American history, black culture, and society.

> To provide students with an understanding of the various social, cultural and

historical forces that gave rise to the particular structure of the Afro-American life-style.

To establish the kind of program which will provide the greatest possibility for exposure to and enhancement of the literature, culture, art, politics, aspirations, and major struggle of Afro-Americans for purposes of achieving self-perspective and dignity through awareness of and respect for Africa as a motherland as well as the creditable heritage built in this country, and as a corrective for the historical denial of this heritage.

To provide systematic study of the experiences, conditions, and origins of black people, their living conditions, their philosophical, religious, and social values, their various modes of artistic expression, and the way in which each of these cultural aspects is interrelated.

To provide the student an opportunity to gain knowledge and understanding of the history, social organization, current status, and problems of black Americans and of black contributions to the American heritage.

The Department should concern itself with a wide range of problems pertaining to the history and present setting as well as to the future aspirations and needs of black America. This means that the work offered in the Department must run across the usual boundaries of the various disciplines, including studies in history, social science, literature, religion, the arts, and other aspects of the black experience.

To establish a Black Cultural Center that will provide the focus for preserving, developing and presenting the literary, graphic, and performing black arts.

To bring together students and faculty interested in studying the political, social, economic, intellectual, and aesthetic impact made by those of African descent on American society.

To evolve a solid series of academic offerings that will give students exposure to black culture not only in the United States context, but from non-United States traditions in South America, the West Indies, and Africa.

In the vast majority of the programs more space is given to a third category, the need to promote sympathetic interest and dedicated involvement in the improvement of the black community (local, national and world-wide), than to any other single concern. It seems that the intense passion for personal identity at the beginning of the thrust for Black Studies has been transformed into a passion for raising the *black awareness* level of the black community. The goal of the most ardent disciples of Black Studies, those who are satisfied with nothing less than a full major for themselves (most black students confine their involvement in the program to from one to two courses, which is also the case of a considerable number of white students), is to seek stronger ties of identification with the black ghetto than they previously possessed. Instead of planning to escape the ghetto as most of their predecessors have done, they are determined to tie their future success to all-out efforts for improvement of the quality of living in the black community. They demand that a reasonable portion of the college and university resources be allocated to community development in the local black ghettos. In cases where there are no local black communities, such as Dartmouth College in Hanover, New Hampshire, and the University of Montana in Missoula, black ghettos in other states and cities serve as their laboratories. In some instances programs require students to spend at least one semester at a black college in the South or in black Africa.

To provide for black undergraduate majors a comprehensive understanding of black culture and society in Africa and America that will enable them to provide service roles in their own communities.

To educate large numbers of minority youths who possess the will and the potential to become leading citizens within their own communities, to alleviate contemporary social and economic problems and, in so doing, to provide public benefit to our society at large.

To provide instructional and learning situations which will contribute to the task of meeting the Center's overall objectives:

   a. To provide the participants with a clear perception of the forces in our society and in the world which contribute to the oppression and underdevelopment of our communities;
   b. To make participants aware of the forces and resources available for ending conditions of oppression and underdevelopment;
   c. To generate well-planned and effective projects which will meet specific needs in our communities—all such projects will be oriented toward the development of black self-reliance;
   d. To utilize the facilities and technical services available.

To implement involvement at the national level. Thus arrangements will be made for some students to spend at least a semester at a predominantly black college in the South.

To provide services to the community and its organizations by jointly identifying and analyzing problems, offering consultation and establishing a channel into diverse resources of the university for the community.

To meet the needs of students who are seeking information concerning the backgrounds, life-styles, aspirations and potential of blacks and Puerto Ricans; who wish to develop their own ideologies and goals based on study of Third World peoples in the United States and elsewhere; who (as students in a prefigurative culture) wish to act in concert with so-called ghetto communities in achieving commuity goals.

To develop a sense of awareness of the areas where applied science can be used to improve the economic and social conditions of African peoples, a view which sees technology as the inner workings, the power which turns the wheels of society.

To provide students a firmer basis for service in the Afro-American community.

To offer the student the opportunity to supplement his classroom work with field activity which will take him into the community, whether it be local, national or international. For example, students in a Black Studies course may visit New York or Washington to do serious research on the problems and growth of black business, or North Carolina to work together with others involved in the building of Soul City, a new concept in town development.

To offer a growing orientation with regards to black community research and practical involvement. Accordingly, the program of the Department involves both the traditional approaches of study and analysis (within a critical and innovative framework), and the direct practical participation of the student within the structure of the black community.

To collect from a variety of sources information about the technical problems and environmental needs in black communities throughout the world.

To establish an institute which would bring together the growing black talent in the scientific fields; collect, analyze, and evaluate the wide range of technological and related information pertaining to Black communities; and provide specifications, as a result of these investigations, in courses and projects in curriculum areas for students from all parts of the African world.

To provide a comprehensive approach to the black experience and its intellectual formulation, calling for consideration not only of the black community in the U.S., but also of its relation, past, present, and future, to the experiences of the black people in other parts of the world, especially in Africa.

To educate citizens who will be committed to the solution of the grave problems in the U.S. and in the world, who will learn to analyze them objectively, and who will acquire the technical competence to cope with them.

To involve Afro-American Studies majors in research and creative work-study programs in black communities in the United States, the Caribbean and/or Africa as an integral part of the program.

The radical reformation of American education by attacking its basic racist assumptions and making it truly democratic and relevant to the current needs of blacks and whites is representative of another category under which many specific objectives may be classified. Of course, such a reform was long overdue according to the militant black youths who risked their very lives by physically assaulting the seemingly impregnable bastions of entrenched intellectual arrogance represented by a bureaucracy that had refused to even listen to the wisest of its own members who sought meaningful reform. Naturally, the inexperienced and unsophisticated students sometimes fought badly, occasionally overshooting the mark and thus providing greater leverage for the entrenched enemy, but they never surrendered. Although the main object of the battle has not been completely won, the bitter physical confrontations have ceased, and a new respect between the combatants has developed which lifts the conflict to higher levels. Many colleges and universities have admitted the falsity and immorality of the previous assumptions upon which their educational practices were based and are striving to atone for the failures of the past. It was within this framework that the following specific objectives were conceived and are being implemented:

To remedy the total indifference of the American system of education to the needs of black people.

To provide an opportunity to deal with subject matter which until recently has been seldom presented in college texts at all, or presented with biases which are supportive of the racism that the Kerner Report describes.

To correct the pathological racist behavior that is unconsciously built into our society.

To develop a curriculum based on the historical and cultural background of Afro-Americans and current issues in American society that are relevant to race.

To serve as an indispensable ally in the fight to preserve the nation's Constitution and the democratic principles for which it stands.

To reveal the personal and social consequences of racism and to prepare students for the work which will help destroy that aspect of American society.

To academically scrutinize the entire ethical and economic structure of the United States, exposing the gulf between the ideals of the Constitution and the actual practice of human equality and social justice, and most importantly, developing a portrait of black people that is free of inhuman stereotypes.

To assist students in acquiring the information and attitudes necessary for living and working effectively in a multi-racial environment.

To create an awareness of the need for greater emphasis on African and Afro-American materials in tutorials and other offerings in departments and universities.

To graduate students who can work efficiently and effectively, whether inside or outside the black community, for a just society, in an era of history which will be increasingly dominated by technology, and in which moral ambiguities and contradictions as well as social injustice will abound.

To create new educational processes more compatible with the life-styles of black people and more in tune with the social, political and economic aspirations of black people.

To prevent black education from becoming so chauvinistic in scope as to divorce itself from keeping abreast of what is going on in the white world: its technology, science, economics, and politics; in this same regard it must also be stressed that black education does not preclude the involvement of white students and/or faculty, but the nature and extent of such involvement must remain the prerogative of black people.

To provide access to Black Studies orientation toward subject matter so that as many white students as possible can be affected to the extent that the major reasons for white racism in this country, such as the misunderstanding of the black struggle, ignorance of the black heritage, and the consequent deprecation of black culture, may be counteracted by exposure to the facts of the black experience in an academic manner.

To provide for white undergraduate students an understanding of black culture that will help them promote greater understanding in the white community.

To provide students and faculty, both black and white, an opportunity to develop deeper appreciation and understanding of the contributions of black men and women to American culture, the varied problems of a multi-racial society, the social and psychological difficulties embodied in second-class citizenship, the pain and suffering endured by black Americans over decades of social and economic ostracism, and the effect of racism and racist institutions on America's growth and development.

To train black students in the philosophy and strategies of revolution as a prelude to black liberation is the aim of another category of objectives for Black Studies. However, "revolution" in this context is defined by Harold Cruse as follows:

> For the first time since the 1930's Americans of more than ordinary social insight are openly discussing the possibility of social revolution in the United States. We know that during the 1930's "revolution" implied the overthrow of capitalistic institutions—a real threat which the more enlightened wing of American bourgeois wealth successfully defeated by the implementation of the various New Deal policies. But unlike the 1930's, when it was reported that some of the idle rich were so fearful of revolution that they had their yachts readied in the harbor for a fast getaway just in case, the talk of revolution today has little to do with conflicts in labor-capital relations or the imminent collapse of the capitalistic system. It has to do with the present state of American race relations which some people (hopefully or fearfully) describe as the "Negro revolution."[1]

The Research Commission of the California Association for Afro-American Education has also commented on the revolutionary aspect of Black Studies programs by warning its institutional members not to attempt to build skills for community development and community survival "from a reactionary rather than a creative, Nation-Building perspective." After quoting Kwame Nkruma, the exiled former leader of Ghana, who said, "Revolution is a revolution against an old order," the Commission suggests that Black Studies must cease to offer what may be pure reactionary, "anti-white" programs and begin to place primary emphasis upon the "emerging social order."

To assess and to build on past and present theories of the black experience
and the strategies and tactics employed in the liberation of black people.

To provide black students with the skills, knowledge, and perspective
necessary to fashion a collective solution to the problems of Afro-Asians
everywhere.

To analyze the past and present political, economic, social, and psychological
conditions of black people in the United States, and to plan and develop
strategies for change in the political, economic, social and psychological
conditions of the black people in the United States.

To base black education on the principles of mutual respect, mutual sharing,
mutual work, mutual responsibility, and the collective endeavor of self-
determination.

To aid in building a nation of black people where people of color will be
united and accepting each other . . . a nation where empty rhetoric will not
be substituted for genuineness, where brothers and sisters can love one an
other for themselves, thus enabling each to contribute to the growth of the
other . . . a nation based on the foundation of power, liberation, and love.

To maximize the relationship between students and people in the community,
while keeping always in the foreground, our concern for the three basic aims
of the struggle (here and throughout the world): Independence, Separation,
and Nationhood.

The development of an African-American major degree program which will
provide the educational resources for the positive maintenance of a black
family, and the eventual building of a black nation.

To promote the development of the concept of Pan-Africanism and the
internalization of our African heritage. Realizing that we are an African
people, we are dedicating ourselves to liberation through Pan-Africanism. We
define Pan-Africanism as (a) black people defining themselves and (b) the
unifying acts of African people wherever they are.

Another category of objectives, which is seldom thought of by
persons who condemn Black Studies as leading into a blind alley,
concerns *preparation for career opportunities, including the professions.* Unfortunately, those who severely criticize the general
concept of Black Studies as a viable educational discipline do not
seem to know that a very small percentage of black students at any
college or university is interested in a major in the field. The question
"What can a student do with a major in Black Studies?" is no more
relevant or reasonable than a similar query about a major in
philosophy. In either case the student so equipped can enter graduate
school or technical institutions for training for a career of his choice,
or he can enter a professional school of law, medicine, dentistry, religion, social work, and so on. At least eighty-five percent of all of the

programs I have observed require students specializing in Black Studies simultaneously to earn a major, concentration, or minor in another discipline as a requirement for the baccalaureate degree. Thus a student with a Black Studies major is better equipped for job competition than one with a major in some other discipline which does not require a second specialty.

Furthermore if a graduate with such a major chooses to teach in the field, there are more than enough vacancies now waiting to be filled by qualified applicants. In fact, on the basis of current indicators more than ten years will be required to fill the present gap between supply and demand.

> To provide training for students who intend to do graduate work in Black Studies or allied areas in the social sciences, humanities, and arts.
>
> To provide preparation for students planning careers in community service.
>
> To provide meaningful humane study-experiences which in themselves might serve as a career or complement the professions in the fields of sociology, psychology, social work, politics, economics, education, and law.
>
> To prepare the student for further academic study or to enter a vocation upon graduation.

The final category of objectives offers evidence to refute the contention of critics that Black Studies programs are designed to offer black students shallow, anti-intellectual courses. Although the unfavorable criticism cannot be dismissed, no one can truthfully deny that the best of these programs is as rigorously intellectual and scholarly as the average program in its particular college or university. The quality and tone of instruction are usually set by the director. Teachers who do not agree with the director's philosophy do not remain long in the program, and directors who are not in sympathy with the intellectual requirements of the college or university administration and/or majority of the teachers in the program soon resign or are fired. The rapid turnover in positions of leadership in Black Studies programs is the most serious weakness. Despite the fact that most directors say the most undesirable tendency they have to combat is that of some of their students to insist upon the right to monopolize class sessions with "rapping" rather than informed discussion based on hard and systematic study, it is encouraging to note that many of the programs include among their major objectives the determination *to encourage and actively develop intellectual growth and broad scholarly interests in their students.*

> To legitimize and intellectualize the black experience through scholarly study and research.

To provide a broad, multidisciplinary liberal education—whereby "liberal education" means the traditional academic concept of freeing or liberating students from the parochialism which may limit their potential contributions to self and society—in much the same manner and intent as any baccalaureate program in the liberal arts or humanities proposes to do. This objective is therefore related to the historic purpose of higher education, preparing free men to live and function critically, creatively, and responsibly in a free society.

To provide scholarly correction of the historical and cultural myths about blacks.

To provide a good general education that will equip students with the basic tools of academic inquiry, a command of the substantive knowledge of various fields of systematic study, and a broad general awareness of human issues, values, and their interrelations.

To further research and teaching in the area of black culture and to encourage increased faculty and student involvement.

To institute and develop a high-quality program of teaching and research in the area of Black Studies.

To provide a foundation for in-depth research by future scholars in the social sciences and humanities.

To create a center for research as well as scholarship, providing the atmosphere and resources for established professionals to expand their knowledge and sophistication.

To provide the student with a valid and intellectually rigorous exposure to the study of the Afro-American experiences in the world, and, to a lesser extent, the linkage between those experiences and their antecedents of the African continent.

To promote traditional approaches of study and analysis, as well as to directly involve the student in research into the structure of the black community.

The California Association for Afro-American Education, in its 1970 report on Black Studies programs in institutions of higher learning in the state, includes the following summary statement concerning "Research, Scholarship, and Development of Intellectual Skills" in seventy-two state colleges and universities:

> Contrary to the belief of many academicians, several academic proposals highlight research, scholarship, and the development of intellectual skills as major purposes. These proposals together discuss five priority areas: (1) "comprehensive analysis of the historical and contemporary Black experience;" (2) intensive analysis and re-evaluation of research (basic and applied) conducted by white researchers; (3) internal evaluation of Black Studies Programs; (4) establishment of Black standards of value and achievement; and (5) development of "respect for intellectual approaches and achievement."
> These proposals stress the importance of reviewing and re-evaluating existing data on the Black experience and the searching out of new data in

unexplored academic domains. Among other things, they emphasize providing skills for the assembly, examination, and evaluation of data relevant to historical and contemporary Black existence. They also stress analyzing contemporary political, economic, and social policies which influence Black existence and which establish guidelines that virtually control the lives of Black people. Almost all focus upon the analysis of Black life-styles from a Black intellectual perspective and call for a rigorous evaluation of prevalent theories about Black social institutions, attitudes, values, behaviors, and life-styles.

Several institutions consider particularly important an on-going internal evaluation for purposes of developing new approaches to teaching Black Studies, developing appropriate materials, "experimenting with the meaning of Black Studies for the Black community," and training Black Studies scholars. Another thrust is the stimulation of research oriented towards the establishment of Black standards of values and achievement. (One institution, for example, is giving attention to survival techniques among African-Americans). A few institutions are attempting to develop a "respect for intellectual approaches and achievement," to provide examples of "competence, integrity, and intellectual honesty," and to thwart what may be a pattern of anti-intellectualism among Black Students.[2]

6
Organizational Patterns

There are three major organizational patterns, with some variations, that characterize most Black Studies programs. The interdisciplinary pattern usually requires that the director, coordinator, or chairman of the Black Studies Committee be responsible for the administration of the program with the provision that regular departments of the college will cooperate in supplying qualified faculty members in their fields to offer the approved courses. When new teachers are needed, they are recommended to the chairman of the appropriate department by the program director and a joint appointment is made, with the teacher's tenure to be established in the department of his major specialization. One variation is the provision in some instances for a new teacher whose teaching load is entirely in core courses required for the Black Studies concentration to be responsible solely to the Black Studies Committee rather than to the department of his professional major.

Approximately 75 percent of all programs operate basically in accordance with the plan described above. One argument in its favor concerns the facilitation of recruiting competent faculty members. Although young inexperienced teachers who are not troubled by the lack of guaranteed tenure or the temporary nature of a prospective position might be attracted by an appointment not anchored in an established department, most directors of Black Studies programs testify that the most desired faculty prospects for such positions refuse to consider appointment without assurance that if their services are mutually satisfactory there will be no reason to doubt the eventual attainment of tenure at the institution. I have talked with a number of professors exceptionally qualified as teachers of Afro-American literature who have refused appointments in departments of Black Studies because of the problem of insecure or nonexistent tenure, but have accepted appointments in interdisciplinary programs with tenure in the English department.

The counter argument to this point of view is that divided loyalty which results from teaching in such a program can weaken the authority of the Black Studies director to the point of ineffectuality. It can be argued that any new program, which is by nature controversial, has a better chance of successful survival if the director has firm authority to hire, fire, and supervise (with, of course, the necessary safeguards against abuse of power) the teachers assigned to the program. I have talked with some directors who have complained bitterly of the handicaps of divided authority for them and divided allegiance of their teachers. Consequently, some directors advocate an interdisciplinary approach with the right of the director and his Black Studies Committee of faculty and black students to hire and fire teachers participating in the program.

Another argument in favor of the interdisciplinary approach is that it is the most logical way to force students and teachers to see Black Studies as an integral part of the whole educational process. It insists that an acceptable college curriculum must provide for the inclusion of the black experience in every course that can legitimately include it, either by integrating it into the subject matter of the basic course or by organizing a separate course as a supplement or an alternative. Some directors believe that unless this approach is adopted individual departments will feel no pressure to participate in an institutional effort to reorganize as many of their courses as possible to reflect appropriate racial and minority awareness effectively.

Several directors suggest that even though independent departments of Black Studies should be the ultimate goal, the interdisciplinary pattern should be used until the idea has been largely accepted by the institution. They argue that programs in American Studies have been accepted by most college administrations and faculties as a viable concept which evokes very little controversy; consequently, a Black Studies program organized on such a basis would be likely to profit by the comparison. However, at least one experienced director insists that in the beginning independence should be the guiding principle. Once the curriculum is established and accepted by the administration and faculty as a regular part of the educational program, the interdisciplinary pattern can be established without as much chance for sabotage by other departments.

Opponents of the interdisciplinary approach agree that teachers in the program are continually at the mercy of hostile administrators for evaluation of their performance—an evaluation for which these administrators have neither the special knowledge or sympathetic understanding as valid bases for judgment. If teachers need special training in and appreciation of ethnic history and culture as a basis for employment, why should administrators without these qualifications be capable of evaluating their performance?

The independent or semiautonomous department is preferred by more than thirty percent of all current directors, although less than twenty-five percent of current programs are organized in this manner. One proponent suggests that such an organization "gives focus, thrust, and a sense of duration, while minimizing problems of coordination." Another proponent suggests that an independent department "facilitates the hiring of competent teachers without adhering to rigid, unrealistic requirements in respect to academic degrees." But many critics regard this latter contention as a major argument against departmental status. They complain that the "lowering" of academic qualifications for teachers and directors is detrimental to the prestige of the program and encourages the widespread belief that the entire thrust of the movement is anti-academic and therefore does not deserve equal status with other departments. These critics insist that departmental status encourages undue emphasis on ideological goals inimical to rigorous scholarship, which would be minimized by the interdisciplinary approach. They assert that although some autonomous departments have achieved a high quality of performance, there is still a larger percentage of inferior programs with departmental status than any other organizational category. It is even suggested that some universities have acquiesced in the establishment of autonomous Black Studies departments in the hope that scholarship and the quality of instruction will prove to be so far below the normal standard of the university that evaluative reports by outside agencies will justify the withdrawal of financial support entirely.

For some the most convincing argument for department status is the fact that such an organizational pattern signifies that the college or university recognizes Black Studies as a legitimate academic field that deserves the same rights and privileges as any other academic department. Those who use this argument consider it to be an overriding consideration. They believe that anyone who denies the validity of the basic demand is either skeptical of the ability of black people to direct their own lives responsibly or has been so brainwashed by white society that he can accept as genuine and appropriate only white values and white standards.

An interesting variation of this pattern is the Institute of Afro-American Affairs at New York University, an autonomous structure within the university that coordinates a wide variety of courses for college credit which are offered through regular divisions and departments of the university. Although the director admits that an autonomous institute functioning in cooperation with the various colleges presents some problems in logistics, he is satisfied that this interdisciplinary endeavor creates a climate that makes possible a high quality of achievement. A major element of the program is the establishment of several joint professorships between the institute and various departments in the schools and colleges of the university. The decision as to who will hold these chairs is made by a mutual agreement between the institute and the faculty of the appropriate schools. Other faculty members may be appointed directly to the institute. This means that the permanent members of the university faculty concerned with Black Studies are those with joint appointments and those appointed directly to the institute.

Another pattern of organizing and administering a Black Studies program is through a semiautonomous school with the same privileges and responsibilities of other such units in a university, municipal, or state system. We shall briefly examine some of the problems and possibilities of two major examples of this type of organization.

On August 2, 1971, *Newsweek* published a feature article entitled "Monument to Blackness." The first two paragraphs contained the following graphic description of Malcolm X College, a new educational concept in relation to the vast possibilities of the meaning and goals of Black Studies programs in American higher education:

In full view of thousands of commuters who daily navigate the busy Eisenhower Expressway, an enormous rectangle of steel and glass towers incongruously over the dilapidated buildings of Chicago's teeming West Side ghetto. Sprawled massively across three full city blocks, the gleaming edifice looks for all the world like the misplaced headquarters of a booming insurance company. But from high atop a flagpole defiantly flutters the red, black and green pennant of the black liberation movement. And before the building's main entrance, an indestructible concrete and steel sign boldly serves notice that this ultramodernistic monument to blackness is the home of Malcolm X Community College, probably the most innovative educational institution for Negroes in the U.S. today.

Every corner, cranny and corridor of Malcolm X bespeaks the school's emphasis on black awareness and pride. Within one glass-walled hallway rests the shiny black Oldsmobile that once belonged to Malcolm himself, and student portraits of the murdered black leader hang throughout the airy halls and plushly decorated offices. Indeed, the entire four-story building is a vast repository of black art, and many of its Afro-haired inhabitants regularly sport colorful dashikis and resplendent African robes.

A visit to the campus on October 28, 1971 confirmed the accuracy of *Newsweek's* description. From the moment I entered the huge hall bathed in sunlight from the unbroken line of windows extending almost the full length of the building until I closed the heavy doors behind me as I left four hours later, I was continually aware of a new kind of educational experience. Upon entry a courteous young security guard seated at a table with a walkie talkie before him requested my name, my business, and the possible duration of my visit. He then directed me to the far end of the hall where another young security guard further interrogated me and cleared me for entrance to the office of the president's secretary. When I asked the reasons for such tight security, I was told that it was necessary to protect the students from dope pushers, enemies of the school seeking to create internal disturbances, and process servers looking for suspected criminals. I learned later that the college offers counseling advice to students who have run afoul of the law and has been successful in saving many students from the grip of unscrupulous lawyers and ruthless bondsmen.

Until 1969, Malcolm X College was known as Crane College, the oldest two-year college in Chicago. After World War II it was abandoned by its predominantly Jewish clientele who moved from the West Side to surburbia, leaving it to black newcomers, many of them from the rural South. When Dr. Charles Hurst became president in 1969, his first important act was to re-name it Malcolm X despite bitter objection from the Chicago Junior College Board. It moved into its $26,000,000 new home recently. College promotional announcements now declare: "Malcolm X College is named after a man who has become for black youth the greatest hero of modern times. . . . [His] goal was freedom for oppressed people. When he said 'by any means necessary' he meant he believed in any means necessary to correct unjust conditions—political, economic, social, and physical—as long as it is intelligently directed and designed to get results. . . .The college is named after this great man, and the college operates within the framework of the ideal expressed in one of his most famous quotations. . . 'Education is an important element in the struggle for human rights. It is the means to help our children and people to rediscover their identity and thereby increase self-respect. Education is our passport to the future, for tomorrow belongs to the people who prepare for it today."

I have cited the information about the naming of the college to substantiate the fact that despite the lack of its official designation as a school of Black Studies by the Chicago Junior College Board, it is regarded as such by the president, the faculty, the students, and the community. If further proof is needed, consider the comment by President Hurst quoted in *The Christian Science Monitor* (May 7, 1971): "We had to create an image of the ability of black people to develop and administer an institution. Our faculty is now around 65 percent black and heading very rapidly toward 80 percent. The administration is 85 percent black and will probably stay right about there. I would say this, it's 100 percent black in thinking and ideology." Among the 6,000 students only a few white faces can be occasionally glimpsed in a sea of black.

Promotional announcements state the creed of the college as follows:

(1) Unity—in the family, community, nation, and race.
(2) Self-Determination—to define ourselves, instead of being defined by others.
(3) Collective Work and Responsibility—to build and maintain our community together.
(4) Cooperative Economics—to build and maintain our own stores and shops and to profit together from them.
(5) Creativity.
(6) Faith—to believe with all our heart in our parents, our teachers, our leaders, our people and the righteousness of our struggle.

Further statements of institutional policy insist that although it does not discriminate on the basis of color, "Malcolm X College is a black institution—one in which educational services are designed to serve in a unique way the goals of black people. College programs are designed to promote the black agenda—to prepare our young people to play dynamic and constructive parts in the development of a society in which progress is measured in terms of human well-being.

Our kind of college, with a black-oriented curriculum and philosophy, is in a unique position to deal both with the ills of our society and the human consequences of its derelictions."

The advantages and disadvantages of the autonomous organizational pattern of Malcolm X College, which is followed to a lesser degree in a few other institutions, naturally depend upon its ability to promote or thwart the implementation of the stated goals, provided the evaluator accepts such goals as desirable. Probably the best method of arriving at a judgment is to examine some of the specifics of this program which could not be attempted under the previous patterns we have discussed.

The proponents of the Malcolm X program cite as innovative and significant the following services:

(1) "The only "week-end college program" in the nation which permits students of all ages who cannot attend classes during the week to earn an A.A. degree by attending classes only on week-ends. During the fall of 1971 classes were held eight hours each Saturday and Sunday with an enrollment of more than 800. This service is intended as an accomodation to lifestyles of many black urban dwellers.

(2) A college program for parolees that provides financial assistance through work-study and other arrangements.

(3) College programs for prisoners by mail and also direct contact.

(4) An assistance program for drug addicts with expert counseling available.

(5) A "street academy" for high school dropouts.

(6) An organized community recreation program two nights a week in college facilities.

Of course, Malcolm X is a two-year college and cannot be judged by the standards of four-year institutions. However, several of its programs are unique for two-year community colleges and are tailored primarily to the needs of the black community. It is the only college in the country that does not limit registration to a particular time period; a student can officially register and begin classes at any time during the calendar year. No failing grades are given: The grade of R (incomplete) is given to students who need more time to achieve the required objectives of the course. The college offers a two-year academic program to those who later wish to earn a bachelor's degree at a four-year college, and a variety of vocational curricula to train for careers in business and paraprofessional health services. Harvey Badesch, the white dean of the school's community-services program, confides, "I believe we're more representative of the American dream than any other college in the U.S."

But black educators in Chicago who have observed "from afar" the operations of Malcolm X College have mixed reactions. Although all admit that the programs are innovative, some discount the genuine educational value of the innovations, claiming that they represent acts of self-serving showmanship rather than educational statesmanship. Many charge the president with flaunting democracy in his desire to build a monument to his own ego. They say he demands of his faculty and administrative personnel unqualified and unreasonable loyalty to his own concept of inferior education for blacks which the white establishment is glad to approve despite its accompanying anti-establishment rhetoric of black nationalism. Thus, according to this appraisal, the spirit of free inquiry and healthy criticism is discouraged.

On the contrary, some educators and a much larger percentage of nonprofessional members of the black community consider the college program to be more relevant for blacks than any other they know or have heard about. They point to the "strong" uncompromising leadership of the president as an asset to the black community. They maintain that the president's political clout disarms white enemies and forces the city fathers to give the college a proportionally larger budget than any other municipal college receives. They claim that no other college in the city has been transformed so rapidly (in less than three years) from the most run-down, dilapidated physical plant to the most modern and impressive at a cost to the taxpayers of $26,000,000. They point to the president's ability to maneuver "uncooperative" white teachers against their will and the objections of union officials from Malcolm X to other college faculties with the approval of the Board of Education of Junior Colleges.

As to college morale of students and teachers, proponents of the program cite the fierce pride and virtual rage for personal decorum, institutional order and cleanliness, and mutual helpfulness which characterize students and faculty alike. These partisans are impressed by the fact that all male faculty members and the great majority of male students wear ties and pressed suits or dashikis every day rather than rumpled blue jeans and soiled open-collar shirts which are the hallmarks of their black and white counterparts in other colleges and universities. They praise the studious atmosphere within and outside the mammoth building where no posted signs are necessary to prevent loitering.

To all criticism, favorable and unfavorable, the president points to a letter in his possession, dated August 11, 1971, which announces: "It is a pleasure to inform you officially that the North Central Association of Colleges and Secondary Schools, at its meeting on July 30, voted to continue the accreditation of Malcolm X College as an Associate's degree-granting institution, and to remove the institution from private probation." Then, adding his own comments, the president calmly states: "Now that we've started building a black institution, nothing's going to get in our way."

In 1971 an article entitled "San Diego Third College Seen Threat" appeared in the well-known syndicated column *Inside Report* by Rowland Evans and Robert Novak. The first two sentences of the article, which set the tone for a curious mixture of unfounded assertions and biased opinion, stated the thesis as follows: "On the peaceful, sun-washed San Diego campus of the University of California is evidence that there were worse, though less obvious, threats to higher education than a rock through the window or a building in flames. The threat here, hidden behind the character-istically languid surface of today's American campus, is the fledging Third College—a new semiautonomous institution designed to give Negro and Mexican-American students a special break."

California leads all other states in its determination to incorporate ethnic studies into the curricula of all colleges and universities within its domain. Every state insitution of higher education either has an organized program in each of the major ethnic cultures or a series of individual courses in each culture. During 1971 the State Board of Community Colleges ordered all institutions under its jurisdiction to establish such programs in Black Studies without delay.

All of the programs in the state institutions except one are organized in accordance with the interdisciplinary or departmental patterns. The one exception is the semiautonomous Third College, referred to in the opening quotation from Evans and Novak, which is a part of the University of San Diego. Although Third College is not officially designated as a school of Black Studies, like Malcolm X College, it is unofficially considered as such by the black and white public, since it has been agreed that for the foreseeable future the largest one of its ethnic components shall consist of blacks. At present the provost is black, as well as 50% of the students and 50%

of the teaching faculty and administrative personnel. The other 50% of the student population is divided among Mexican-Americans, American Indians, Asian-Americans, and white Americans.

The San Diego campus of the University of California will eventually comprise twelve interrelated colleges, separate but cooperative, each with a student body of approximately 2,300 students. At present only three of these proposed colleges are in operation —Revelle College, John Muir College, and Third College—each with its own faculties, administration, buildings, and laboratories, and *each with its own graduation requirements.*

The Third College accepted its first students in the fall of 1970. It was the intention of the student and faculty planners that its central thrust be the education of minority students and the study and alleviation of social problems. It was also the intention that its life-style and character encourage the maintenance of the student's ties to his nonacademic community. The core of the curriculum emphasizes the studies of the peoples which make up the racial minorities of the United States, as well as the Third World experience in the context of economic, social, and political phenomena with the aim of giving the student both a local and international perspective. The college offers interdisciplinary majors in Urban and Rural Studies, Third World Studies, Communications, and the physical sciences with a concentration on the health sciences and pre-medical studies. Traditional majors are also offered with an orientation toward those areas which are of particular significance to minorities and to urban and developing societies.

The three colleges differ not so much in subject matter taught as in their philosophical approach to education. One major difference lies in the nature of the breadth requirements (or general education requirements) developed to meet the graduation requirements of each college. These courses are usually open only to students in the particular college in which they are taught. Although a student may take courses in a college other than that in which he is enrolled, he must meet his college's breadth requirements for graduation. These requirements for the Third College are three 4-unit courses in each of the following: *Third World Studies* (ethnic cultures), *Communications* (speaking, reading, and writing), *Urban and Rural Development* (exploration of the dimensions of the moral, economic and social crisis, with efforts to provide intellectual tools necessary for coping with specific problem areas); four 4-unit courses in *Science and Technology* (introduction to modern biological and physical sciences with laboratory demonstrations); and two 4-unit courses in *Mathematics*. A total of 180 credit units are necessary for the A.B. degree.

For a major in Third World Studies the student must concentrate in one of the following areas: Black Studies, Chicano (Mexican-American) Studies, Latin America, Africa, Asia, American Indian, or comparative Third World History and Institutions. Seven Third World courses are necessary in addition to the first and second year breadth requirements. It is expected that most students in the Third World major program will do field work in their particular geographical area. In addition a junior-senior thesis in the area of concentration is required.

Third College has been severely censured by white critics from its inception. Prior to its scheduled opening date, a California assemblyman labeled it a "wild and wooly experiment in racism," insisting that its courses range "from straight Mickey Mouse to thinly veiled racism, with a smattering of legitimate courses thrown in." The 1971-72 Bulletin of the University of San Diego offers this description of the Third College academic program, along with information about the programs of the two other colleges:

> The academic plan of the Third College gives particular emphasis to the special problems of racial and ethnic minorities in present-day American society and to the very difficult questions posed in contemporary higher education by the commitment to grapple with these problems rather than to stand aloof from them. It should be observed that in addition to stressing the acquisition of skills, courses in the lower division general education program of Third College would draw heavily upon library resources and historical materials not often studied in existing college curricula. It is believed that these courses will prove attractive to students outside Third College [scholarly American whites] as well as to those in it since many students on the campus are eager to comprehend the pluralistic society which characterizes America in this decade.

In this official description by responsible officials of the university there is no hint of a "wild and wooly experiment in racism" nor of any "straight Mickey Mouse" course. Furthermore the official list of subjects to be taught in 1971-72, published by the college, contains no hint to substantiate the assemblyman's charge. It may be that the semiautonomous nature of the Third College under black leadership invites such false charges that interdisciplinary or departmental status subject to overall white control would not provoke.

Likewise the same reason might be applicable to the charge by Evans and Novak in the article referred to earlier, that it is "not surprising political conservatives most abhor the Third College as an alleged training ground for revolution. For example, *Third World,* a university-subsidized student publication, demands the release of Angela Davis and exhorts students to 'attend the revolutionary meeting of your choice.' " In my visits to campuses from Maine to California I have seen dozens of student publications subsidized by white-oriented colleges and universities whose angry protests against the Angela Davis case make the *Third World's* comment sound like baby talk. But there was no attempt to condemn the institution as a "training ground for revolution."

But Evans and Novak suggest, "The heart of the problem is admission of black and brown students to the Third World College who do not qualify under strict standards applying to the rest of the University of California." This charge reveals either monumental ignorance of the new admission policies of white-oriented universities or a determination to condemn a black-governed semiautonomous college for doing exactly what hundreds of American colleges and universities are doing from Maine to California. It is indeed difficult to find a college or university in this nation that will admit that it does not lower its previously unrealistic admission standards to admit more black students to all of its academic programs.

Unlike Malcolm X College, located in the heart of Chicago's West Side teeming with multitudes of prospective black students, Third College is situated in La Jolla, a nonblack suburb of San Diego, with a nonglamorous campus of temporary frame buildings for offices and classrooms. Consequently, recruitment of minority students is difficult. Harlem-born Provost Joseph W. Watson admits that freshman enrollment during the second year of operation fell short of the allotted quota.

Although most of the published criticism against Third College emanates from whites, some blacks have expressed displeasure at the inferior buildings and facilities of the college compared to the beauty and elegance of the two adjoining campuses. They complain that it is a glaring example of "separate and unequal," a condition which black people should no longer tolerate. Some traditional black scholars, as well as white critics, while admitting that students should have an opportunity to participate in the formulation of policies by which they are governed, deplore the extent to which the provost shares his administrative powers with students. Third College is governed by a Board of Governors composed of three students, each elected by his ethnic group, and three faculty members including the provost. All decisions require consensus rather than majority vote. To criticism of this policy the provost replies that relevant education must prepare students for a meaningful role in a democratic society.

7
Basic Course Offerings and Essential Rationale

Although there are hundreds of different courses offered in the total aggregation of Black Studies programs examined in this study, there are only fifteen basic offerings according to departmental classification. For example, for the basic course classified departmentally as black literature there may be more than a dozen varieties offered by one program: Survey of Afro-American Literature, African and Afro-American Folklore, The Afro-American Novel, The Harlem Renaissance, Richard Wright, Black Essayists, New Black Poetry, Afro-American Drama, The African Novel, African Drama, The Literature of Afro-American Blacks, Fiction by Black American Women, etc. The fifteen basic courses listed in the order of their preponderance percentagewise are history, 20.5%; sociology, 19.3%; literature, 16.6%; political science, 11.9%; anthropology, 6.2%; art 5.2%; psychology, 4%; music, 3.5%; economics, 3.4%; African languages, 2.8%; speech:rhetoric, 2%; religion, 1.8%; geography, 1.3%; philosophy, 0.9%; mass media, 0.5%; others, 0.5%. It can be seen from this tabulation that the three most popular courses which account for 56.4% of the total offerings are history, sociology, and literature. Approximately two-thirds of the offerings are in the area of the social sciences, with the remainder in the humanities except such odd listings as Social Biology of Blacks and Black Cosmology and Aesthetics.

Since history and literature, which account for approximately a third of the offerings, are subject to misunderstanding and biased interpretations by nonblack teachers and students and consequently provoke more controversy than any of the other courses offered, I shall consider some of the problems involved in the teaching of each.

79

Black History

Despite the constant pressure since 1968 on officials of American schools and colleges to establish adequate programs in black history, the public still has not accepted the urgency of the demand. In September, 1970, a letter to the Editor appeared in the *Baltimore Sun* condemning the Baltimore School Board for wasting the taxpayer's money by allocating $250,000 to the initiation and support of an experimental program in the subject. The female correspondent wrote as follows:

> Sir: How can we possibly believe there is a wolf at the door of our financially embarrassed public school system, when the School Board allocates $250,000 for a disputed black history program, sight unseen and cost unknown? How chilling it is for the despoiled providers of public funds to see signs of another social experiment in the boondoggle area!
>
> It seems to the mystified bystander who comes in contact with living proof of the present inadequacy of public school education that there is little hope for the future when a confused School Board is unable to distinguish between essentials and non-essentials—a fatal weakness when funds are really short.
>
> Social and political experiments are costly in any field but especially so when substituted for improved public school education. A more realistic examination of values might divert some of that unbudgeted $250,000 to more productive channels.
>
> Is there any reason for an optional black history course—not program —exclusive of political and social frills, to cost more than the actual price of necessary text books?

Answers to such letters as the foregoing are contained in a brochure published by the Urban Education Corps of the New Jersey Department of Education which lists thoughtful answers to a number of questions pertinent to the subject. I am reproducing eight of the questions and answers which were prepared by Robert F. Engs and Frank M. Updike, departmental consultants.

Why should black history be taught in the schools?
The experience of black Americans is a legitimate and necessary part of the American past. That it has been ignored in the past was due to the widespread feeling that the Negro had no history worth mentioning and an equally widespread reluctance to confront the negative elements in American history.

What value does black history have for the black student?
Teaching black history in the school demonstrates to the black student that his experience, problems, and past are an important part of learning in the school. It may, therefore, improve his attitude toward the school. More importantly, by giving him greater knowledge of himself, his people and his

past, he will gain greater self-respect and self-esteem.

What value does black history have for the white student?

The study of black history, for the white student, builds a greater knowledge and awareness of black people and their role in the growth and development of this country. It is one of the first steps in creating empathy and bridging the gap between black and white young people. Moreover, both white and black students can make more intelligent choices about the causes and solutions of racial conflict if they know the background of such conflict.

What should be the content of units on black history?

The contents of a unit on black history should include, at minimum, discussion of African past and the slave trade, slavery, emancipation and reconstruction including such aspects as the Negro's role as a soldier, the period of political disfranchisement and the great debate between Booker Washington and W. E. B. DuBois, the migration to the North, and early civil rights movements (1954-63), current urban problems, and the debate between nationalists and integrationists. It cannot be stressed too strongly that black history should not become a mere recitation of black accomplishments and heroes, as is so often the case now with the teaching of American history. Black history serves no purpose if it leads to misplaced pride in oversimplified heroes rather than to a more sophisticated understanding of American race relations and race prejudice.

What materials are available on black history and how can the teacher make intelligent choices among them?

The materials on black history are now almost overwhelming in volume. Unfortunately, many of these materials are seriously deficient in quality. They tend to avoid conflict and to promote mythical figures rather than deal with issues. Several selective bibliographies are available or in progress. The New Jersey State Library and the Schomburg collection at the New York Public Library can supply many of these. The most effective materials are those prepared by teachers or by teachers and students together. The experiences of students often supply the content on which excellent studies of black history can be based. In addition, the local community often can provide unexpected sources.

Should black history be integrated into the regular history program or taught separately?

The content of black history is highly emotional. Ideally it should be taught in conjunction with other history topics. Unfortunately, the tendency of most history instruction in the schools is to avoid the conflict and emotion implicit in all history. The student can gain no intelligent understanding of any history, but particularly of black history, in such circumstances. Where the inclusion of black history accompanies a general revision of the history curriculum with the aim of increased relevance and utility to the students, then black history can be easily incorporated. In other situations, teaching black history separately is wiser and more effective.

Who should teach black history?

Selection of the teacher for black history is essentially a pragmatic decision based on the peculiar circumstances of each school. In entirely black ghetto schools, a black teacher, for obvious tactical reasons, is preferable. In other situations the criteria for selection should not be based on race. Rather, the essential ingredients are: (1) sufficient knowledge of black history to offer a course designed to meet the needs of the students and to counter the mythologizing that surrounds so much discussion on black history these days, and (2) a skilled and sensitive teacher able to handle the volatile situations which discussion of race creates.

Won't use of controversial topics and subject matter make black students more alienated and angry?

The introduction of controversial topics and subject matter in the schools will naturally bring with it open admission of feelings which are presently excluded from the school situation. It is important to remember that such feelings exist in the student in any case. If the student's only source of information and only forum for discussion are the streets, his understanding will be seriously distorted. It is the responsibility of the school to help the student deal with issues of race in intellectually rigorous and valid ways. While this does not guarantee that students, especially black students, will not remain angry, it does provide a chance that they will make thoughtful, reasoned decisions and actions.

C. Van Woodward, a native of Vandale, Arkansas, and professor of history at Yale University, says:

All who write or teach American history are aware by now of the demand for more attention to the part that Negro people have played. It may come quietly from a distressed college dean, or it may come peremptorily and noisily from militant student protest. In any case the demand is insistent that we move over and make room. With whatever grace they can muster and whatever resources they command, historians as teachers are responding one way or another. New colleagues are recruited (black if humanly possible), new courses listed ("Black" or "Afro" in the title), new textbooks written, new lectures prepared. Or in a pinch, old colleagues may have to be pressured and reconditioned and old lectures hastily revised. The adjustment is often awkward and sometimes rather frantic, but American academic institutions are responding, each after its own style and fashion—clumsily, belatedly, heartily, or half-heartedly, as the case may be.[3]

American history, the white man's version, could profit from an infusion of "soul." It could be an essential corrective in line with the tradition of countervailing forces in American historiography. It was in that tradition that new immigrant historians revised first-family and old-stock history, that Jewish scholars challenged WASP interpretations, that Western challengers confronted New England complacencies, Yankee heretics upset Southern orthodoxies, Southern skeptics attacked Yankee myths, and the younger generation since the beginning assaulted the authority of the old. Negro historians have an opportunity and a duty in the same tradition.[4]

In an article entitled "What the Historian Owes the Negro" originally published in the *Saturday Review*, Benjamin Quarles calls attention to certain facts and implications that all teachers and students of history, especially black history, should understand and constantly remember. The following excerpts are presented with the author's permission:

> Much of history is interpretation. Its most trusted interpreter is, of course, the professionally trained historian, his name trailed by clusters of letters. Guardian of the sacred word, he knows that he is expected to bring an objective intelligence to his work—to winnow and sift sensitively and then to relate what it was that actually happened. This is a tall order. For despite his professional training, the historian's own values and beliefs are likely to be intrusive. His own social outlook may give a "personal equation" to his reconstruction of the past. This tendency, however natural, poses a real problem. One who works from what Oliver Wendell Holmes called an "inarticulate major premise" may well wind up with something less than the whole truth. History then becomes image-making with footnotes, its brush strokes blurred by what logicians call the fallacy of initial prediction.
>
> Such historical introspection has inevitably worked to the detriment of the various minority groups in America—the Asiatics, the Spanish-speaking peoples, and immigrants from southern Europe—all of whom have been treated as "out-groups." Negroes, especially, have been the objects of this narrow-mindedness on the part of historians. Speaking in 1840, Henry Highland Garnet, then beginning a long career as a militant clergyman, clearly stated the problem: "All other races are permitted to travel over the wide fields of history and pluck the flowers that blossom there—to glean up heroes, philosophers, sages, and poets, and put them into a galaxy of brilliant genius; but if a black man attempts to do so, he is met at the threshold by the objection: 'You have no ancestry behind you.' "
>
> A researcher is often engaged in a subconscious mission, his conclusions already lodged in the back of his head. He has, in Herbert Butterfield's words, "a magnet in his mind," one that impels him to extract from the documents such data as fits into a framework already fashioned. When, as he combs the sources, this researcher comes across a reference to Negroes, he turns the page as though it were blank. When one goes fishing for facts, writes historian Edward Hallett Carr, what he catches will depend partly on chance, but primarily upon other factors, such as "the part of the ocean he chooses to fish in," the kind of tackle he selects, and the kind of fish he wants to catch. And, to take Carr's figure a step further, an unwanted specimen is likely to be quickly thrown back into the water.
>
> As often as not this mind-set of the historian takes the form of glorifying his own. Historians are not immune to ancestor worship. To puff up one's own ethnic group is not the exclusive province of a Hitler (whose favorite subject was history). As practitioners of the dictum, "Be to her faults a little blind,/ Be to her virtues very kind," historians tend to reflect rather than to correct the group mores. This ethnocentric attitude has had serious implications for the Negro. Since American history has been written, in the main, by men of old English stock, the role of the Negro could hardly come in for a rounded appraisal. Such a historian felt no kinship with the colored

people, no identity. To glorify one's own is certainly no sin, but in a many-faceted culture such as America's this in-group emphasis may amount to a denigration of other component population elements. . . .

An almost complementary refrain to group glorification has been the historian's tendency to take his cue from the civilization or culture that is currently dominant. For the past five centuries the dominant peoples and nations have been of Germanic-tribes origin and have been located in Europe. Nobody can touch the historian for hindsight—he knows to begin with "where the bodies are buried." He knows that for half a millennium the nations of Western Europe were destined to predominate. Thus, it is natural for him to have a Europocentric view of the modern world, to believe that non-Western cultures were below par if not permanently inferior. Less blatantly, but no less surely, writers of history have shared Tennyson's belief, "Better fifty years of Europe than a cycle of Cathay."

The fact that these dominant nations of Europe were white was bound to make a deep impression on observers. Europe was equated with white, which in turn was equated with civilization and progress. Non-European was equated with non-white, which in turn meant outside the pale—stagnant if not primitive, lesser breeds standing in long-time tutelage to Western man. These assumptions, reflected in the writings of generation after generation of historians, certainly did the Negro no service.

The belief in white superiority has been fully shared by historians. No less than other Americans, they have found it possible to subscribe simultaneously to the all-men-are-created-equal dictum of the Declaration of Independence and the theory of "divine-right white." Hence, the historian's treatment of the Negro has been more of a conditioned reflex than of an examined premise.[5]

Black Literature

In November, 1968, I presented a paper at the annual convention of the National Council of Teachers of English on the subject "The English Department and the Challenge of Racism." This paper was published in September, 1969, in the *ADE Bulletin*, official organ of the Association of Departments of English in Colleges and Universities comprising approximately a thousand of the most influential members of the professsion. In the process of preparing my paper I carefully examined the contents of six college anthologies of American literature, edited and/or coedited by thirteen of the most distinguished professors in the field.

My findings were summarized as follows: *Anthology No. 1*, first published in 1934 and revised in 1947 and 1957, more widely used in colleges and universities than any other, includes in a two-volume edition the works of 93 authors covering 1,659 pages, *with not one black writer. Anthology No. 2*, first published in 1956 and revised in 1957 and 1961, includes in a two-volume edition the works of 80 authors covering 3,158 pages, *with not one black writer. Anthology No. 3*, copyright 1961, one volume with the works of 58 authors covering 853 pages, *with not one black writer. Anthology No. 4*, copyright 1961, one volume with the works of 84 authors covering 1,007 pages, *with not one black writer. Anthology No. 5*, copyright 1961, one volume with the works of 99 authors covering 1,020 pages, *with not one black writer*. The most remarkable fact about this anthology is that it advertises the inclusion of 30 poets born between 1900 and 1920 but fails to include black Langston Hughes born in 1902 and black Pulitzer Prize winner Gwendolyn Brooks born within the period designated for coverage. *Anthology No 6*, first published in 1962 and revised in *1968*, includes in a four-volume edition the works of 102 authors, *with not one black writer*. Although one volume was devoted entirely to 50 writers of the twentieth century, it fails even to mention such distinguished black writers as Langston Hughes, Richard Wright, Ralph Ellison (whose *Invisible Man* received the National Book Award for 1952 and won first place in a *Book Week* poll in 1965 as the most distinguished American novel published in the period 1945-65), James Baldwin, or Gwendolyn Brooks.

I stated that I could not understand how a professed specialist in American literature could possibly ignore all the above-named black writers of national and international distinction and not be guilty of gross ignorance or blatant racism. I suggested that it was my hope that these disclosures would so shock the consciences of all fair-minded members of English departments that the current sanction of white racism by this sector of the profession would cease.

On April 24, 1969, I organized and moderated a symposium on black literature at the Annual Conference of the College Language Association (an organization of English and foreign language teachers at predominantly black colleges) which was co-sponsored by the ADE. In 1970 a transcript of this symposium was published by the *ADE Bulletin* and by the *CLA Journal* (official quarterly of the College Language Association). I am reproducing here excerpts that are pertinent to this discussion. My colleagues, both black, were Professor Charles A. Ray, chairman of the department of English, North Carolina Central University at Durham, and Donald Gibson, associate professor of English, University of Connecticut.

Ford: Our subject, "Black Literature: Problems and Opportunities," lies at the bottom of the greatest crisis that has confronted American higher education in this century. Unless it and the companion question of black culture in general in our curricula are satisfactorily solved, there will be no peace, and consequently no fitting climate for higher learning for Americans in this generation. Unfortunately, as of now, attempted temporary solutions have been based principally on advice from one major group, which, by experience and scholarly perspective, is obviously unprepared to be the sole architect of such vital revamping of the college curriculum. I refer to militant black students and their inexperienced advisers whose understandable impatience and courageous challenge triggered the crisis. It is high time for another group, amply prepared by training and long years of experience, to offer advice and guidance to the profession. I refer, of course, to the large number of competent black professors at predominantly black colleges, such as those represented by CLA, whose inspired and relevant teaching over the years has revealed to their students by precept and example the black man's part in the making of America. It is in this spirit, Ladies and Gentlemen, that we undertake this symposium.

We have agreed to center our discussion around several major questions that are asked most often by teachers who suddenly find themselves responsible for organizing and teaching new courses in black literature or integrating this material into the corpus of existing courses. The question that seems most trivial, but recurs most often, is concerned with an appropriate designation: Should such courses be designated by the adjective *Negro, Black,* or *Afro-American?*

Gibson: The most neutral of these terms is "Afro-American," and if one desires to foster "neutrality" (I cannot go into all the meanings "neutrality" has in this context), to choose the term least likely to be offensive to anyone regardless of his politics, I suggest using "Afro-American." "Black," the term I use in the title of my own course, is intended to suggest a more firm, personal commitment to the ideals to be served by the very fact of instituting courses of the nature under consideration. I suggest that the term "Negro" may (not necessarily *will*) mean a lack of desire on the part of a teacher to understand many of the reasons both psychological and sociological for having such courses.

Ray: The designation should depend upon the objectives of the course. At North Carolina College, we designate our graduate course (which has been going for more than twenty years) *Poetry and Prose by American Negroes.*

Ford: The most elementary course at Morgan State College is a survey entitled *Introduction to the Negro in American Literature*; the other, open to advanced undergraduates and graduates, is entitled *The Negro in American Prose.* Although we attach no significance to the differentiating adjectives, we are aware of the psychological nuances in the minds of some black students.

Another question that is high on any list is: Should courses primarily concerned with black literature include works written by whites?

Gibson: Courses dealing with black writers should not include works written by whites simply because such courses will be unable to focus specifically enough on black writers. There is not time enough in a semester to include works by whites dealing with subjects, themes, and characters related to black people. When such courses are offered, they should be considered as having different functions from the exclusively black writers course. A course including white writers might be a second offering (or a third) *after* the exclusively black writers course, but by no means should it substitute for the exclusive course.

Ray: I agree.

Ford: The decision to include or exclude white writers should be based entirely upon the objectives of the course and the interest and competence of the instructor. An inexperienced instructor should not attempt the combination, but I can see extraordinary opportunities to develop deep insights into the differences and similarities of black and white writers in their treatment of comparable experiences. For instance, in my own course, *The Negro in American Prose*, I find the comparative study of Styron's *The Confessions of Nat Turner* and Arna Bontemps' treatment of the slave revolt led by Gabriel Prosser in *Black Thunder* a most rewarding experience for students interested in the varied possibilities of the historical novel. Recently, a well-meaning skeptic challenged me to justify the offering of separate courses in black literature by a college which has no courses in the literature of other ethnic groups, such as Jews, Indians, and hyphenated Americans. What is your reaction?

Ray: Ideally, courses in world literature should deal as nearly as possible with the literature of all ethnic groups, particularly those groups which have produced representative literature. Practically, the upsurge among nonwhite peoples throughout the world suggests that attention should be paid to their way of life. In the United States, the general neglect of literature about black people in the past makes it mandatory to pay particular attention to this literature now, both as a means of inspiring pride in the black experience and as a means of interpreting to the nonblack world the real aspirations (and frustrations) of black people. A widespread airing of the literary expressions of the black experience should prove cathartic to a society that has ignored or degraded this experience in the past.

Gibson: Literature by "hyphenated Americans" is not generally unknown to the extent that literature by black writers is. Most writers of foreign descent, if they have been excluded from general courses, have not been excluded for the same reasons that black writers have been. In any case, the problem is simply a theoretical one and is often used as a means of avoiding the real issues. There is only a problem when large numbers of Irish-Americans, Italian-Americans, etc., begin asking for ethnic courses. When they do, it is high time to begin instituting such courses, especially if it can be clearly demonstrated, as in the case of black writers, that ignorance of such writers indicates the limitations of the academic establishment.

Ford: Furthermore, writers of other ethnic groups are already included in the mainstream of American literature. Jews, Irish-Americans, Italian-Americans, etc., are included in courses in fiction, poetry, and drama with no emphasis on ethnic origins. But it has been a universal practice over the years to omit the contributions of black writers from anthologies. Recently, I made a study of the contents of six of the most popular anthologies for courses in American literature which had a combined total of 10,259 pages, with an average of 86 authors each; not one even mentioned a black writer.

During a professional conference in which the subject of Black Studies was discussed, one discussant insisted that the introduction of separate courses in black literature and history was racism in reverse. He insisted that whatever attention is given to Negro life and culture in the school or college curriculum must be in an integrated frame of reference. He admitted that his institution had done nothing concrete to correct the imbalance, but assured the group that he and his colleagues would have no part in the promotion of separatism. Until integrated courses could be established, he argued, his college would not join the current trend toward Black Studies. What is your reaction to this attitude?

Gibson: Institutions of higher learning should be concerned with instituting separate courses in black literature. At the same time attention should be given to integrating courses. While the eventual end is to integrate courses, there must be a widespread knowledge of black writers. Neither of these alternatives, however, can be a substitute for the other. Colleges and universities need be concerned with both matters until such time as it is no longer necessary to separate the materials. In integrated courses students simply cannot learn enough about black writers.

Ray: The obvious and unfair exclusion of black literature in the past should be corrected on as widespread a basis as possible. Ideally, colleges and universities should be concerned with correcting past inequities in all courses. However, in view of the demand by so many students for in-depth courses in black literature, it would appear reasonable to meet this demand—as long as it lasts. Moreover, there is enough intrinsic literary merit in the literary expressions of black people throughout the world to justify special black literature courses for people who desire to specialize in this area.

Ford: The ideal way is to demand that all required courses in literature and history include the most significant contributions of all ethnic groups to the national culture. But required general education courses are generally for freshmen and sophomores, and if we could begin next fall with all such courses instantly integrated in an effective manner we would still deny almost half of our current college population the opportunity to become aware of the many cultural contributions of the largest racial minority in the nation at a time when racial understanding is the key to the re-establishment of a peaceful existence at home and abroad. I, therefore, agree that both separate and culturally integrated courses must be instituted on all campuses immediately.

When I speak of "separate courses" in black literature, however, I do not mean courses exclusively for black students. Under no circumstances do I advocate or even approve such courses.

Ray: Colleges and universities should continue to open courses to qualified students, rather than qualified or unqualified black students. Emphatically "No" is my answer to the question of the exclusiveness of black literature courses for black students only.

Gibson: Emphatically No! There should not be courses in black literature exclusively for black students. I can envision the possibility of occasional meetings with only black or white students for various reasons, but the exchange between black students and white in the classroom situation can be stimulating, educational, and a means of sensitizing whites to the intricacies, the nuances, the complexity of the situation of black people—not only the black people in books, but in life too.

Ford: Many teachers new to the field will want to hear your opinions concerning standards for the selection of black literature to be taught in college classes.

Ray: In view of long-standing prejudices against the inclusion of black literature, initial standards for selecting literary works of black people should be largely *genre.* An objective study of the various genres produced by black artists will reveal varying degrees of aesthetic merit. Those with the highest aesthetic merit should be selected for study.

Gibson: The standards employed for selecting black literature to be studied in college courses should be the standards used for selecting any other writers. We should bear in mind, of course, that writers are selected for many reasons. We teach the Puritan writers for cultural, historical, and philosophical reasons; we teach Thoreau and Emerson for similar reasons; we teach Henry James (at least ostensibly) for aesthetic reasons. So much of what we teach is used for the teaching of literary history. Ultimately we teach what we *desire* to teach and for whatever reasons we choose. If the teacher applies whatever criteria he uses to teach the literature of any period or genre, he will have no difficulty finding black writers who measure up to his standards.

Ford: Would you like to extend your consideration of this question by commenting on the problem of emphasis in the teaching of such courses? Should the primary emphasis be literary or sociological?

Ray: In teaching black literature, or any literature for that matter, one often finds it difficult to separate life and art. I believe that black literature should be examined primarily in light of its aesthetic merit. Because the art is so much a part of its milieu; however, it would be unfortunate to exclude the milieu.

Gibson: The emphasis that any given teacher will give to the artistic or sociological matters will probably depend upon his prior bias. Neither, however, should be ignored. If one of these is to be neglected, I should hope it would be artistic, for in the past the so-called aesthetic consideration (insofar as it has been related to the "new criticism") has been largely responsible for the neglect of black writers. Much of what seems to be current critical theory is positively hostile toward social, political, and economic themes in literature partly for political reasons and partly because our methods of approach to the understanding of literature are not adequate. We, for example, have yet to deal adequately with Thoreau in other than political (and to some extent philosophical) terms. Any narrow artistic approach to black literature may very well result simply in misinterpreting it. I would prefer a broad approach which would not exclude either approach, but would include each in proper relation to the other and to the texts.

Ford: Let us now consider one of the most significant and crucial questions underlying the whole subject—the question of teacher qualifications. Black militants have demanded and won in some colleges the right to select teachers they want for these courses regardless of academic training or experience. These students seem to have decided that unqualified commitment to the cult of blackness, acquiescence in student aims, and willingness to serve are major tests. They insist that no white person is qualified to teach the black experience. They believe a black teacher without a college degree will be a more effective teacher of Black Studies than any nonblack with the highest academic degree and a most distinguished teaching record. How valid are these assumptions? If they are not valid, what can be said to refute them?

Gibson: Teachers of black literature should have the same qualifications expected of anyone who teaches any other area of literature.

White teachers can theoretically teach black literature satisfactorily. What students mean when they raise this question is that they are wary of the attitudes which might be held by the teacher. If the teacher's attitude is right, if he does not feel superior to his students (racially superior), if he respects the material and the students, then he may certainly teach black literature. A teacher who has been infected with the racism of the society and who does not recognize his infection may be unable to see the materials of a black literature course with sufficient sensitivity and awareness. White teachers who are presently not fit to teach black literature may become fit if they are willing to become sensitive to the literature and to the needs of the students through the experience of teaching the course.

Ray: The same high standards and the same thoroughness of preparation that should characterize teachers generally should characterize black teachers particularly. Of course, thoroughly trained and knowledgeable white teachers can teach black literature.

Ford: I fully agree with your sentiments.

By November 26, 1970, when the Board of Directors of the National Council of Teachers of English adopted "Criteria for Teaching Materials in Reading and Literature," recommended by the Task Force on Racism and Bias in the Teaching of English which it had appointed earlier, at least three of the anthologies I had condemned in 1968 for failing to include any black writer had been revised with the inclusion of a token number of black authors. But the problem is still acute and continued pressure must be exerted on the publishers and the profession. *Searching for America* (1972), edited by Ernece B. Kelly and published jointly by the Conference on College Composition and Communication and the parent body, the National Council of Teachers of English, contains the following admonition:

Because conventional English courses and reading programs constitute the bulk of the Language Arts taught in elementary and secondary schools and colleges and because they are frequently organized around an anthology, a basic text, or a single learning program, it is to the publishers of such texts, and to the designers of systems approaches to learning, and to the bodies that adopt them, and to the teachers who use them that the following criteria are addressed:

A.   Literature anthologies intended as basic texts and having inclusive titles and/or introductions must commit themselves to fair (more than token representation) and balanced (reflecting diversity of style, subject matter, and social and cultural view) inclusion of the work of nonwhite minority group members. This includes, but is not limited to the following:

      Collections embracing the whole of American literature
      Collections of generic materials
      Collections of materials from a given historical period
      Collections of materials from a given geographic region

    To do less than this is to imply that nonwhite minority groups are less capable, less worthy, less significant than white American writers.

B.   Nonwhite minorities must be represented in basic texts in a fashion which respects their dignity as human beings and mirrors their contributions to American culture, history, and letters. This means that hostile or sentimental depictions of such groups must be balanced with amicable and realistic ones in an effort to present a balanced and nonprejudicial picture.

C.   In collections and parts of collections where a writer is represented by only one selection, the basis for its inclusion must be explained.

D.   Illustrations and photographs must present as accurate and balanced a

picture of nonwhite minorities and their environments as is possible in
the total context of the educational materials.

E.   Dialect, when it appears, must not be exaggerated or inconsistent, but
appropriate to the setting and the characters. Where the risk is courted
that the preponderance or exclusive appearance of dialect materials,
including representations of the speech of bilingual Americans, is
suggestive of cultural insensitivity, it should be balanced with an
explanatory note which effectively places that dialect in accurate
historical-linguistic context.

F.   Editorial and critical commentary must not ignore the role played by
nonwhite minority writers in the continuing literary development.
Literary criticism, whether short quotations from critical writings or
collections of critical essays, must draw as heavily as possible from the
critical writers of nonwhite minorities. This is equally important in
discussing works by or about members of the same group.

G.   Historical commentary and interpretations must not present an
idealized or otherwise distorted picture of the social and political
history out of which Americans have written and are writing. Nonwhite
minority group members should be included. where appropriate, in any
commentary on writers active during significant literary periods.[6]

Although it is imperative that anthologists and publishers reevaluate their bases for selecting authors to be included in anthologies, it is even more obligatory for teachers and critics of
literature to reconsider their criteria for evaluation. If black literature
is to be truly accepted by the profession as legitimate material for
literary study, the current criterion of aestheticism must be
repudiated as the privileged test for all literature worthy of classroom
study. It must become only one of the criteria among several. In fact,
aestheticism is the product of an elitist society in which only the
leisure class was expected to be concerned about literature and art;
consequently, literature and art were expected to be primarily
concerned with beauty in content and expression. The coarse, the
ugly, and the mundane were not to be encouraged. Actually the
emphasis on aestheticism is an emphasis on the formal, the
nonhuman, the determination not to become involved in the sordid
aspect of the human condition, the preoccupation with con-
templating the stars while bogging down in the muck and mire of
the terrestrial terrain. Consequently, in an article in *College English*
(February, 1971) I proposed that all literary scholars and critics
seriously consider, individually and collectively, the urgent need to
revise drastically traditional norms for evaluating literature according
to the WASP pattern. I quoted John H. Fisher, then executive
secretary of the Modern Language Association, who had recently

declared, "The subject of English in this country has been used to inculcate a white, Anglo-Saxon, Protestant ethic. This was our principal and most valuable inheritance from the mother country. The most important people in 'English' in this country have traditionally been those who outdid the British at their own game—did better scholarship on Chaucer, Shakespeare, or Milton; brought over the most English books to found Folger or a Huntington, or a University of Illinois library . . ."[7]

I suggested that aestheticism no longer be allowed to remain as the privileged criterion for literary evaluation, and that other criteria be accepted as supplements of equal value. I recommended that one such acceptable criterion could be the test of *significant human experience,* which would assume that any literary work that offers significant insight into the cultural and racial background of the civilization that produced it is valuable. Another criterion might be the test of *relevance* to an understanding and appreciation of contemporary life.

Because of the refusal of teachers of literature to abandon the theory of aestheticism as the determining factor in the selection of literature for classroom study, most of the younger black writers and critics have demanded that black literature be judged by separate standards.

In an article discussing the current "Black Arts Movement," Larry Neal, black poet and critic, explains his idea of how black literature differs in aims and methods from the standards of White-Anglo-Saxon-Protestant aestheticism. He declares:

> It is radically opposed to any concept of the artist that alienates him from his community. Black art is the aesthetic and spiritual sister of the Black Power concept. As such it envisions an art that speaks directly to the needs and aspirations of Black America. In order to perform this task, the Black Arts Movement proposes a radical reordering of the western cultural aesthetic. It proposes a separate symbolism, mythology, and iconology . . . The two movements postulate that there are in fact and in spirit two Americas—one black, one white. It is the opinion of many Black writers . . . that the western aesthetic has run its course: it is impossible to construct anything meaningful written in its decaying structure.[8]

Although I do not subscribe to all of Neal's fears and dire predictions as of this moment, all available evidence points to the conclusion that unless the literary establishment takes seriously the need for a reordering of evaluative standards and procedures *now,* without further subterfuge, many of us who still believe in the "humanity" of our discipline and those who practice it will be forced to acknowledge a great betrayal. I conclude with pertinent advice from the eminent English critic, David Daiches, who warns:

In the lower ranges of literature are all sorts of mixed kinds, partly documentary, partly sociological, partly historical, and one of the problems of defining the task of the literary critic is precisely that literature is so wide-ranging, often so "impure," with the spectrum ranging from the almost wholly documentary to the wholly imaginative. One must find a technique of description that enables one to do justice to these mixed kinds, to demonstrate the effectiveness of the literary devices which make the documentary element so much more vivid and persuasive. The novel in particular tends to be a mixed form. In calling these mixed forms "lower" I am not so much implying a value judgment as suggesting a scale between the high visionary and the low documentary, with every kind of combination in between ... It can be easily argued that the purely visionary is not by any means the greatest and that a grip on contemporary social fact, however indirectly or obliquely demonstrated, is the mark of the greatest writers.

8

The Personal Equation

The problems and opportunities of Black Studies programs seem to be significantly affected by personal traits, attitudes, and relations. Although the personal element influences to some extent the degree to which any educational program succeeds or fails, its influence is more pronounced in its application to Black Studies.

The Administrator

The administrator (chairman, director, or coordinator) of a Black Studies program is more responsible for its success or failure than any other single influence except, of course, the financial budget. It is important, therefore, that a college or university use every means possible to select an administrative officer with the personal character traits and educational philosophy that are consonant with the institution's philosophy of and commitment to Black Studies.

More than 100 current chairmen of Black Studies programs answered the following question in my questionnaire: "Based on your experience with the demands of the position, what would you consider to be the most desirable qualifications (academically and otherwise) for a chairman or director of a Black Studies program?" The one qualification that everyone stated or implied was that he must be black. Even the few white acting chairmen unequivocally insisted upon color as the first prerequisite. Several insisted that he be more than black physically; he must have had some experience in black-related teaching and some knowledge and experience of life in the black community. He must possess a strong sense of the black experience and be able to relate it to the total educational process, but he must also be able to relate objectively to *all* students.

The second most insistent demand, although not a unanimous one, is that he possess an academic background equivalent to that required of all department chairmen in the institution. Some respondents suggest the Ph.D. in an academic discipline or the active pursuit of the highest degree in his specialty. Others indicate a willingness to substitute scholarly publication or unusual administrative experience in a college or university. It was pointed out by some that unless his credentials include a strong academic background he cannot command the respect of his academic colleagues.

I am reproducing below a variety of characteristics that respondents consider important.

(1) A willingness to challenge outmoded structures and the imagination to project new, viable alternatives.

(2) A familiarity with other ethnic studies programs.

(3) A special capacity to verbalize concepts in a clear, concise manner and to communicate effectively with black students.

(4) An understanding of the sensitive nature of the program and ability to work with people in a respectful and persuasive manner.

(5) A good broad knowledge of all things affecting black people; a strong, determined personality, not necessarily militant but able to make reasonable and forceful demands on the institution, as well as the program staff and the students.

(6) A person of definite opinions, but open-minded and willing to accept suggestions and change.

(7) A sense of perspective, not easily discouraged by criticisms from black students or colleagues.

(8) Patience and diplomacy in juggling the contradictory demands of administration, faculty senate, and black students.

(9) Solid academic standing and good rapport with faculty, administration, and students.

(10) A thick skin, wide multidisciplinary experience, strong research orientation, political sophistication, balanced contacts in the black community, and strong black consciousness.

The Faculty

To the question: "What is your professional attitude toward all black versus integrated staff?" sixty percent of directors expressed preference for an integrated faculty, while forty percent preferred all black teachers. Some comments supporting each viewpoint are reproduced below:

(1) "I oppose an all black staff under any conditions, except where qualified integrated staff is not available."

(2) "I have no objection to whites teaching Black Studies, provided they have the necessary training and unbiased attitudes towards black students."

(3) "Most teachers probably should be black; however, there should be room for competent well-informed white teachers with the appropriate system of values."

(4) "The staff should be integrated, but certain courses should be taught by blacks only."

(5) "I favor all-black staff mainly because most black students can relate better to black teachers. Also white students prefer black teachers for these courses."

(6) "I prefer an all black staff because whites have their vision turned directly toward their own survival as masters of the world. At present everything they touch will be tainted with racism."

To the question "Should academic requirements for black faculty members for Black Studies programs be lowered in order to increase the short supply of available personnel?" respondents divide into two approximately equal groups. Those who demand the same standards required for other programs argue that to do otherwise would be to admit the inferiority of the Black Studies program, an admission that would reduce the prestige of Black Studies in the thinking of the administration, faculty, and students. It is argued that such practices in some institutions are responsible for the current skepticism concerning the quality of Black Studies as an academic discipline.

Some who disagree with the foregoing philosophy assert that they believe in the necessity of "changing" the academic requirements for teachers of Black Studies, but that "to change" does not mean the same thing as "to lower." They insist that current academic requirements do not effectively measure teaching ability, intellectual capacity, or creativity. They suggest that "broadening" not "lowering" is a more accurate explanation for the refusal to be bound by the often stultifying requirement of the Ph.D. degree.

Others say that they are willing to accept lower academic qualifications provided that such qualifications are compensated for by more intensive personal experiences which can be useful in the classroom. It is urged that Black Studies should develop new criteria for selecting its faculty which should consider minimum academic requirements as only one factor.

One director, who has a Ph.D. degree, confides, "I do not see non-credentialism as the lowering of requirements. That is a white academic argument. The criteria should be high standards and in-depth experience. Good courses dealing with black workers or community organization may be almost valueless *unless* taught by indigenous non-credentialed people."

Students

The average black student who enrolls as a dormitory resident at a predominantly white college or university is faced immediately with a crisis of identification. He discovers that he is in a large group of people of his own age and educational attainments but not fully a part of it. He seldom feels at ease until he discovers another person of color with whom he can identify. Even if he finds a compatible white roommate, he often feels some restraint in sharing his inmost thoughts. His problem is more acute if there is no black community nearby. Thus black students in a white college or university wish to have a dormitory room or a black culture center where they will have opportunities to relate personally with other students of color without conscious inhibitions. This innocent desire for identity often leads to irrational demands for separate courses in Black Studies limited only to black students and separate dormitories for blacks only. In an institution such as the University of Montana at Missoula, where there is no black community (and reportedly less than 100 blacks in the entire state), or at Dartmouth College at Hanover, New Hampshire, the desire for a campus haven such as a special culture center (but no separate dormitories) reserved primarily for blacks is not abnormal or irrational.

During campus visitations I have discovered that informal social activities in a special facility such as that suggested above have revealed no stronger manifestations of abnormal separatism than comparable activities in a fraternity or sorority house. I have found no serious sentiment among black students during my travels (1970–72) in favor of all-black institutes of Black Studies similar to the 1969 project at Antioch College which black psychologist Kenneth B. Clark condemned in his letter of resignation from the Board of Directors of the college which warned, "To encourage or endorse a separate black program not academically equivalent to the college curriculum generally, indeed to endorse any such program, is to reinforce the Negro's inability to compete with whites for the real power of the real world."

Of more than 100 directors who expressed an opinion on the question of providing on-the-campus "separate facilities of any kind" for the *exclusive* use of black students, only two expressed absolute disapproval. On the contrary, three expressed absolute approval with no reservations. One explained: "They are desirable and necessary for most white institutions that are in the process of understanding the values of non-white students and their needs." A second advocate said, "I agree with the concept of pluralism. Black people must create and control institutions, even if it is no more than the black wing in one dormitory." A third argued, "Since there are still many facilities (exclusive clubs, fraternities, etc.) for whites, I am not adverse to separate facilities for blacks as long as it is by their choice that they affiliate with such facilities." Another suggested that for publicly financed institutions separate facilities cannot be legally justified but that black students usually appropriate territory for their own separate use in an informal fashion; consequently, the need for separate facilities per se is disguised under the headings of special interests, student committees, Afro-American Student Press, and so on. One respondent believes it is unnecessary for the institution to provide separate facilities, "since black students will migrate to each other especially on large white campuses, thus informally creating various black enclaves."

The overwhelming view of directors is that academic separation such as the exclusion of whites from classes is unacceptable, but separate facilities such as lounges or culture centers for social and cultural activities and relaxation are a necessary part of an effective Black Studies program. It is suggested by some that such facilities should not be designated as "off limits" for other members of the college community, since the nature of the activities carried on there automatically limits the participants. Although in some programs black students have refused to attend sections of classes with whites, unrestricted sections of all courses are open to interested whites. Only rarely is it necessary to set up separate black sections of a course. At one institution I discovered that black students set a precedent in one class taught by a popular black teacher by arriving early each class period and occupying all the front seats making it necessary for the much larger contingent of white students to find seats in the rear. After this ritual was repeated so constantly in the first weeks of the course, the whites understood and accepted it, having now become reconciled to leaving the choice seats to their black classmates.

At one highly rated university the black professor and his assistant found that the popular black course had attracted an enrollment of 200 students, three-fourths of whom were white. Instead of immediately dividing the class into four sections, the senior professor decided to meet the entire group in a small auditorium for two weeks (three sessions per week) hoping to establish some degree of rapport between the two races. At the end of the period he announced that he was now ready to establish four sections of fifty each according to the following pattern: Section A exclusively black, Section B exclusively white, and Sections C and D racially mixed, and that each student must indicate his choice on special cards. When the cards were returned and tabulated, every black student had chosen the all-black section and every white student had chosen the racially mixed sections. The white students begged for some black students to join their sections and for some of them to have the privilege of registering for the all-black section in order to make the experience valid and meaningful. But not a single black student would agree to abandon the section he had chosen. In desperation the professor finally persuaded a few black students to visit the all-white sections informally once every two weeks to participate in the class discussions.

One of the reasons black students offer for not wanting whites in their black courses is that whites are so ignorant of the most elementary facts of black life and culture that half of the class period is wasted in explaining the elementary facts which the average black teenager has known since puberty. A second reason often advanced is that certain analyses and interpretations of racial materials are often passed over by the knowledgeable black professor because of the embarrassment it may cause the black student in the presence of unsympathetic and insensitive whites.

On campuses where the black student population is less than 100, the crisis of identification is especially acute. The white faculty and student body tend to regard a small group of blacks as more homogeneous than they do a larger group. Because of the need for protection against the vastness of "the enemy" each individual finds it more important to appear to conform to the group norm. Whereas under normal circumstances personal preferences in dress, manners, and speech are exhibited without fear, under conditions of pressure one finds more security and protection by suppressing differences in order to present a unified front to "the enemy."

In a special meeting with a group of sixty black students on a white campus with 3,000 non-blacks, I sought to discover their most basic problem. With little dissent I was informed that the basic problem was the smallness of their number. The white students were either hostile or indifferent, and to maintain the necessary rapport with their group for protection each had to sacrifice his individuality to the requirements of group solidarity. In a private conference one girl who had decided to transfer to another institution at the end of the semester confided that she was forced to associate closely with other members of the group with whom she had nothing in common except color because there was not a wide enough variety of blacks to find a reasonable number of associates of similar tastes and life-styles. Consequently teachers had misjudged her by the company she was forced to keep, and the personal tension created by the situation was driving her into a state of neuroticism.

Another complaint of black students is directed at the failure of many colleges to provide an effective remedial program for those whose high school training is inadequate in such skills subjects as reading, writing, and mathematics. The policy of open admissions recently adopted by a number of institutions permits the recruitment of the quota of black students set by the college, but it proves to be a cruel hoax rather than a blessing when it is not implemented by a sufficient number of trained and concerned counselors to give the necessary remedial aid so that the open-door policy will not become simply a revolving door that pushes the student out at the end of a year or less with the stigma of a failing record. Most of the black colleges have had effective programs of this kind from the beginning of their existence; consequently, their drop-out rate has been fantastically smaller for students entering with substandard skills in reading and writing than the rate for typical white colleges.

At predominantly black Morgan State College, where I was chairman of the English department for twenty-three years, as early as fifteen years ago we abolished all noncredit courses in Freshman English, substituting for them five-hour attendance sections for three hours of credit on the assumption that noncredit courses for freshmen lacked the motivative power to insure success. In addition we added a two-hour attendance course in reading skills for one-hour credit with exemption for those who demonstrated satisfactory competence. During the first year, performance scores on objective tests increased approximately twelve percent. At the same time we changed our grading policy for Freshman English from the standard *A, B, C, D, F* to *A, B, C, U, F.* The *U* was not a grade; it indicated unsatisfactory achievement without penalty and permitted the student to continue the course for another semester, with the understanding that failure to achieve satisfactory performance during the second chance would earn an *F.* We reasoned that in the area of reading and writing a *D* grade was not acceptable since success in all other subjects depended to a large degree on satisfactory skills in reading and writing. Our graduates who had entered four years before with substandard scores in reading and writing found no extraordinary difficulty when they entered graduate schools of the highest ratings, some earning Ph.D. degrees with distinction.

In *The New York Times Magazine* (May 8, 1971) in an article entitled "Report Card on Open Admissions: Remedial Work Recommended," Solomon Resnik, assistant professor at Queens College, CUNY, and Barbara Kaplan, staff member of the Cooperative College Center, SUNY, raise some pertinent questions concerning the current dilemma of open admissions. They say: "The old, traditional view assumes college is a privilege granted to a relatively few talented students, the B.A. degree is a rare and coveted prize, and the university is under no obligation to reach larger numbers of people; it is thus the responsibility of the student to meet on his own, the rigorous requirements for graduation and a degree. According to the new view, it is the university's responsibility to provide an education for as many students as possible, though, ideally, not at the expense of standards. To do so it must be active in recruiting students and in helping them live up to its standards. In place of the old 'ivory tower,' the university is seen as a force in the struggle for social equality."

The authors argue that critics of open admissions insist that this practice involves the lowering of standards for a college degree. But the fact is that admissions and graduation are entirely different ends of a process separated by four or more years. There is no necessary relation between the two. Indeed a student may enter college with an excellent command of fundamental skills and graduate four years later with no evidence that he has sharpened or refined those skills. Likewise a student may enter the four-year cycle deficient in the basic skills necessary for effective learning and emerge four years later with evidence of a mastery of those skills far greater than a student who was in a more fortunate position four years earlier. In many cases a student's failure to develop satisfactory learning skills in high school is the result of lack of interest, lack of effort, or lack of a satisfactory teaching and learning environment as is generally the rule in the black ghettos.

The best Black Studies programs offer formal or informal remedial aid to students who need it. In almost all cases black students with well-developed learning skills and superior backgrounds in basic fields of study serve as tutors for the less prepared. The Center for Afro-American and African Studies at the University of Michigan provides an effective remedial and enrichment program under the title Coalition for the Use of Learning Skills (CULS) which is described as "not a program *for* black Students. Rather, it is a program *of* black people and other people in the University who have experienced the oppressive effects of racism and exploitation and are determined to contribute to changing those effects through improving and using their skills." (For further description see Chapter 9. pp. 123, ff.).

There has been some unfavorable criticism of black students for demanding and being granted the right to have the controlling voice in the selection of the director and faculty of the Black Studies program in their college or university, the nature and manner of organization of the courses, and the methods that teachers must use for evaluating student achievement. Although some institutions have yielded to these demands, others have resisted and refused to grant some of these prerogatives. In some institutions the students have vetoed the appointment of teachers whom the director and the college administration considered desirable. Students argue that they are more capable of making these decisions because they know better than any other individual or group what learning experiences are relevant to them, how these experiences should be organized and presented, and what teacher has the racial philosophy and point of view that they can respect. Furthermore, they believe that they (or at least their immediate generation) are entirely responsible for forcing the colleges and universities to establish these programs and that without their efforts there would be no programs to administer; therefore, they have earned the right to dictate the rules by which they are to be governed.

Some directors accept the students' arguments as valid and support the right of the students to have the controlling voice in administration. Others do not accept the idea of student control, but are willing to share equally with the students all administrative powers. Most agree that students should participate in governance of the program but should not have the controlling voice. One director charges, "There are courses that no nonblack Ph.D. can structure. In an institution where ninety-nine percent of the teaching staff is white, it is obvious that the black students must sit with the white to draw up the program. This does not mean student control." Another suggests, "Black students should participate in program development and have some power over hiring faculty and designing the program." A director at a community college declares, "Universities and colleges are for students to learn, faculty members to teach, administrators to administrate, and community to give financial support. All should be involved in crucial decision making."

Thomas Sowell, black associate professor of economics at U.C.L.A., charges in an article in *The New York Times Magazine* (December 13, 1970), "Intimidation and physical assaults on non-politicized black students by their 'brothers' with messianic (or simply hoodlum) instincts are resolutely ignored by college administrators. To white activist faculty members, it is either something to be blotted out of the mind or an incidental unhappy eddy in the backwash of the wave of the future. Compulsory indoctrination programs for entering Negro freshmen have been a demand of black militants on some campuses, and while it has not been formally granted in most cases, arrangements have been made which amount to the same thing *de facto*. Recruitment, prescreening for admission, and even control of financial-aid funds have been put into the hands of the politicized minority on many campuses, including some of the highest prestige institutions in the country . . ."

9
Significant
Representative Programs

The purpose of this chapter is to present seven significant Black Studies programs that are operating effectively in five classes of institutions of higher learning. The reader is exhorted not to assume that these programs are the seven best in the estimation of the writer. But the reader may rightly assume that each is among the best in its classification and that all are among the most effectively organized and administered that the writer has seen or read about during his two years of study. *Class A* includes two-year community colleges, *Class B* includes four-year predominantly white colleges, *Class BB* includes four-year predominantly black colleges, *Class C* includes predominantly white universities, *Class CC* includes predominantly black universities.

For the most part, programs are described in the language of the college publications where they appear in greater detail. No program is outlined here which the author has not discussed with the program director or his representative and about which the author has any doubts concerning its successful use in the context described. The author is grateful to program directors and other college officials for permission to reproduce pertinent descriptions of organizational patterns and activities representative of significant practices in their institutions.

CLASS A
Wayne County Community College

Wayne County Community College, located in Detroit, operates on the theory that a community college is obligated to base its priorities on the most basic needs of the community it serves. The philosophy of the Black Studies program, according to its published announcements, rests on a concept that includes a major consideration of the past, present, and future of black people in America. The prime intent of the program is to equip its students with a knowledge and understanding of the past essential to their survival and the improvement of the present and future conditions of the race. It is concerned with providing knowledge and skills necessary for the enhancement of the situation of a black minority in a highly technological society.

According to the administrators and faculty the basic courses have been designed to meet the immediate and future needs of a disadvantaged minority which has been ignored completely in the designing and implementation of educational programs operated at public expense. An examination of the rationale for some of the innovative courses offered by the Black Studies program at this college can be both interesting and enlightening.

Course Offerings

All courses in Black Studies count as credit toward the two-year A.A. degree at the college and are accepted for transfer credit by all state-supported colleges and universities in Michigan.

Course Title	Course No.
Inner-City Business: How to Organize — How to Finance	BKS 101
Techniques and Principles of Urban Salesmanship	BKS 102
Exploitation and the Black Consumer	BKS 103
Repercussions of Illegal Drug Traffic: Its Growth and Development in the Black Community	BKS 104
Urban Home Management	BKS 107
American Government and the Black Struggle	BKS 131
Black Psychology	BKS 140
Psychological Nature of Struggle	BKS 240
Black People in Michigan History	BKS 150
Social Action, Television and the Black Community	BKS 169
Basic Black Art	BKS 170
Theory and Technique of Black Art	BKS 171
History of Jazz on Records	BKS 175
Comparative Government (Africa)	BKS 180

Course Title	Course No.
International Relations (Africa)	BKS 181
Race Relations for Law Enforcement Officers	BKS 235
Introduction to Afro-American Literature	BKS 247
Black Rhetoric	BKS 248
Major Afro-American Authors I	BKS 249
Major Afro-American Authors II	BKS 250
Afro-American Poetry	BKS 251
Afro-American History I	BKS 261
Afro-American History II	BKS 262

Rationale of Course Construction

The course BKS 104, *Repercussions of Illegal Drug Traffic: Its Growth and Development in the Black Community,* was decided upon after a consultation with the Inner-City Drug Coalition of Detroit composed of several community groups concerned about the problem. The City of Detroit is currently treating 1,800 addicts at a cost of more than a million dollars. It is generally believed that there are from 30,000 to 50,000 addicts in the community. Surveys by faculty and students in the Black Studies program indicate that this problem needs study not only as to the underlying causes of addiction but as to the best methods of rehabilitation.

BKS 102, *Techniques and Principles of Urban Salesmanship,* was developed and is offered through the cooperation and assistance of the director of the Small Business Development Center and the president of the Economic Development Corporation. The course offers an up-grading mechanism for blacks already employed as salesmen. Instruction is organized and tailored to fit the needs of each student. Some companies are not only paying the tuition for their workers but are permitting the students to attend classes on company time.

BKS 235, *Race Relations for Law Enforcement Officers,* is designed to prepare policemen to function more effectively in minority communities.

Community Projects

In order to enhance the total education of students in the Black Studies program the department requires that the academic setting of the classroom be complemented by practical exposure to specific projects in the black community. This requirement forces *all* Black Studies courses and community projects to be mutually conceived by the instructor and the class. Some special projects on which departmental interest is now focused are (1) a paraprofessional program in consumer education funded by Title I with an enrollment of 30 students who will eventually be employed in industry and public institutions; (2) an Inner-City Business Improvement Forum which offers training in innovative methods of preparing personnel for inner-city industry; and (3) the planning of a state-wide Black Studies conference consisting of workshops and problem-solving sessions.

According to published statistics more than half of the student body at the college is white, but the black enrollment is larger than that of any other college in the state. Approximately 80 percent of the students are employed, and the average student is registered in two classes. Because of the nature of the problems and the needs of the students enrolled in Black Studies, the chairman believes that the role of community activists must be accepted by the faculty and administrators of the program. A perusal of the chairman's records of his activities relative to his role as academician and community activist during a semester reveals the breadth of his concerns. I am reproducing a memorandum typical of one week's activities of the chairman of Black Studies at Wayne County Community College:

MEMORANDUM

TO: George Bennet and Quill Pettway
FROM: Lonnie Peek, Chairman of Black Studies
DATE: 22 November 1971
RE: Weekly Report

For the week of November 15th, Black Studies chairman participated in the following events:

—Mon., Nov. 15, spoke on program at Central High School sponsored by the Afro-American Club.

—Attended meeting with Betty Reynolds, her assistant, and Bernard Webb of Model Neighborhood. We are in the process of putting together a program for Model Neighborhood and Wayne County Community College. After our next meeting we will have a full, written report.

—Attended State of Emergency Meeting.

—Attended meeting at Wayne State University's medical research component. They heard of our endeavor at DeHoCo and are interested in developing a program with the local jails whereby they can offer medical assistance.

——Attended meeting with the President of ICBIF, Walt McMurtry. We are in the process of revitalizing our endeavors in the area of economic development. ICBIF is very favorable and is in the process of putting together an outline for a joint meeting with EDC, ICBIF, and President Wilson.

——Attended Board of Directors meeting for Black Causes Association.

——Tues., Oct. 16, attended meeting at Highland Park College conducted by Mr. Homer Smith, State Director of HEA, to learn possible ways to acquire refunding under Title I for Consumer Education program.

——Evaluated Afro-American History class (BKS 261) taught at Ford on Tues., by Mrs. Gloria Pitts.

——Oct. 17, attended Student Services Committee meeting, which made final plans for student meeting on Oct. 20, at Garfield Building.

——Sent correspondence to Mr. Rhoads Murphy, Director of the Center for Chinese Studies at University of Michigan, and Mr. Gumecindo Saalas, Director of the Chicano Studies Program at Monteith College, Wayne State University, requesting information on course outlines, programs, and personal contacts in these areas. We are attempting to gather information for the development of an Ethnic Studies Department here.

——Sent memo and attached outline to Dr. Wilson regarding program development with Channel 56, dealing specifically with our class "Mass Media and the Black Community." This program will attempt to incorporate a working knowledge of the technical aspects of mass media, TV in particular, with the social aspects already built into the course.

——Sent up-to-date report to Dr. Wilson, per his request, on the progress made and problems incurred by our attempt to have Wayne County Community College courses offered at Detroit House of Correction.

CLASS B

San José State College

The Black Studies Department of San Jose State College has sought to build a rich educational program with the aims of academic excellence and relevance to community needs. The department is geared to provide its students with the best possible academic training and also to invest them with practical skills that can be advantageously employed by the communities they will be serving after graduation.

Curriculum

This department offers instruction in one major curriculum leading to the baccalaureate degree: Black Studies. Subject matter includes education, sociology, economics (all three focusing on black community development).

Professional training in this department is offered in the junior and senior years. General education and Black Studies lower division core courses should be completed during freshman and sophomore years.

Junior college transfers must consult with a Black Studies advisor before registration.

B.A. Degree with a Major in Black Studies

	Semester Units
General Education Program	40
Physical Education	2
Requirements in the Major	30
Minor or Electives	52
Total Units Required for Degree	124

Minor Program

A minor in Black Studies is offered for students majoring in other departments of the College, and requires fifteen semester units in the minor.

Limitations and Explanations:
1. A program should be planned in consultation with an advisor to meet the needs of individual students. (A program leading to the Standard Teaching Credential is being developed by the Black Studies Department).
2. General education courses should be selected with consideration of supporting courses in Black Studies.
3. A minor program should be considered from a supporting field of study. A minor in an academic subject matter area is required for the Standard Teaching Credential.
4. For further explanation and guidance, students are urged to consult with advisors or the department chairman.

Lower Division Courses

1A, B. Black Experience in the United States
40.   Black Origin

Upper Division Courses

100A—The Black Community Before 1900

100B—The Black Community After 1900
101—Black Diaspora
102—Afro-American Music
103—Afro-American Art
104—Art Education in the Black Community
105—Black Community Health
110—Education in the Black Community
120—Sociology of the Black Community
121—Seminar in Social Problems
130—Psychology of the Black Community
140—Economic Development of the Black Community
141—Seminar in Economic Problems in Africa
142—Law and the Black Community
143—Politics of Poverty and Welfare in the Black
      Community
144—Politics of New African States
150—Black Urban Politics
153—Contemporary Black Thought
155—Communication in the Black Idiom
156—Black Nationalism
157—Religion in the Black Community
158—Survey of Black Literature
159—Racism and Capitalism
197—History and Development of the Black Theatre
160—Seminar in Techniques in Community
      Development
161—Seminar in Black Curriculum; Problems and
      Design
170—Community Research Methods
171—Seminar in Social Change
172—Political Problems of the Black Community
180—Individual Studies
184—Directed Reading
190—Internship in Community Development

Summer Institute

As an outgrowth of the demand that public school teachers and personnel become more aware of the history and culture of the various ethnic groups in our society and culture, the Black Studies Department has developed a summer program designed to increase knowledge, widen perspectives, and deepen understanding of these groups, particularly black Americans. The specific purposes of the courses are to provide information and materials, develop intergroup relations techniques, improve teaching methods, facilitate innovative programming, and create individually designed curriculum.

The courses are open to college students and instructors, public school teachers and personnel, as well as professionals and individuals in the community.

Ten courses are offered during the summer session, which include: B1S 112, Black Experience in the United States; B1S 111A, African History; B1S 110, Education in the Black Community; B1S 120, Sociology in the Black Community; B1S 140, Economic Development in the Black Community; B1S 141, Political Economy of Southern Africa; B1S 144, Politics of Development in Africa; B1S 156, Black Nationalism, B1S 161, Black Curriculum—Problems and Design; and B1S 196, Ethnic and Minority Cultures.

Field Study Seminar in Black America and Africa

One of the department's most innovative programs was conceived by black students and faculty in classroom discussions. Students frequently expressed a desire to give a concrete dimension to their learning experience. As one student put it: "It seems that for us to get really thorough understanding of what Black Studies is about we should go where black people live in America and Africa to study their communities and experiences."

Gradually a plan was developed for a traveling field study seminar in the black world as part of the department's 1970 Summer Institute. The idea was to visit black communities in this country and Africa to study first-hand the problems of community development. Academically, the plan called for the participating students—majors and minors in Black Studies—to enroll in four courses each: B1S 160, Techniques of Community Development; B1S 196, Special Problems in Black Community Studies; B1S 190S, Political Development of West Africa; and B1S 191S, Art and Culture of West Africa.

The first seminar began in June with an orientation session at San Jose State College. The program was divided into two sections: black America and Africa. After the orientation twelve students and four faculty members traveled throughout black America visiting such communities as San Francisco, Oakland, Nairobi (East Palo Alto), Los Angeles, Watts, Compton, and Carson in California; Jackson and

Crystal Springs in Mississippi; Tuskegee and Macon County in Alabama; Atlanta, Georgia; Washington, D.C.; Newark, New Jersey; and Harlem in New York City.

Thirty people participated in the second section of the seminar: fifteen students, six faculty members, and nine community people, including a black minister and his wife, a black doctor, an African student from Uganda in East Africa, and several public school teachers. The seminar traveled throughout West Africa studying communities such as Abidjan, Locodjoro, Aboisso, Yamossoukro, Abengourou in the Ivory Coast; Kumasi, Tema, Accra in Ghana; Conakry, Kindia, Mamou, Labe, Dalaba in Guinea; Dakar and the island of Goree in Senegal.

The traveling seminar broadened the students' understanding of the roots of the black experience and introduced them to the present-day life and conditions in the black world. The students developed skills in field research techniques, and collected, and/or copied folk music and art in the black communities visited.

The students received eight units of course credit, if they participated in both sections and completed a project, i.e., a comprehensive paper or special project worked out with the instructor. They received four units of course credit if they participated in only one section of the seminar.

CLASS BB

Morgan State College

The Bachelor's Degree Program in Black Studies

Formally launched in 1970, the undergraduate "major" in African-Afro-American studies is officially known as "a program leading to the bachelor's degree with an emphasis in African-Afro-American studies." The degree requires 128 hours of credit, including the general education requirements for the college. The program is open to any qualified student. There are no other prerequisites for the program.

The program is interdisciplinary. Although it does concentrate mainly in those courses offered by the Department of History and Political Science and the Department of Geography, it does leave the student free to take courses of similar interest from many other departments within the college.

Required courses in the program: 80 credit hours, as follows:

General education courses	50
African-Afro-American studies required courses	30
Elective hours of the program	48

As for the African-Afro-American *required* courses, the student must select from the following array of courses the indicated number of hours:

3 hours in political science (one of the following 3-hour courses)
    Black Politics, or
    Government and Social Welfare, or
    The Supreme Court and Civil Rights
3 hours in geography (one of the following 3-hour courses)
    Introductory Geography, or
    Geography of Africa
3 hours in sociology (one of the following 3-hour courses)
    Cultural Anthropology, or
    The Negro in the United States
3 hours in economics:
    Economic Activity in the Black Community
12 hours in history
    History of Civilization (6 hours)
    6 hours selected from among the following 3-hour courses:
        The Negro in United States History
        The Reconstruction Period
        The Nineteenth Century South
        History of Latin America and the Caribbean Area to 1823
        History of Latin America and the Caribbean Area Since 1823
        Sub-Saharan Africa to 1875
        Africa since 1870
3 hours in Music (one of the following 3-hour courses)
    The Afro-American and His Music
    A Survey of Jazz
3 hours selected from the following 3-hour courses:
    Philosophy of Protest
    Negro in American Literature
    Psychology of Black Awareness

Graduate Program in Black History

A graduate student at Morgan State College may earn the Master of Arts degree in history in one of three programs—with an emphasis in European history, Negro history, or United States history. The Negro history graduate program is two years old. Some twelve students are working toward degrees.

For the M.A. degree in history with emphasis in Negro history the following courses (all exclusively graduate courses) are required:

> The United States, 1850–1877
> The Antebellum Free Negro, 1800–1860
> The Negro in the Twentieth Century
> Pre-Colonial Sub-Sahara Africa
> Colonial and Contemporary Sub-Sahara Africa
> Historiography and Historical Method
> Thesis Seminar

Three of the following courses (all exclusively graduate courses except the one marked with the asterisk) are required, one of which must be a history course:

> The American Negro in Art
> The Traditional African Art
> *The Negro in American Prose
> Geography of Africa
> The Negro in the United States prior to 1915
> History of American Urbanization
> History of Popular Culture in the United States
> Latin-American History
> American Political Parties and Pressure Groups
> Urban Politics and the Negro since 1950
> Sociology of Deprivation

As with the undergraduate program, the master's degree program in Negro history is taught by full-time tenured black and white faculty, its courses designed and approved by the Department of History and approved by the Graduate Council.

As for the remaining 48 credit-hours (sixteen three-hour courses) which the student in this program may elect, he may choose from among the following (as well as from those above):

> The American Negro in Art
> The Traditional African Arts
> The Negro in American Prose

African Literature
Work-Service Community Cooperative
  (Social Science 301: a pass-fail
  option course involving work-service
  experiences with community programs,
  projects and affairs)
Social and Cultural History of Africa
Social and Cultural History of Africa
  since 1870
Urban History of the United States
Contemporary Africa (Political Science)
Urban Geography
Minorities
The Urban Community (Sociology)
Introduction to Social Work

By vote of the faculty, the program is coordinated and supervised by the chairman of the Department of History and Political Science. All of its courses are designed and approved by the respective instructional departments and further approved by faculty vote. A variety of teaching methods, including forms of independent study, field work, seminar technique, and reports of investigations are utilized.

Post-Doctoral Programs in Black Culture

Although the master's degree constitutes the upper limit of the college's formal offerings, its course work in Negro studies at the advanced undergraduate and graduate levels, the research-writing concerns of its faculty in such subjects, the strength of its library holdings in African and African-American materials, and the special urban thrust of various other corollary college activities together provide an unusually rich setting and opportunity for postgraduate study. In the school year 1970–71 the college became involved in two post-doctoral programs in Black Studies.

The college was invited to be one of the participating institutions in the Danforth Foundation's Post-Graduate Fellowships for Black Studies for 1970–71. Other institutions in the same program are Yale, Chicago, Howard, and Stanford.

The National Endowment for the Humanities in selecting the Institute of Southern History at the Johns Hopkins University as a post-doctoral center in Black Studies asked that institution to seek arrangements whereby Endowment Fellows would have access to personnel, materials, and programs at Morgan State College. The proposal was mutually agreeable and the two institutions have therefore cooperated in a variety of planning activities, including Morgan's participating in the nominating of the Fellows.

The major role of Morgan in these post-doctoral enterprises consists of providing access for Danforth and Endowment Fellows to the Special Negro Collection in the college library and to consultation and courses (as auditors) with Morgan faculty who are deeply involved in research and writing on the Negro; and in informal seminars involving Fellows and faculty of the two institutions.

CLASS C

Chicago State University

Black Studies at Chicago State University is an all-encompassing multifaceted program of activities and instruction which emphasizes black culture and black thought. It includes undergraduate and graduate concentrations, workshops, lectures, an annual festival of black arts, tutoring, counseling, research services, and community projects.

Philosophy

The Office of Black Studies has adopted the philosophy of the African Association for Black Studies. It states:

> We are dedicated to the development of the concept of Pan-Africanism and the internalization of our African heritage. Realizing that we are African people, we are dedicating ourselves to liberation through Pan-Africanism. We define Pan-Africanism as (a) Black people defining themselves and (b) the unifying acts of African people wherever they find themselves. Black Studies is the means of implementing this objective by the development of skill and professional expertise through an interdisciplinary educational process.

Black Cultural Center

The headquarters of Black Studies on campus is the Black Cultural Center, which was dedicated November 13, 1970. Here events are planned and implemented and the staff is housed. The center provides an atmosphere where persons with a common heritage can gather for intellectual exchange, seminars, exhibits, and educational events.

Programs of Study

The University currently offers an undergraduate "concentration" in Black Studies in which students in any degree program may elect 15 credit hours of Black Studies courses as electives. Courses in anthropology, art, education, English, geography, history, music, political science, and sociology are included in the concentration. Students electing these courses develop skills in comparing historical events with current trends and thus acquire a comprehensive view of the black man and the black psyche.

On the graduate level, a concentration in black literature and history as part of the Master of Arts degree program is offered at the university. A student may elect to concentrate in black literature and history if he is enrolled in either the Master of Arts program in English or the Master of Arts program in history.

Planning of an undergraduate major in Black Studies is now in progress.

Resource Service

A Black Resource Service has been developed at the Black Cultural Center devoted to collecting information on topics related to Black Studies and community services. The service supplies students, faculty, administrators, and members of the community with information and special materials for research in Black and Urban Studies. The service has gathered data and stored documents usually unavailable to the black community. Newspaper files, pamphlets, microfilm, and college and university catalogs are stored in limited-access files at the Black Cultural Center. The service also makes available artifacts and paintings either from the Black Cultural Center collection or on loan from museums or private collectors.

Black Arts Festival

Each year the Black Cultural Center sponsors a Black Arts Festival which is designed to expose the entire university community, through workshops, lectures and other events, to the work of black artists of local and national importance. The week-long festival features black leaders in such fields as art, drama, mass communications, music, politics, etc.

Cultural Enrichment

A number of guest lecturers appear on campus each year as part of the Black Studies program. Speakers have included Adam Clayton Powell, Stokely Carmichael, Charles Evers, Nathan Hare, James Turner, and Barbara Sizemore. A symposium of student leaders from Kent State University, Jackson State College, and Northwestern University was held during Black Martyrs Week in 1971.

Special Activities

Activities sponsored by the Black Cultural Center include a film workshop for elementary school students, a counseling center, a tutoring service, a drama group, and two summer projects.

The history workshop is designed for elementary school students between the ages of 6 and 12. Through the use of movies, film strips, slides, records and story telling, the workshop recounts the history of blacks throughout the world. Students are taught how to develop and produce their own film scripts.

The Black Cultural Center also serves the needs of Afro-Americans in the areas of career planning, educational assistance, and curriculum counseling. "Careers Unlimited" is designed to channel black students into meaningful careers through student-to-student counseling.

The tutorial service is designed to assist students from the university community and the community-at-large.

The Black Arts Theatre exists to give black university students opportunities to perform works in drama and poetry written by blacks.

During the summer the Office of Black Studies directs two summer cultural and enrichment programs for neighborhood youths. Project Overdue enrolls more than 200 youngsters from the Englewood community. In operation since 1968, the program began with high school students, but has been adapted for eight to twelve year olds. Students enrolled in the program are provided with experiences in art, music, mathematics, English, history, and home economics. Project Right-On enrolls more than 200 students of the West Garfield community in activities designed to improve basic skills in reading and mathematics by means of a variety of educational, cultural, and recreational experiences.

Courses Offered During the Fall 1971 Trimester

Anthropology 310–Analysis of Cultural Patterns
Education 361–Educational Issues in the Community
English 291–Afro-American Literature
English 323–Three Contemporary Writers: Wright, Ellison, and Baldwin
English 361–Language and Culture
Geography 316–Urban Geography
History 271–The Negro in the U.S. Since 1619
Music 215–Afro-American Music
Psychology 351–Psychological Problems Related to Afro-Americans
Psychology 352–Testing of Afro-Americans
Sociology 202–Community Organization and Community Problems

Other Black Studies Courses Offered at the University

Anthropology 215–Africa and Afro-America
Anthropology 302–World Ethnology
Art 202–African Art
Art 281–Black Art Workshop
Biological Science 301–Biology of Africa
English 322–Black Poetry
English 333–The Negro Novel
English 334–The Image of the Black Man in American Prose Fiction
Geography 334–The Geography of Africa
History 350–The Negro in the U.S. to 1900
History 351–The Negro in Twentieth Century America
History 445–Seminar in the Negro in America
Music 323–Afro-American Music
Philosophy 305–Special Seminar in Black Philosophy
Political Science 350–Black Politics in America
Sociology 255–Racial and Cultural Minorities

Sociology 257—Group Dynamics
Sociology 302—The Urban Community
Sociology 303—The Black Power Movement

University of Michigan

The Center for Afro-American and African Studies at the University of Michigan is the result of the joint planning and continuing cooperation of the University (largely guided by black faculty and students) and the black community of Ann Arbor. It serves as a focal point for the educational, informational, and community activities consistent with the objectives jointly agreed upon by the university and the black community. The basic administrative structure provides for the following positions: director, administrative associate, academic director of African Studies, academic director of Afro-American Studies, research area director, services area director, and head librarian.

The academic program includes individual courses, degree programs, workshops, seminars, film presentations, lecture series, and cultural exhibits. The underlying objective of the academic program is to provide an understanding and appreciation of the nature and genesis of the cultural and philosophical foundations of black life.

Undergraduate Degree Program

Through the College of Literature, Science, and the Arts, the Center for Afro-American and African Studies offers an inter-disciplinary baccalaureate degree with a concentration in Black Studies. Students are permitted to plan course sequences which will emphasize their particular interests and life objectives. For example, one student may wish to choose courses which will provide preparation for a career in the administration of community projects and services, while another may desire courses oriented toward broader analyses and research into the dynamics of more specialized experiences in the sciences or the humanities. The requirements for the degree are the completion of Afro-American Studies 201 through 204, and 24 credits of additional upper level courses, including at least six hours of involvement in a project that directly benefits the community.

Course Offerings

100—Black Encounter
105—Community Projects

201—Survey of Afro-American History, I
202—Survey of Afro-American History, II
203—Issues in Afro-American Development
204—Cultural History of Afro-Americans
213—Technological Change in the Black World
333—Perspectives in Afro-American History
360—Arts of Black Folk: African-Contemporary, I
410—Supervised Research
411—Tutorial Reading
422—Anthropology: Precolonial Africa
423—Anthropology: African Peoples in the Americas
430—Alternative Approaches in Black Education
450—Black Communities and Legal Rights
455—Seminar on Project and Research Planning and
        Funding
465—History of Afro-American Music, I
466—History of Afro-American Music, II
475—Early Literature by Afro-Americans
476—Contemporary Afro-American Literature
536—Tropical Africa from 1800 to the European
        Conquest
540—Comparative Decolonization
560—Pan-Africanism
577—Black Political, Social, and Cultural
        Developments of the 20th Century
598—Black Politics in the New World
615—Seminar on Problems in African Ethnology
616—Seminar on Contemporary African Societies,
629—Historiography of the Lacustrine Region of
        East Africa
687—Studies in Black History
699—American Cultural Philosophy and Its Historical
        Determinants as Related to Race and Ethnic
        Differences
781—Seminar in Black American History
786—The Conquest of Africa: Background to Modern
        African Nationalism

Non-Degree Program

In addition to courses designed for credits toward a degree, the center offers special courses intended to develop and illustrate the use of varied skills that will contribute to the effective participation of black people in industry and other areas of employment for nonprofessionals. Workshops are held throughout the year which are open to all interested members of the larger community. Discussions and demonstrations are organized around such topics as "Legal Rights," "Neighborhood and Housing Problems," "Community Health and First Aid," "Project Planning," "Basic Business Methods," and "Topics in Black History."

Other types of community service in which students of Black Studies as well as black people in the community are encouraged to participate are community educational projects such as the Liberation School where children between the ages of 6 and 13 are given tutorial help as well as awareness instruction in black history and culture; the legal research and awareness program led by students and knowledgeable adults who assist in general and specific investigative work on class actions beneficial to the black community and who assist in the preparation and dissemination of information describing the legal rights of the poor and the uninformed; and the medical aid service program intended to help publicize information about free medical services to the community such as innoculation against childhood diseases and general physical examinations including chest x-rays.

The most important aid, however, to the effectiveness and success of the Black Studies program is the operation of the Coalition for the Use of Learning Skills (CULS) which offers several academic options to black students who feel the need of special help in the improvement of their learning skills. A description of the program is presented below in the words of its chief spokesman:

> What is CULS? Is it some kind of tutorial or compensatory program for Black students at the University of Michigan? Is it another paper organization with paper solutions to real problems?
>
> The above are common questions at the U-M today. This flyer is an answer to these questions and an appeal for you to become a part of CULS.
>
> CULS, the Coalition for the Use of Learning Skills, is not a program *for* Black students. Rather, it is a program *of* Black people and other people in the University who have experienced the oppressive effects of racism and exploitation and are determined to contribute to changing those effects through improving and using their skills.
>
> The members of CULS are its staff and the students who are committed to active participation in its projects. The people of CULS are united by the recognition of several things:

1. We realize that solid education is essential for the future of our people as a united and moving body and as individual members of that community. We know that to get out of our situation, we must be able to *think*.

2. We realize that the education needed must be the best available; our communities can not afford, nor do they deserve, second-rate workers. We also know that to be functional for us, education must incorporate the truth about Black and other oppressed people and the truth about how the nation and the world operate in the lives of our people, and it must show how our skills can be put to the best use for our community.

3. We realize that all of us—students, staff, and others—must adopt a new stance and approach to education. We must cooperate rather than maliciously compete with one another to *make certain that each and everyone of us in CULS learns and uses what he learns.* Combining the implied attitude with effective methods of learning, the academic problems expected by any student can be either headed-off or easily handled if they arise.

Projects

Following are the major activities undertaken by CULS:

Orientation

Throughout the summer CULS counselors provide assistance and information of particular interest and importance to incoming Black students. During the first week of school the Coalition sponsors a series of workshops, presentations, and social activities to facilitate the transition to the U-M scene and to give students an opportunity to join in the work of local Black organizations, including CULS itself.

Counseling

Incoming students have an option of working with a CULS counselor who is an upperclassman or graduate student. The counselors can provide assistance, advice, and insights into course selection, choices of majors and careers, and a wide range of school-related and personal problems. In addition, the counselors can offer valuable information to all Black students, regardless of level, as to job and future educational possibilities.

Course Study Groups

CULS maintains study groups in a wide range of courses in the sciences, social sciences, languages, mathematics, engineering, and other areas. The groups, which are conducted by CULS study group leaders, center on all the group members (the students) assisting one another in learning materials and preparing for evaluations in associated courses. The group leader is an advanced student or faculty member in the field who can provide help with the course material when the group members can not provide it themselves. The leader also provides guidance as to effective ways to learn the materials and prepare for tests, papers, work, etc. The group is, finally, intended as a setting in which the members can attempt to criticize and relate course materials to the lives and goals of Black people.

General Study Groups

Each term, study groups including students from a diverse set of courses in a general category, e.g. social science or physical science, are organized toward the goal of building skills in handling the materials in courses within these areas. For example, through the group leader's direction and focusing on requirements of their courses, group members can acquire such things as facility in reading, organizing, using library research materials, taking analytical notes, preparing for tests, etc.

Course Sections

CULS sponsors discussion-recitation sections of several courses in the College of Literature, Science, and the Arts. These sections differ from other sections of the courses in that besides introducing concepts and providing the usual clarifications of lectures, an attempt is made to achieve the same ends as CULS course study groups. That is, learning methods are introduced, stress is placed on students cooperating with and teaching one another, and implications of the course content for Black people are discussed.

CULS English 123

A special case of the CULS sections are the CULS English 123 sections. These sections not only are intended to build skills in writing of a broad range of types, but can provide insights into the reading process and a variety of other skills such as analytical note-taking, using library research materials, preparing presentations, and preparing for and taking examinations.

Writers' Clinic

The CULS Writers' Clinic consists of several staff members who are experienced in a wide variety of writing tasks and types as well as assisting others in writing. They can provide direct assistance on specific writing assignments and offer suggestions as to how writing difficulties can be corrected for future work.

Individual Assistance (Tutorials)

When a student has a special difficulty with a particular course and he, for various reasons, cannot receive sufficient assistance in the context of a study group or section, CULS will attempt to arrange individual assistance for him. In contrast to most tutorial situations, the assistants provided by CULS are instructed to not only aid the student in dealing with the problem at hand, but to provide concrete suggestions as to how he can learn more effectively on his own in the future.

Recruitment Assistance

The Coalition staff, in conjunction with the Black Union and the Office of Admissions, organizes recruitment trips by current U-M Black students to Michigan high schools. The objectives are to provide interested Black high school students with: (1) general information and advice on job and further school possibilities, (2) "inside" viewpoints on what college and, specifically the U-M involves, and (3) direct assistance and encouragement in gaining admissions to the U-M or some other institutions if the students desire to further their education.

Faculty and Staff Orientation and Consultation

CULS is well aware of the backlog of misguided attitudes and dispositions present in any faculty of a predominantly white institution. We also know that many, perhaps most, of the members of such faculties are unprepared to offer the kind of education demanded by Black people. With the objectives of alleviating these two problems, CULS maintains conferences with individual faculty members and groups.

General Services

The members of CULS are always prepared to offer assistance to others who are attempting to achieve the same objectives as we. We can provide copies of materials we have, consultation, and, when necessary, people.

Research and Support Projects

To provide the foundations for our work, CULS maintains several research and information gathering projects. These include a project concerned with developing new and effective learning approaches, an evaluation project for evaluating the progress of students and the effectiveness of CULS work, a course content project for developing more useful, stimulating, and relevant courses in all areas, and, finally, a job and labor trends research project to gather and analyze information on post-graduate education, job openings, and economic and labor trends in the Black and the general economies.

Yale University

In the spring of 1968 Yale University sponsored one of the first conferences in the United States to examine the nature of Afro-American Studies. As a result of that examination and the exchange of views between the conferees, an Afro-American Studies program was established at Yale in September, 1969, after considerable planning by several committees, unanimous endorsement by the Yale College faculty, and the receipt of grants from the Ford Foundation and the Rockefeller Foundation.

Major Requirements

The major ordinarily requires twelve terms of course work including Afro-American Studies 20a, 20b, 80a, 90a, 91b and one specialized seminar in the Afro-American Studies 80 series. These courses represent the core of the program and most of them serve as sounding boards for ideas and problems which may originate in many fields but which have the single common aspect—the black experience. The more specialized seminars in the 80 series are designed to explore more profound relationships between the black experience and a specific discipline.

The other six terms of course work are electives in Afro-American Studies and should show some signs of interrelationship either by way of the discipline of concentration or theme of interest that the student wishes to pursue as an Afro-American Studies major.

In addition to the twelve terms of course work constituting the

Afro-American Studies major, a student must have an area of concentration or major in one of the traditional departments such as economics, political science, sociology, anthropology, music. English, history, or one of the sciences. Though a great deal of flexibility is permitted in the choice of courses in the non-Afro-American field, students are encouraged to take a number of upper division courses and especially those centering on research and methodology in the traditional departments. Model programs for each department with recommended courses are available in the Afro-American Studies Office.

Each student must work out his particular course of study in consultation with the Director of Undergraduate Studies, or one of the designated advisers from the faculty and, if necessary, with the help of the Director of Undergraduate Studies in the student's discipline of concentration.

Freshman and Sophomore Years

Afro-American Studies 20a, Comparative Studies of Black Revolution, Decolonization, and Liberation Movements
> An analysis of the historical development of black liberation movements in the United States, Africa, the Caribbean, and Latin America.

Afro-American Studies 20b, Classic Studies of the Black Experience: Introduction to Afro-American Studies
> An interdisciplinary approach to the "great books" dealing with the Afro-American experience. Among the works to be discussed are Frazier's *The Negro Family in the United States,* Myrdal's *An American Dilemma,* Cruse's *The Crisis of the Negro Intellectual,* Ellison's *Shadow and Act,* Toomer's *Cane,* and others.

Junior Year

Afro-American Studies 80a, Interdisciplinary Seminar in Afro-American Studies
Afro-American Studies 82, Afro-American Literary Tradition
Afro-American Studies 82a (American Studies 62a), Black Autobiography
> The black experience—its traumas and triumphs—as reflected in a number of representative autobiographies by black writers

from slavery to the present.
Afro-American Studies 86a and b (American Studies 60a and b),
Comparative Black Literature in the Twentieth Century
Afro-American Studies 83a and b (English 77 - 4a or b) Prose Writers'
Workshop
Part of each class session is devoted to related readings
exclusively from black literature.
Afro-American Studies (English 77-6a or b), Creative Writing
Workshop

Senior Year

Afro-American Studies 90a, Senior Colloquium
Seminar enabling students to discuss progress of their own
research with specialists in various disciplines. *For majors only.*
Afro-American Studies 91b, Senior Essay
(Independent research on senior essay. *For majors only.*
Afro-American Studies 99a and b, Individual Research

For non-majors.
General Courses

Anthropology 43b	Maroon Societies
Anthropology 61b	Anthropological Approaches to Folklore
History 31a and b	Afro-American History
History 65a (Sociology 63a)	The Cuban Revolution: Historical and Sociological Perspectives
History 69b	Race Relations in the Portuguese and Spanish Colonial Empires in the Sixteenth and Seventeenth Centuries
History 70a and b	Introduction to African History
History 91-2b	Slavery and Anti-Slavery
History 91-33b	Research Seminar on Cuba and the Caribbean
History 78b	From the Guinea Coast to the Black Americas
Music 14	Afro-American Music
Psychology 65a	Interpersonal Dynamics and Racism
Psychology 62b	Field Workshop in Intergroup Relations and Psychology

Psychology 83b   New Approaches to Teaching the Inner
                          City Elementary School Student
Sociology 16b   American Racial and Ethnic Groups

Graduate Courses in Afro-American Studies

181 History of Black and White Americans
184b Slavery from the Revolution to the Missouri Compromise
201a History of the South to 1861
201b History of the South since 1861
202a History of American Race Relations
202b Reconstruction and the Gilded Age
208a History of Brazil
140a Carribean Culture
141a Topics in Afro-American Ethnology

Afro-American Studies introduces students to a great variety of
approaches to human problems. Students whose interests are broader
than the usual major within a specific department can learn about
some of the key issues in the humanities and social sciences and
discover ways to adapt their specific knowledge to some of the most
vital needs of society in Afro-American Studies (See Combined
Science Major). Afro-American Studies prepares students for graduate study and a variety of careers by developing special competence
through systematic training in the methods, materials, tools, and
interpretations of several disciplines as they relate to the black
experience in the United States, Latin America, Africa, and Europe.
Afro-American Studies trains students to view contemporary issues
from the perspective of several disciplines and in relationship to
many cultures as part of general liberal education.

Since one of the objectives of Afro-American Studies is to
encourage students to re-examine old theories and uncover new data
about the black experience, majors are eligible for special summer
research grants. Five Afro-American Studies majors received summer
grants to do research on their senior essays in 1970 and 1971: Don
Roman for a historical and sociological study of Richard Wright's
Memphis as portrayed in *Black Boy*; Cecelia McDaniel for field work
in Trinidad, Venezuela, Grenada, and Jamaica to examine African
religious survivals; the late Gerald Edwards for fieldwork in Nevis and
Trinidad to analyze the educational experiences of West Indian

emigrants to New Haven; Larry Thompson for travel to examine the manuscript collections of black writers active during the Harlem Renaissance; and William Farley for a psychological analysis of Pan-Africanism and interviews with contemporary exponents of the concept.

With one of the most distinguished special collections of books and manuscripts on Afro-Americans in the world, Yale University provides a unique opportunity for systematic study in the arts and literature. The James Weldon Johnson Memorial Collection contains thousands of rare books, pamphlets, and manuscripts which are of interest to scholars throughout the United States.

Senior Essay in Afro-American Studies

Early in his junior year each major in Afro-American studies should begin seriously considering a topic for a Senior Essay. Often a student will decide to investigate a subject related to his readings and research in one of the junior seminars. Once the student has found a topic in which he is interested, he must write a brief statement (5 to 10 typed pages) describing the topic, availability and location of sources, demonstrating his general awareness of the literature on the subject, and discussing any special methodology involved. One copy of the prospectus and the name of the faculty member the student wishes to advise him should be given to the Director of Undergraduate Studies on or before May 1. Submissions of the prospectus on or before May 1 is a prerequisite for admission to the Senior Colloquium. Any student who wishes to obtain a summer research grant to work on his essay topic must submit a copy of his prospectus and an itemized statement of expenses on or before April 15th.

The objective of the Senior Essay is to enable a student to collect and evaluate evidence relating to the black experience and to write a concise, fully documented report of his conclusions, assessment of significant controversies, and analyses of the issues involved. Whatever the topic, the essay must be interpretive, critical, and analytical rather than a mere assemblage of facts. At the same time, the essay must meet the general standards for research in the student's major discipline (e.g., in history a student is expected to concentrate on primary rather than secondary sources; in political science, on the formulation of original questions and research designed to answer them). The student should demonstrate a clear knowledge of the general bibliography and methodology of his discipline and the relationship to each of his areas of interest in Afro-American Studies.

The literary quality of the essay should be high. Gaucheries of style, grammar, typographical errors, and incorrect footnoting in the final draft of the paper will not be acceptable. In general the student should try to write an essay comparable in literary quality to those which appear in the journals in his field. In as much as the best papers will be submitted to the various university committees awarding prizes, it is especially important that the essays be typed clearly on good bond. The title page should contain the date on which the essay was submitted, the student's name and that of his advisor, and the words: "An essay written in partial fulfillment of the requirement of Afro-American Studies, Yale University."

In the academic year 1969–70 Yale University faculty approved seventeen Ph.D. dissertation subjects dealing with the life and culture of black people. The subjects are listed here by departments:

American Studies
"The Emergence of Black Political Leadership during Reconstruction"
"A. Philip Randolph and *The Messenger*"
"W. E. B. DuBois"
"James Weldon Johnson"
"Langston Hughes"
Anthropology
"Social and Cultural Feature(s) of Religious Variation in a Trinidadian Town"
Art History
"The Architecture of Djenne"
History
"Adaptation of Negro Personality and Culture in the Emancipation Era: Hampton Roads, 1861–1876"
"Plantocracy, Peasants and Power: Post-Emancipation Colonization– Jamaica, 1838–1865"
"Social Change in a Georgia County, 1850–1880"
"The Suffrage Restriction Movements in the South, 1890–1910"
"The Rise of Residential Segregation in the Urban South, 1860–1930"
"Mirror of Possibilities: Americans View Slavery, Anti-Slavery and the Negro Abroad, 1830–1870"
"Archibald Henry Grimke: A Biography"

"Industrial Workers in Birmingham, Alabama, 1871–1908"

Religious Studies

"Francis James Grimke, Portrait of a Black Puritan"

Sociology

"The Career of an Innovative Project" [A case study of the establishment of a clinic in a mainly black area]

Since 1969–70 nineteen Danforth Post-Doctoral Fellows in Afro-American Studies have chosen to matriculate at Yale for their year of intensive independent research, a larger number than any other university has attracted. Evidence in the university files indicates that they have not been disappointed. In 1972 a Yale Black Studies major was selected as a Rhodes Scholar.

At Yale it is customary for most students to choose double majors to increase their options for later graduate study or for immediate job opportunities. Consequently, the regulation that all Black Studies majors are required to select an additional discipline for a second major or concentration is considered normal. A model program is listed below to indicate in a general way how the program of a Black Studies major might look if he chose literature as his traditional discipline.

Literature Concentration

The majors in Afro-American studies with concentration in literature are advised to supplement the study of AFAM Literature with work in the basic forms and modes of general literature (especially fiction and poetry) and/or the study of specific literary movements and periods (i.e., Romantic, Twentieth Century, etc.)

Freshman

First Semester
English 25–Major English Poets (or English 15)
Foreign Language I (or III)
Natural Science Elective (Biology 10 recommended)
AFAM 20a–Comparative Studies of Black Revolution
English 29–The European Tradition

Second Semester
English 25–Major English Poets
Foreign Language II (or IV)
Natural Science Elective
AFAM 20b–Classic Studies of the Black Experience
English 29–The European Tradition

Sophomore

First Semester
Foreign Language III (or elective)
Math 10a—Analytic Geometry and Calculus I
History 31—Afro-American History
AFAM 82—Afro-American Literary Tradition
English 56a—American Literature (19th Century)

Second Semester
Foreign Language IV (or elective)
History 31—Afro-American History
AFAM 82 Afro-American Literary Tradition
English 59b—Twentieth Century American Literature (before 1945)
Elective in English

Junior

First Semester
AFAM 80a—Interdisciplinary Seminar in Afro-American Studies
English 66a—Aspects of Fiction
English 71a—Contemporary Poetic Theory and Practice: The Eliot Revolution
Elective in English and/or AFAM
Free Elective

Second Semester
AFAM 80 Series Elective
Elective in English
Elective in English or AFAM
Elective in English or AFAM
Free Elective

Senior

First Semester
AFAM 90a—Senior Colloquium
Elective in English and/or AFAM
Elective in English
Free Elective
Free Elective

Second Semester
AFAM 91b—Senior Essay
History of Art 78b—From Guinea Coast to the Black Americas
Elective in English and/or AFAM
Free Elective
Free Elective

CLASS CC

Atlanta University

Afro-American Studies have had a long and respectable history at Atlanta University—a history that extends back to the mid-1890's. Under the leadership of the distinguished scholar W. E. B. DuBois, the university as an undergraduate institution sponsored a series of annual conferences on the "Negro in the Cities." By 1910, these conferences had spawned twenty monographs dealing with many significant sociological, educational, and cultural aspects of the Afro-American urban experience. A second period of major emphasis of Afro-American Studies began when the university became a graduate school in 1929 and DuBois rejoined the faculty in 1933. Thus, in the light of the history of Atlanta University, Afro-American Studies are not new but actually part of a long and distinguished university tradition.

The program in Afro-American Studies, which was inaugurated in 1970, is a cross-disciplinary academic program leading to the Master of Arts degree. Essentially, the program involves an interdisciplinary blend of black content courses in the humanities and in the social sciences. Specifically involved in the program are the Departments of English, History, Political Science, Economics, French, and Sociology and Anthropology. In all of the courses the major objective will be to explore, both diachronically and synchronically, the many dimensions of the black man's experience. Not only will the American black man's African roots and his American past be studied, but there will be an attempt to discover the myriad ways in which the black man's past impinges on his present.

To secure a degree in this program, a student must complete twenty-four semester hours of course work, maintaining a B average throughout; pass a comprehensive examination; and prepare and submit an acceptable thesis. The criteria for admission to the program are:

1. All candidates must hold a baccalaureate degree from a standard, four-year institution.
2. All candidates must have earned a B average in an undergraduate major (21 to 24 hours) in either history, political science, American or English literature, sociology, economics, or Afro-American studies.

Although an effort will be made to offer a varied and flexible program adjusted to the needs and interests of the students, all Afro-American studies degree candidates will be required to take a six-hour core of courses as follows:

1.   Proseminar—Introduction to Afro-American Culture
2.   The Peoples of Africa or The History of West Africa
     Other courses which the student may elect to take can be selected from the department course offerings listed herein.

Course Offerings

510—Black Economic Development
530—The Black Worker
532—Afro-American Dialect
534—Black Poetry
538—Contemporary West African Literature
545—Methods of Research
590—Seminar: Women in Afro-American Literature
482—Poetry of Negritude
662—Seminar: History and Culture of Francophone Africa
478—The South and the Negro
462—African History
463—The Negro in the United States
          Music: Survey of Afro-American Music I
                  Survey of Afro-American Music II
441—Public Opinion and Propaganda
452—Constitution and Racism in the U.S.
453—Blacks and American Political System
529—Politics in Developing States
490—Racial and Cultural Relations
575—Introduction to African Anthropology
647—Decision-Making in the Black Community

With the aid of a Ford Foundation grant a Ph.D. program in Black Studies is now (1972) in the planning stage.

10
Workshops, Institutes, and Conferences for Administrators and Teachers

When pressures for inclusion of Black Studies in the curricula of American colleges and universities were vehemently applied by black students during the 1967–68 academic year, the administrations and faculties of these predominantly white institutions were totally unprepared to react intelligently. Very few institutions had even one black teacher on its staff, and the thought of hiring qualified black faculty had not reached the level of consciousness. But black student power accelerated so rapidly that before the end of the second semester it had become apparent that positive remediation was inevitable. Consequently, administrators began to encourage white faculty members who seemed sympathetic to black student demands to prepare to offer some token black courses the following fall. To this end administrators and faculty joined forces in a search for the best means of preparation for the inevitability.

Fortunately, three years earlier the U.S. Congress had enacted a bill known as the National Foundation on the Arts Act, designed to offer support for educational and public programs, research, and fellowships in all areas of the humanities. On the basis of this mandate the National Endowment for the Humanities was founded in 1965 and by the summer of 1968 was prepared to support a limited number of workshops and institutes in the South and Northeast, with a $10,000 grant for each to defray costs not covered by participants' fees. Seven institutes devoted to various aspects of Black Studies were granted aid by the Foundation and served to assist approximately 350 teachers, most of whom were white, to prepare themselves for token courses which colleges and universities were forced to offer the following fall. Four of the institutions conducting these learning experiences were predominantly black, and three were predominantly white. Each participant was nominated for attendance by the chief academic or executive officer of his institution, with the provision that the nominating institution would pay travel and living expenses for each participant. The names, dates, and specialties of the workshops are listed below.

Southern University, Baton Rouge, Louisiana, August 12–16. Director: E. C. Harrison, vice-president for academic affairs. The focus was on literature, criticism, and the visual arts in the context of American Negro culture, designed to produce extensive and annotated bibliographies.

Howard University, Washington, D.C., July 22–26. Director: Dorothy Porter, librarian of the Negro Collection. This workshop provided opportunities for participants to meet and discuss with specialists problems pertaining to the improvement of library collections dealing with the American Negro, to help to produce working documents in the field, and to consider such topics as securing and/or producing pertinent audiovisual materials, indexing and microfilming, and securing and handling manuscript collections.

Boston University, Boston, Massachusetts, August 5–17. Director: John Cartwright, Afro-American Coordinating Center. The major consideration was to determine how existing courses in the social sciences could most effectively incorporate materials on the Afro-American experience. Also areas of research which could produce valid new courses dealing with Afro-Americans were explored.

Fisk University, Nashville, Tenessee, August 26–31. Director: George N. Redd, dean of the college. The main objective was to formulate a model interdisciplinary program which would effectively incorporate the black experience in American civilization.

Morgan State College, Baltimore, Maryland, August 5–9. Director: Roland C. McConnell, chairman of the Department of History. The purpose of this workshop was to provide an extensive chronological review of the Negro in American history and to introduce participants to relevant resource materials on the subject.

Duke University, Durham, North Carolina, August 18–24. Director: Richard L. Watson, Jr., Department of History. The purpose of this workshop was to provide assistance to teachers of new courses in the history of the American Negro. Major topics included: "African Backgrounds for American Negro History," "Slavery," "The Civil War and Reconstruction," "Capitulation to Racism,"

"School of Negro Thought," "Urban Problems," and the "Harlem Renaissance."

Cazenovia College, Cazenovia, New York, August 18–24. Director: Lionel R. Sharp, Department of Languages and Literature. This conference, which attracted 100 participants representing every geographical region of the country, was co-sponsored by the National Council of Teachers of English, a professional organization with a membership of more than 150,000, covering the various levels of instruction in language and literature from the elementary through the graduate school. However, participants were limited to college and university teachers. The stated objective was to assist the participants (eighty percent white) to gain an understanding and appreciation of the most effective methods of organizing and teaching courses in Afro-American literature on the college and university level.

Although each institute or workshop had its own methods of achieving its objectives, the reader might be interested in seeing the operational plan of one such group. I shall, therefore, present here the most important aspects of the Cazenovia plan as set forth in the mimeographed guide for participants.

Summer Institute on Curriculum Development
Resources on the Negro in American Literature
Consultants

The following specialists will be present throughout the week to conduct the Institute:

Dr. Nick Aaron Ford, Chairman of the Department of English and Speech, Morgan State College; author of *American Culture in Literature;* editor of *Language in Uniform;* co-author of *Basic Skills for Better Writing;* contributor to *College Composition and Communication, College English, The English Journal, Teachers College Record;* member of Administrative Committee of MLA's Association of Departments of English and of NCTE's Board of Directors; former president of College Language Association; former consultant for USOE and the Ford Foundation.

Mrs. Elizabeth Postell, Assistant Professor of English, Chicago City College, Woodrow Wilson Campus; presently on special leave as a Fellow at the Innovations Center of Chicago City College to prepare a syllabus for a course in American Negro Literature.

Mr. Ishmael Reed, novelist; author of *The Free-Lance Pallbearers* and of the forthcoming *Yellow Back Radio Broke-Down;* guest lecturer at the University of California at Berkeley; contributor to *Arts Magazine, Ikon, The Urban Review, The Writer.*

Dr. Darwin T. Turner, Dean of the Graduate School, North Carolina A & T State University; author of *Katharsis,* a volume of poems, and of the forthcoming *Negro American Writers;* co-editor of *Images of the Negro in America*; contributor of articles and reviews to *CLA Journal, Journal of Human Relations, Journal of Negro History, Massachusetts Review, Negro History Bulletin, Southern Humanities Review*; consultant at NDEA Summer Institutes, 1965, 1966, 1967; former president of College Language Association.

Program

Through a series of lectures, discussion groups, and individual study sessions during the week, the program will include:

Consultations with specialists on materials by and about the Negro in American literature.

Consideration of standards for selection of relevant materials.

Examination and evaluation of bibliographies and other lists of materials.

Examination and evaluation of curriculum materials: books, pamphlets, periodicals, tapes, recordings, films.

Examination of course and unit outlines on the Negro in American literature.

Distributions and discussion of selected materials for use in the development of curriculum resources.

The 100 participants were divided into four sections of 25 each, and each section met 75 minutes per day with each consultant from Tuesday (August 20) through Friday (August 23) between 9:00 a.m. and 4:30 p.m. This meant that each participant had 75 minutes of group contact with each consultant every day, which is a total of five contact hours with the four consultants daily, as well as individual conferences when requested. Each consultant was concerned primarily with a particular specialty but was free to consider for discussion questions of any kind with which he felt qualified to deal. For instance, the general divisional areas were fiction, poetry, drama, and curriculum organization. During the first day, August 19, each consultant presented an introductory lecture on his specialty, attended by all participants. In the evenings from 8:00 to 10:00 p.m. the following films dealing with black life and culture were presented with full attendance of participants:

"The Game" (17 min.). Cinema 16 Film Library, Inc.

"Harlem Wednesday" (10 min.). Cinema.

"Sunlight" (9 min.). Cinema.

"The Cry of Jazz" (35 min.). Cinema.

"Malcolm X: Struggle for Freedom" (22 min.). Cinema.

"Black Spring" (30 min.). Jihad Productions.

"Dutchman" (60 min.). Jihad Productions.

"Nothing but a Man" (92 min.). Brandon Films, Inc.

"Portrait of Jason" (105 min.). Film Makers Distribution Center.

A special lecture was delivered by Saunders Redding, distinguished black scholar and writer, who was at that time an official of the National Endowment for the Humanities. The concluding presentations on Saturday consisted of readings by poet Naomi Madget, a forum of participants including Alfred H. Grommon, president of the National Council of Teachers of English, and a panel discussion by the consultants with the addition of Ernece Kelly of Chicago State College.

During the summer of 1969 the Ford Foundation joined the National Endowment for the Humanities to increase the number of subsidized workshops in Black Studies from seven to fourteen and to extend the coverage to the Midwest and to the West. The cost to the home institutions of participants was reduced from the entire expenses for travel, tuition, and living costs required in 1968 to one-half of the previous amounts.

The workshops were as follows:

Brooklyn College of C.U.N.Y., June 10–20. The purpose was to prepare the faculty members to incorporate Negro history and culture within existing courses and to set up new programs in Black Studies.

University of California at Los Angeles, July 14–August 1. The major concern was with materials and methodology in the teaching of Afro-American culture and history.

Ferris State College, Big Rapids, Michigan, August 17–23. The major objective was to examine the image of the Negro in films and to explore ways in which films can be used to improve college instruction in the humanities and social sciences.

Fisk University, Nashville, Tennessee, August 4–15. The purpose was to acquaint social science and humanities teachers with available materials in Black Studies and the several approaches for their incorporation within the liberal arts curriculum.

Morgan State College, Baltimore, Maryland, August 4–8. The aim was to afford faculty members an opportunity to increase their knowledge of the black experience and to prepare themselves to strengthen or redesign their college curricula to reflect the increasing demand for Afro-American studies.

North Carolina Central University, Durham, July 21–August 1. The objective was to provide bibliographical and other vital information to enable participants to continue individual research on Negro history in order to qualify to teach the subject more effectively.

Northwestern University, Evanston, Illinois, August 4–10. The purpose was "to provide curriculum materials on and a deeper understanding of contemporary race relations for college faculty members" in order to strengthen existing courses and prepare to introduce new courses stressing "the historical context of American race relations."

Pitzer College and *Claremont Graduate School,* California, June 22–July 4. The focus was on the validity of the black experience as an academic pursuit with special emphasis directed toward the development of materials, courses, and curricula for teaching Black Studies.

Roosevelt University, Chicago, June 23–August 1. The focus was on the American Negro's history, social organizations, and contributions in the arts.

Southern University, Baton Rouge, Louisiana, August 9–24. The aim was to provide intensive attention to the teaching of Afro-American literature and art at the college and university level. Vital issues included the role of whites in relation to black literature, black students, and the cultural revolution; the political implications of Black Studies; and the relation of Black Studies to racial identity.

University of Texas, Austin, June 23–August 1. The workshop was designed as experience spanning the total area of Black Studies. Sensitivity sessions and confrontations were provided with panels of blacks from various levels of the community along with black and white college and high school teachers.

Cazenovia College, Cazenovia, N.Y., August 3–23. The experience included a concentrated study of black literature and an exploration of innovative curriculum concepts and their application to the design of multi-media literature programs.

University of Iowa, Iowa City, July 1–August 8. The major objective was to offer concentrated advanced training in the history and culture of the black American designed for college and university teachers and to provide bibliographical aids and manuscript sources for research.

Atlanta University, June 22–August 3. The purpose was "to give substantive direction and academic coherence to the black studies movement."

The summer of 1969 marked the highest point of interest in workshops and short-term institutes for the "training" of teachers of Black Studies. In the summer of 1970 there were only three such institutes sponsored by the National Endowment for the Humanities in contrast to fourteen in 1969. In 1971 the number was four, one of which was limited to junior and senior high school teachers. It appears that the novelty of the thrust for Black Studies has now become shopworn, and college and university faculties have made whatever accommodations they think are necessary. In some cases institutions have sought to fulfill their obligations to the black experience by permitting and occasionally encouraging teachers to integrate it into their regular courses in American history, American literature, and the arts, regardless of the teacher's academic competence or racial attitude. Consequently, some white teachers have used this liberty to exercise their racial prejudices in subtle and offensive ways in the name of democratic coverage of subject matter. In other cases separate black courses have been established on an elective basis with the aid of teachers willing to volunteer for the assignment. It is assumed that there are now enough books and articles in educational journals to satisfy the needs of teachers who wish to prepare themselves to teach these courses.

Furthermore, after the first series of summer workshops and institutes in 1968 the tension between whites and blacks and between "separatist" blacks and "integrationist" blacks became so intense and intransigent that constructive accomplishments were limited. Objective observers of the fourteen 1969 "training" experiences reported:

> Discussion and even heated confrontation arose over the issue of whether whites could or should teach black studies. The desire of many whites to authenticate themselves as "Negro experts" was repugnant to certain black participants . . . .
> It appeared that some black participants viewed the workshop as an occasion requiring a militant posture. One reason might be the fact that approximately seventy percent of the participants were white (although blacks outnumbered whites about five to one on the faculties and consultant staffs of the workshops) . . . .White participants, on the other hand, complained of the paucity of black participants and the hostile atmosphere. They had come with the intention of "mixing" with black faculty members and felt they had been short-changed, rejected and excluded by the behavior of the blacks.

There were, of course, sufficient accomplishments to consider all workshop experiences of considerable value. Of foremost importance was that they emphasized the fact that the black experience, which had been ignored entirely in the curricula of predominantly white institutions, could not be introduced into the educational programs of colleges and universities without proper orientation and that the proper persons to direct this orientation were black scholars who were experts by nature, scholarship, and experience. The workshops dispelled the myth concerning the insufficiency of scholarly materials necessary to warrant the establishment of legitimate courses in Afro-American life and culture. They also shattered for white participants the stereotypes of all blacks being alike. They permitted the whites to see that blacks often differ among themselves as widely and as bitterly as the general American population and that black students must be understood and taught as individuals rather than as white-conceived stereotypes. In addition, they provided opportunities for frank exchanges of opinions between white and black teachers concerning basic inequities, inadequacies, and inconsistencies in American educational practices directly related to institutional racism.

Probably the most significant of all the institutes held thus far was the Institute on Richard Wright, sponsored by the Afro-American Studies program at the University of Iowa. Its special significance is in the fact that it was the first time a prestigious American university had chosen to recognize the worth of an American black writer as a subject for rigorous and exhaustive study in a two-week institute for mature scholars and teachers with an M.A. degree or its equivalent as the minimum requirement for admission. Seminars were organized for the close textual study of Wright's five novels, two volumes of short stories, and autobiography, led by recognized Wright scholars, black and white. The morning seminars were led by Charles T. Davis, University of Iowa; Donald B. Gibson, University of Connecticut; Nick Aaron Ford, Morgan State College; George Kent, University of Chicago; and Edward Margolies, Staten Island Community College. Lectures, scheduled in the afternoons and evenings, were delivered by Ralph Ellison; Margaret Walker, poet, novelist, and director of the Institute for the Study of History, Life, and Culture of Black People, Jackson State College; Allison Davis, University of Chicago; Kenneth Kinnamon, University of Illinois; Martin Kilson, Harvard University; Michel Fabre, University of Paris; Robert Washington; and Daniel Aaron. Organized and unorganized discussion groups added to the engrossing pleasure and excitement of the unprecedented experience.

There have been three national conferences on Black Studies whose announced purpose was evaluation. The first one was sponsored by the Institute for the Study of History, Life, and Culture of Black People, Jackson State College, February 17–20, 1971, and funded by grants from the National Endowment for the

Humanities, the Ford Foundation, and the Cooperative Project of Binghamton-Harpur College-Jackson State. The announced purpose of the conference was threefold: (1) To discover the nature, philosophy, and method of Black Studies programs as they exist in the various types of colleges and universities; (2) to evaluate the educational worth of such programs as revealed by the extent and nature of the changes they effected; (3) to consider the formulation of a broad spectrum of criteria to serve as guidelines for acceptable programs of Black Studies.

The evaluative process was implemented by means of lectures, workshops, committees, and questionnaires. Eight workshops, each consisting of four two-hour sessions, were organized as follows: *Workshop I*—Directors of Black Studies programs considered the following topics: (1) Philosophy, Purposes, and Directions of Black Studies. (2) Black Studies, an Academic Discipline or a Corrective Program? (3) Some Criteria for Future Black Studies Programs. *Workshop II*—For teachers of Black History. *Workshop III*—For teachers of Sociology, Psychology, and Anthropology. *Workshop IV*—For teachers of Afro-American literature. *Workshop V*—For students of Black Studies. *Workshop VI*—For Teachers of the Black Man in Art. *Workshop VII*—For Teachers of the Music of the Black Man. *Workshop VIII*—The Black Church. Discussion in each workshop was initiated by the presentation of a position paper and a reactor paper prepared by selected participants prior to the conference. Six lectures were presented covering such topics as "Political Life Styles," "The New Black in Search of Self," "Education and the Government," "Black Collections in Libraries," "Research in Black History and Family Styles," and "The Current State of Black Studies."

The following paragraphs present a summary of the final report of Dr. Margaret Walker Alexander, director of Jackson State College's Institute for the Study of History, Life, and Culture of Black People and organizer and director of the conference.

(1) It was agreed that on black and white college campuses there is a divided philosophy concerning Black Studies. One philosophy insists that Black Studies are a revolutionary concept whose guiding purpose must be allied with the political need of blacks to establish black nationhood within and without current national boundaries. The other philosophy views Black Studies as a potent instrument for a massive attack upon the very foundation of racism in American

education and all American life by the use of the democratic methods that the white majority professes to respect. The latter philosophy insists that Black Studies must conform to reasonable standards characteristic of a valid academic discipline.

(2) There is irreconcilable disagreement among blacks concerning the control of Black Studies programs. One group believes that black students, with the assistance of black faculty members of whom they approve, should be in control. The other group believes that black students should serve in an advisory capacity only in respect to the administration of the program.

(3) There is no agreement on the extent to which community involvement should be required of participants in the program. Some strongly believe such involvement must be compulsory, and others believe with equal fervor that it should be optional.

(4) It was the general consensus that most white institutions have made no real commitment to Black Studies. Government agencies and Foundations are "phasing out" their concern and the whole movement stands in jeopardy through "benign neglect."

Sixty-five colleges from thirty-seven states were represented. Although the experience was considered by most to be enlightening and useful in many ways, it did not succeed in achieving to any appreciable degree the goal of meaningful evaluation.

Approximately a month after the Jackson State conference a second conference with a similar aim and with an equal number of participants representing institutions not represented at Jackson convened at Rutgers University, New Brunswick, under the auspices of the A. Philip Randolph Educational Fund, to consider "Problems of the Afro-American Studies Curriculum." The organizational pattern and method of procedure differed markedly from the Jackson State College plan. The two-day discussion centered around the presentation of a so-called model Afro-American Studies program prepared by the director of Black Studies at a black college. The participants focused on the strengths and weaknesses of the model. As was true of the earlier experience, there were so many irreconcilable points of view about every aspect of specific programs that no agreement could be achieved even on minimum essentials. As to philosophical attitudes concerning the basic objectives of a Black Studies program, the insistence upon academic standards in consonance with the general requirements of traditional concepts of scholarships was more apparent than the separatist political view that dominated the earlier gathering. The conference director, Ernest Rice

McKinney, and Bayard Rustin, executive director of the A. Philip Randolph Institute, were clearly in favor of emphasis on the more traditional standards of scholarship as the desired direction in which the drive toward Black Studies should move.

The third National Conference on Black Studies was held at Gary, Indiana, November 5–6, 1971, under the guidance of Charles E. Mosley, chairman of the Black Studies program at Chicago State University. It was sponsored by the African Association for Black Studies which was founded December 11, 1970, at Chicago State College (now Chicago State University) by representatives of seventeen institutions of higher learning in Illinois and Indiana. The statement of philosophy as set forth in Article II of the Association's constitution follows:

> The African Association for Black Studies is dedicated to the development of the concept of Pan-Africanism and the internalization of our African heritage. Realizing that we are an African People, we are dedicating ourselves to liberation through Pan-Africanism. We define Pan-Africanism as (a) Black People defining themselves and (b) the unifying acts of African People wherever they find themselves. The African Association for Black Studies has chosen "Black Studies" as our means of implementing this objective by the development of skill and professional expertise through an inter-disciplinary educational process.

The conferees ratified the most specific and detailed set of standards and criteria for Black Studies programs that has ever been agreed upon by a voluntary group of representatives of such programs. The statement is reproduced below by permission: [9]

Standards and Criteria for the Establishment,
Recognition and Evaluation of Black Studies Programs
and Their Component Parts

A. The Institution:
   The institution must have clearly defined goals and be committed to the support and propagation of the Black Studies Program and its objectives.
B. Administration:
   The chief administrative officer must be an individual judged qualified through academic training and/or experience by his peers in the field. His duties should encompass not only those normally associated with administrators at comparable levels, but also activities related to the community and students being served by the program. Such duties, lines of communication and authority, and total program scope shall be firmly established and clearly delineated by the institution.
C. Faculty:
   The faculty must give evidence of scholarly achievement and competence

within the area of instruction. Exceptions may only be made if the non-academic experience of a faculty member is of such nature as to provide a particularly enriching quality to the program not obtainable elsewhere. No program should be based upon a fully part-time faculty, and members of the faculty should be specifically assigned to an autonomous academic unit.

D. Budget:

The program should be adequately supported financially with concern being given to:

    a. competitive salaries for faculty, staff and administrators

    b. adequate funds for cultural and academic programs both at the institution and in the community

    c. financial aid for students serviced by the program

    d. supplies, equipment and travel

    e. library acquisitions

E. Curriculum:

The curriculum should reflect the needs of the students and the community. It shall be a degree-granting program with courses systematically and programmatically projecting the theme of Pan-Africanism. The development, additions and deletions within the curriculum shall be the responsibility of the chief administrative officer of the program.

F. Library:

The library shall contain a core curriculum of materials related to the Black experience including filmstrip, reference works, microfilm, microfiche and periodicals. Additionally, a larger collection should provide research support for courses reflected in the curriculum of the Black Studies Program. A sufficient number of contemporary periodicals, newspapers and non-scholarly materials should be included. The academic and geographic community should, periodically, be made aware of new acquisitions.

G. Student Services–Counseling:

There should be an organized program within the institution with staff members qualified through experience to deal with the peculiar problems of minority group and disadvantaged students. The counseling staff should be large enough to provide individual counseling service at each major stage of the student's academic career. Additional counseling service should also be available within the Black Studies Program.

H. Financial Aid:

The institution should commit itself to assisting students financially in their pursuit of an education by providing grants, scholarships, long term loans and deferred tuition. Information concerning additional financial support from outside agencies should be made available to students and widely circulated within the community being serviced.

A unique institute with broader emphases and objectives than the ones previously discussed is the Institute of the Black World, founded officially in 1969 by Vincent Harding, a black scholar and former professor and chairman of the Department of History and Sociology at Spelman College, Atlanta, Georgia. In a statement of purpose it is defined as "an independent research center whose work is based upon the conviction that black people must move to control the definition of our past and our present if we are to become masters of our future." Among its specific aims are the development of new materials and methods for the teaching of black children, the development of a Black Policy Study Center, the establishment of creative links with counterparts in other areas of the Black World, and the preparation of a new cadre of men and women trained in the scholarship of the black experience and fully committed to the struggles of the Black World.

Its first concerted effort to influence the nature and direction of Black Studies was in the fall of 1969 when it sponsored a workshop for Black Studies directors to meet under favorable conditions "to share and analyze their experiences" with the leadership of the institute. Its first annual report, December, 1970, listed among its achievements, active cooperation with the director of the under-graduate Afro-American studies program at Atlanta University in developing an eight-week institute on Afro-American Studies for faculty members from ten black colleges and universities. In addition, it mentioned cooperative working relationships "with the black students and faculties in charge of the Black and African Studies programs at Brooklyn College, Dartmouth College, Cornell, and Wesleyan University." It further disclosed that its staff members have actively participated in conferences and workshops sponsored by other organizations. On several occasions its staff members have been invited by college and university Black Studies programs to visit their campuses for evaluative purposes.

IV

THE FUTURE
1974—

To predict the future is hazardous. Yet the need for predictive insight in respect to possible outcomes is so overwhelming that fortunes are made by those whose predictive powers have been sharpened by the ability to interpret signs and analyze correctly the trends in political polls. Even weather forecasting and the art of predicting success or failure of human activities in accordance with the zodiac sign under which one was born have become prosperous professions. I do not, of course, expect to profit materially by any predictive foresight I may be able to exercise here, but I am tempted to assess the future of Black Studies on the basis of testimony by knowledgeable observers, of trends now apparent from my two years of close observation, and on my intuitive judgment based on the inherent nature of the forces involved in shaping that future.

Of sixty representative directors of Black Studies who agreed to comment on the question, 34 percent predicted a bright future, one asserting that "the program will be around as long as Plato and Aristotle have already been studied." Twenty-three percent thought that there will be a decline in separate courses but an integration of black materials into regular courses in the general curriculum. Twenty percent was pessimistic, suggesting that severe financial problems and outright opposition of administration and faculty cast an ominous shadow over the future. Fifteen percent was afraid "the establishment will turn Black Studies into an antipoverty program unless greater emphases are placed on improving the quality of the programs." The remainder believed that for permanent survival these programs must look to the black colleges for adoption and support.

11
White Colleges and the
Future of Black Studies

I agree with those who believe that Black Studies are here to stay, although the survival will assume different or somewhat modified objectives, methods, and results from most of those now in vogue. In this chapter we shall be concerned with examining the prospects for the survival of Black Studies on the white college or university campus, the possible conditions of such survival, and the effects of the survival on the white institution and the black and white students.

To begin, let us clearly understand that although the term Black Studies is usually taken to mean an organized program, in reality it rightfully means a collection of courses dealing primarily with black life and culture, individually administered or organized into a special program. Thus an institution which offers one or more courses in Afro-American literature or Afro-American history without being a part of an organized program leading to a major or concentration is offering courses in Black Studies. Since the number of students who actually major or concentrate in Black Studies is seldom more than ten percent of the black student enrollment whereas an average of fifty percent of these students as well as a considerable number of their white classmates register for one or two such courses, the college or university with such offerings is playing an active role in promoting the cause of Black Studies.

(1) In the light of this explanation one can confidently predict that Black Studies are here to stay and that although some organized programs with chairmen or directors will be discontinued for many reasons, the trend will be to increase the number and variety of

individual courses by more and more institutions until all accredited colleges and universities will be represented. Reliable evidence indicates that at least fifty percent of all accredited institutions of higher learning now offer one or more such courses. I predict, therefore, that in the future one role of the white college will be to increase the number of its courses in Black Studies until there will be at least one such course in every significant area of black life and culture.

(2) The white college must accelerate its efforts to incorporate educational materials of black life and culture into every course in the curriculum that can appropriately absorb them. Naturally all courses in the humanities and the social sciences are capable of reflecting aspects of the black experience, whereas mathematics and most of the natural sciences cannot. The acceptance of this role means that every course in American literature, American history, music, and the fine arts will include objective information and evaluation of the activities and/or contributions of distinguished blacks. Already trends of this kind have begun in representative institutions. Recently I was invited to serve as consultant to the English Department of one of the largest public junior colleges in the South to assist in the incorporation of the most significant writings of black poets, dramatists, fiction writers, and essayists into regular courses offered by the department.

(3) The white college will begin or continue to make available on a permanent basis interdisciplinary programs (or independent departments) in Black Studies which will provide opportunities for black and white students who so desire to major or concentrate in the field. In addition, institutions qualified to offer the M.A. and/or the Ph.D. degree will begin or continue to encourage (or at least not discourage) black and white graduate students to choose theses and dissertation projects in a wide variety of areas of black life and culture. Harvard University was the first American institution of higher learning to acknowledge this role when in 1896 it accepted W. E. B. DuBois' study, *Suppression of the African Slave Trade to the United States of America, 1638–1870,* as fulfillment of the dissertation requirement for the Ph.D. degree.[1] Since 1896 other universities have occasionally accepted dissertations in the field of black history, sociology, and education, but rarely have literature and the arts been included. When dissertations have been approved in the latter two disciplines, the students involved have for the most part been white.

The phenomenon of discouraging blacks and encouraging whites to undertake dissertations in the area of black literature has resulted from the refusal of the white professors of English to admit that a black scholar is capable of an objective or valid act of literary criticism. Only recently have white journal editors and book publishers been willing to consider for publication an article or a book of literary criticism by a black scholar. In the too recent past, whenever such an article or book on literary criticism was submitted, even though it concerned black literature, the editor or publisher would send the manuscript for evaluation to a white literary scholar who admittedly knew almost nothing about black writers or their writings. The white consultant would suggest certain changes that must be made in the black critic's judgments in order to conform to the white consultant's stereotyped notions. If the black critic rejected the consultant's ill-conceived advice, as was almost always the case, the article or book was never published. Some white colleges have now begun to repudiate this blatant racism, and the number will slowly accelerate in the future.

(4) The white college which now has an organized Black Studies program with a chairman or director will be forced to face up to the problem of granting it equal status with all other programs of a similar nature, or to discontinue it. Of course, it is easier to hold on to an inferior program, make excuses for lack of adequate support, and accept the responsibility for crippling black students who have the misfortune of being affiliated with it. It is easier to offer a self-serving or misguided director a meagre, inadequate budget and give him the privilege of setting his own standards for all aspects of the program regardless of the failure to approximate the superior quality of general college standards. Such abdication of responsibility by a college or university is reprehensible and will lead to the discrediting of the legitimate concept of Black Studies in general. Such an abdication of educational responsibility by an accredited college is legitimate grounds for a protest of that accreditation. It adds strength to the assertion of Thomas Sowell, black professor at U.C.L.A., who complains, "Even where the intellectually oriented black student makes his way into and through college without being directly harmed by all this, he cannot be unaffected by the double standard which makes his degree look cheap in the market and his grades suspect to those concerned with academic standards. Worst of all, he cannot even have the full confidence within himself that he really earned them." A college which does not guard against the

cheapening of its degree, whether by students in a substandard Black Studies program or athletes on a top-rated football or basketball team, deserves the condemnation and scorn of the academic profession.

(5) The white college in the future will be expected to acknowledge Black Studies as the forerunner of interest in various other kinds of ethnic studies, and to recognize the differences among them. Since the insistent demand for Black Studies began in 1967 other ethnic groups have sought similar treatment. Of course, it is a well-known fact that Jewish Studies have been recognized in American education for many years. The Hebrew Bible, which embodies many historical and cultural aspects of Jewish life, is better known by the majority of Americans than the basic facts of American history. Furthermore, in the past three or four decades some of the most distinguished authors and critics studied in American literature have been Jews. Consequently, Jews are not demanding equal educational time and resources as that allotted to blacks because they know they already have enjoyed the limelight to a much greater extent than blacks. But other ethnics such as American Indians, Mexican-Americans, Asian-Americans, and Puerto Ricans are rightly seeking fair treatment for their life and culture in school and college curriculums. Furthermore, the "forgotten American," as described by President Nixon, which means the white lower-middle class worker, is often considered "ethnic" because he is usually the first, second, or third generation of central, east, or south European stock. He is also generally angry, troubled, and alienated for reasons similar to those of nonwhite minorities.

The Ford Foundation *Letter,* December 1, 1970, contains the following significant article concerning ethnic studies:

> Conspicuous absentees from the college and university curriculum include not only the black experience in America but the history and culture of other ethnic minorities as well. The melting pot ideology muted their role, but scholars and teachers have started to make up for past neglect. The aim is not a chauvinistic carving of the pie. Rather, it is to examine ethnic phenomena in order to understand the complex past and the troubled present and to illuminate the varied strands of America's social and cultural fabric.
>
> To facilitate such research, the Foundation has established a program of *Dissertation Fellowships* for Ph.D. candidates writing on the experience of black Americans, American Indians, Mexican-Americans, Asian Americans, and Puerto Ricans. Eligibility does not depend on the candidate's own race or ethnic status. Eighty-seven candidates were awarded fellowships totaling $288,052 for the 1970–71 academic year, and the program will be conducted for a second year.

This series evolved from Foundation assistance for the development of interdisciplinary Afro-American studies at the undergraduate level, for which a total of $2.8 million was granted to twenty-eight colleges and other agencies. Also assisted in this field have been the preparation of college teachers and the collection and cataloging of historic documents and other materials.

In the initial round of the new series, slightly more than half of the doctoral dissertation topics for which awards were made deal with black Americans. Of the rest thirteen deal with American Indians (e.g., "The Federal Indian Policies in the Pacific Northwest, 1940–1960"); eight with Spanish-speaking Americans (e.g., "Pachuco: A Social Dialect"); four with Asian Americans (e.g., "Consequences of the Relocation of Japanese Americans on California Agriculture") and thirteen with multi-ethnic matters (e.g., "The Politicization of Ethnicity: Indians, Appalachians, and Blacks in Chicago").

The recipients are working at fifty-four universities in all regions of the country. They were nominated by their graduate schools and selected by a multi-ethnic and multi-disciplinary committee of scholars headed by Professor J. Saunders Redding of Cornell University.

Harlan Cleveland, president of the University of Hawaii, made the following comment about ethnic studies in 1970: "At the University of Hawaii, we are moving toward an ethnic studies program that includes black studies along with Hawaiian, Japanese, Chinese, and Filipino studies. I would hope that both oriental and white Americans would find their way into the black studies classrooms, and I am sure that some of the black students will interest themselves in Hawaiian and other cultures of the Pacific—that is, indeed, why some of them come to college so far from home."[2]

Black Studies differ from all other ethnic varieties in that the black American was forcibly separated from the African culture of his ancestors almost three hundred years before any scholarly systematic attempt was made to study that culture and to transmit and interpret consciously its meaning to the involuntarily alienated descendants, and that during that interval the leaders of American society were deliberately attempting to suppress and/or distort its true value and meaning for predatory reasons.

(6) The white college in the future will be pressured from within and without to recognize its obligation to the black as well as the white community to which it is bound by the physical environment. The Cox Commission Report on the violent confrontation between Columbia University and the neighboring Harlem community in the spring of 1968 declared, "Columbia cannot flourish in upper Manhattan until it establishes a new and sounder relation with its

present neighbors." Since that controversy, Columbia has sought in part at least to acknowledge some degree of responsibility for helping to alleviate certain community problems by the use of university personnel and resources. Reports have been published indicating that more than fifty projects have been initiated requiring close cooperation between black community groups and faculty and students from Columbia's schools of medicine, law, education, and architecture.

Almost all organized Black Studies programs have in their objectives some reference to community service and campus relations. A common objective is often worded thus: "To do research in and provide services to the black community and its organizations by jointly identifying and analyzing its problems, offering consultation, and establishing service channels into the community from the diverse resources of the college or university." In a commencement address at Southwestern College at Memphis, June, 1970, F. Champion Ward, vice president of the Education and Research Division of the Ford Foundation, explained the need for and cited an example of the kind of community service that can be rendered by a college that recognizes such an obligation:

> But some promising starts have been made recently, designed to reconcile action and direct experience with theoretical studies . . . The first difficulty is in finding the right "mix" of theory and practice within the curriculum; the second is in determining the appropriate contribution of a liberal arts college to the solution of national problems. There is now a widespread effort to develop courses of study that have substantial intellectual content and yet force both faculty and students to lay out a plan of possible action to cope with particular problems of the hour. . . . Take, for example, a group of courses that students and faculty at Stanford University developed around some complex questions of social policy in California. I recently read the product of one of the Stanford seminars, a report entitled "Logging in Urban Counties," produced by a group of eleven students under the supervision of Stanford geophysicist Allan Cox, who reported:
> "We all learned a great deal. The students discovered that it isn't enough to write essays—lawmakers and supervisors require hard facts if they're going to act.'
>   This is what we had to go after—with field trips, in talks with county officials and people in the logging industry, and by reading published research, the students got extremely interested—it really turned them on."
> What is impressive about the Stanford seminar is the way older and younger minds combined established knowledge, reasoned analysis, and fact-getting to move from contrary cliches concerning a controversial social question to an agreed-upon, workable solution. State and county legislators in California are now making use of the group's report.[3]

(7) Already the white college is finding it necessary to modify its

admissions policies to accommodate a larger percentage of blacks and other ethnic minorities than is now possible. It will finally understand, as some institutions of recognized quality have begun to understand and as many black colleges have known for a long time, that the quality of education is measured by the finished product rather than by the initial input. College administrators will learn by forced experience that the combination of native intelligence and motivation, which cannot be accurately measured by culture-bound entrance tests, is a greater guarantee of genuine academic success than any measuring instruments currently in use. Unless some type of open admissions is adopted by all institutions of higher learning, the guarantee of equality of opportunity by the U.S. Constitution will remain an empty mockery. This reasoning does not suggest that a student whose performance indicates, after a sufficient trial period with necessary remedial aid and counseling, that he cannot succeed at that particular college should be permitted to remain. But it does suggest that every high school graduate who so desires should be guaranteed the right of admission to a public institution of higher learning within the city or state of his residence, at least until he has proved by his performance fairly evaluated that he is incapable of pursuing such a course. Naturally, unless black students are fairly considered for college admission, talk of Black Studies is but idle chatter.

Another aspect of black student recruitment and admissions that the white college must thoughtfully consider in the future is a concern for social balance in recruitment policies. Professor Thomas Sowell suggests that it is the present practice of white colleges and universities to devote their major efforts in admissions, financial aid, and counseling to the academically deprived black student because it is believed the good black student outside the ghetto will "make it anyway." He insists that many directors of special programs for black students do not seek to fill whatever number of places exist with the best recruits available. Some officials, he observes, will openly state this; others will be evasive before admitting it, and still others will continue to deny it after the evidence has piled up. Sowell charges: "What constitutes the 'right' kind of black person has varied greatly with the emotional needs of white people, but the great tragic fact of the black man's history in the United States is that his own ability has always been far less important than his satisfaction of white emotional needs. These emotional needs now include the discharge of guilt feelings, and special care for the incompetent and the abusive black student obviously discharges more guilt than the normal application of academic standards to competent and thoughtful black students."[4] White institutions in the immediate future must make certain that their policies do not produce the kind of unfair results of which Sowell complains.

(8) The white college or university must modify its academic and ethnic qualifications for faculty appointments if it intends to provide for its students, black and white, the most knowledgeable and practical guides to the new and relevant education necessary for successful urban living. A particular type of educator is needed to prepare the student of today to cope with the problems of urban life and the problems associated with the vast technological changes; there are not nearly enough Ph.D. holders or candidates with the theoretical and pragmatic competence to fill even half the college and university positions now open or soon to become available.

Benjamin Thompson, associate professor of education at Antioch College, advises, "As individuals, we need to evidence risk-taking behavior and to acknowledge the fact that only the quick will not become the dead, and this applies to the institutionalizing of new forms and programs as well as to individuals. We must give more concern and freedom to styles of teaching as well as learning in the educational establishment, which demands a faculty that knows the world as well as a particular discipline."[5] Black students have led the way in evaluating teachers on their abilities to understand the world and its current problems, rather than on outworn theories that are no longer relevant to living and working in the modern world.

Robert Beller, president of the student body of the University of Iowa, recently reminded the administration and faculty of his university: "The purpose of the university must be to provide the students with access to the latest informational sources and, more importantly, access to the problems themselves for first-hand observation. From this point, the university staff—no longer simply lecturers and researchers but workers and practitioners—must open broad channels for the testing and revision of new knowledge and skills. In effect, the ghetto, smog, and government become laboratories. The explosive growth of knowledge and other problems have resulted in the rapid obsolescence of traditional tools of education. The university has to offer more than second-hand experience drawn from a text if the student is to place himself usefully in the mainstream of society in any role broader than that of breadwinner and if he is to have leverage for combatting environmental, social, and political shortcomings.""[6]

Although Beller is white, his warning recognizes the necessity for the white college to broaden the ethnic base of its faculty as well as its curriculum. It is true that there are not now enough qualified black professors to satisfy the minimum need of white colleges and universities who are seriously seeking such additions to their faculties. Consequently, administrators must devise new methods for fulfilling this need other than on a full-time basis. Black teachers at black colleges who qualify academically as well as pragmatically could be persuaded to serve as visiting professors or lecturers for one or two semesters with options to return to the black institution or to remain longer if there is mutual agreement. Some white institutions have sought mutual exchanges of faculty members with black institutions for one or two semesters but such arrangements are seldom possible because every black college in the nation already has a larger supply of white teachers than it needs (since integration is supposed to be a two-way process) and, therefore, does not choose to exchange one of its most effective black teachers for a second-rate white teacher who would need a year or two of training and experience to perform even on the lowest acceptable level at the black college. Naturally, the average black teacher has almost no problem in adjusting to faculty service in a white institution, since in most cases his advanced degrees were earned at a white university.

Another possibility of bringing black teachers to the white campus for effective service could be the hiring of a black teacher from a nearby black college to teach an evening course once or twice a week. I have observed some satisfactory arrangements on this basis. Still another possibility is the establishment of Black Studies courses that would be coordinated by a white faculty member with a series of distinguished black professors to serve as lecturers.

In addition to the effort to secure black faculty to teach Black Studies, every white college or university should seek to recruit trained and experienced white teachers who are prepared academically and emotionally to teach such courses. On another occasion in answer to the question "Who should teach courses in Black Studies?" I expressed the following conclusions:

> This is a crucial question in any discussion of the inclusion of the black experience in school and college curriculums. Black militants have demanded and won in some colleges the right to select teachers they want for these courses regardless of academic training or experience. In many instances students have decided that blackness, publication of some kind dealing with

the black experience regardless of its nature and quality, loud and uncompromising allegiance to the black revolution as they understand it, and willingness to serve exclusively the needs of the black student population are the basic qualifications. These students insist that no white person is qualified to teach any subject dealing with the black experience. They believe any black teacher with the four qualifications listed above will be a more effective teacher of a course in Black Studies than any non-black with the highest academic degree and a most distinguished teaching record.

Naturally, any reasonable, fair-minded person will sympathize with the above point of view, but in the name of reason and reality must reject it. It is true that there are many highly trained, efficient white teachers who are not qualified by temperament, social sensitivity, and lack of unconscious racial prejudice to teach Black Studies. But some white teachers do qualify in all three of these non-academic essentials. No white teacher should be permitted to teach a course unless he does meet the academic as well as the non-academic requirements. However, having lived through the black experience for twenty, thirty, or fifty years is no guarantee that a black person is qualified to teach in a satisfactory or meaningful manner an understanding or appreciation of that experience. To permit unqualified black teachers to teach a course in, say, Black Poetry or The Black Writer as Novelist for academic credit is to either admit that the course dealing with the black experience is not as important as other courses in the college curriculum or to admit that the requirements for college teaching are not valid. It is becoming more and more evident that the latter assumption may be true, but, if so, it is the duty of the college or university in which such aberrations occur to forthrightly announce its rejection of the validity of current teacher qualifications for its faculty and the basis for the formulation of its new requirements. It must be clearly understood, however, that these objections to the exceptional treatment of teachers of Black Studies are not directed at the normal practice of making exceptions to all rules in cases that involve *truly* exceptional persons of any race. Neither are these criticisms applicable to poets-in-residence or consultants in special programs not involving academic credit.

But beyond logical and emotional considerations, a recognition of the reality of the current situation demands that white teachers who are qualified academically, emotionally, and sympathetically (lack of conscious or unconscious racial prejudice) to teach courses in Black Studies must be encouraged and even urged to accept such assignments. For regardless of arguments to the contrary, it is clear that the black experience must be included in all school and college general education courses in this nation if it is to survive as *one* nation. *And never in the foreseeable future will there be enough black teachers to perform this task.* It is, therefore, necessary for all qualified colleges and universities to inaugurate a crash program, with ample provisions for scholarship aid, for the preparation of prospective teachers, black and white, for this tremendous task ahead.[7]

12
The Black College as Focus for Black Studies

In Chapter 4 I pointed out that Black Studies were a part of the curriculum in some black colleges more than fifty years ago. I predict that in the year 2000 the most innovative and significant developments in the field will be found in whatever black colleges still exist. By that date it is possible that more than half of the current number will have either discontinued the struggle completely or will have lost their identities in mergers with predominantly white institutions or have been transformed by a gradual takeover by white students, white faculties, and white administrators. Such a development will, of course, be catastrophic for American blacks unless by that time, which is extremely doubtful, white racism as we know it now will have disappeared.

The 1971 report of the Carnegie Commission on Higher Education entitled *New Students and New Places* contains the following commentary:

> Higher education in the United States until about 1940 was largely for the elite; from 1940 to 1970, we moved to mass higher education; and, from 1970 to 2000, we will move to universal-access higher education—opening it to more elements of society than ever before.
>
> We do not anticipate a further move to universal higher education in the sense of universal attendance; in fact, we consider this undesirable and believe that public and private policy should both avoid channeling all youth into higher education and create attractive alternatives to higher education.
>
> But we clearly are moving from mass to universal-access higher education. This creates problems.
>
> It also creates opportunities for more nearly equal treatment of all our citizens, for more nearly adequate service to all localities of our nation, for more varied response to the increasingly varied composition of the enroll-

ments in higher education, for a more thoughtful consideration of the future role of each of the major components of our universe of higher education, for a more careful look at the essential nature of each of our institutions, for a more systematic examination of the effective use of resources.[8]

This brief resume of the aims of American education in the past and the future direction in which it seems to be moving should be of some aid to black colleges as they prepare for new roles in the future. Of course, the major deterrent to the growth and expansion of black colleges is now and will continue to be the lack of adequate funds. In 1967 a Task Force on Education, appointed by President Johnson and headed by William C. Friday, president of the University of North Carolina, said in its report published for the first time in 1972, "the federal government should provide substantial aid to pre-dominantly Negro institutions,"[9] but at the same time it urges that this aid should be extended with the understanding that the long-time goal must be the elimination of all segregated institutions of higher education. Until we know the commission's definition of "segregated institutions of higher education" we cannot have a valid conception of how this recommendation would affect current black colleges. Almost all black colleges are already integrated according to the government's definition as applied to the public schools. The Task Force admits that "At the present it is the predominantly black institutions which offer the effective opportunity for an education to Negroes," but it seems to believe that this "effective opportunity" is not truly valid unless the black college is affiliated in some manner with a "non-developing" (white) institution.

In their controversial book *The Academic Revolution*, Christopher Jencks and David Riesman say, "We believe that substantial numbers of Negroes grossly overestimate the academic quality of Negro colleges. We think many Negro undergraduates would be better off in an integrated college—especially one that had enough other Negroes to form a partially self-contained subculture.... We regret this [the publication of this opinion], but we do not think that individuals should be sacrificed for institutions, however worthy the latter may be and however honorable their historical role."[10] They also remind the reader that in an article published earlier they had suggested that instead of being third-rate imitations of Harvard and Berkeley the Negro colleges should reconsider their role and strike out in new directions. "As far as we have been able to discover," they lament, "no Negro college president took these suggestions very seriously. Apparently it is Harvard or bust." They assert that black colleges now are living reminders of how bad most white colleges in an earlier era had been. They admit to only a few exceptions:

> Nevertheless, as we have already emphasized, Negro colleges are not all alike. At the head of the Negro academic procession stands a handful of well-known private institutions, such as Fisk, Morehouse, Spelman, Hampton, Tuskegee, and Dillard, an even smaller number of public ones such as Texas Southern and Morgan State, and that peculiar hybrid [privately controlled but largely federally financed] Howard. By most criteria, these institutions would probably fall near the middle of the national academic procession. They attract a few brilliant students, employ a few brilliant professors, and run a few very lively programs. . . . By almost any standard these [other] 110 colleges are academic disaster areas.[11]

These two eminent white "authorities" on Negro education would undoubtedly agree with the recommendation of the Friday Task Force that the federal government should seek to provide higher education for all minorities in integrated educational contexts, thus promoting the elimination of black colleges and universities (those with predominantly black administrators, faculties, and student bodies). Of course, the Friday report recommends covert methods for elimination, such as the government's furnishing funds to support the operation of a currently black institution with insurmountable financial problems provided that it merges with a much larger white college or university. Naturally, the administrative pattern would be on a cooperative basis similar to the one in the black anecdote of a meat processor who when questioned by FDA examiners about the ingredients in a certain suspect product he was selling declared that he used a fifty-fifty mixture of horse and rabbit meat. When pressed for a more detailed explanation, he said he meant by a fifty-fifty mixture "one horse to one rabbit." Of course, there could be no further doubt about the resultant flavor.

President King V. Cheek, Jr., of Morgan State College presents an enlightened rationale for the black college, present and future, which places its problems and opportunities in proper perspective:

> There is the third demand that black colleges relate more to the black communities—that we become more social-action-oriented. This demand has some legitimacy, but we must carefully define the role.
>
> Colleges are first and foremost educational enterprises. This is all the expertise they can claim.
>
> Their contributions must be in the form of knowledge and data which appropriate agencies in society can use to make alternative judgments and decisions. Second, they must produce the intelligent and skilled manpower and effective agents of change for our society.

Indeed, if these contributions are conscientiously pursued, they will have overwhelming impacts upon problems black people face. This is the way we realize and fulfill our roles as Black Power bases within the black community.

We cannot be expected to go further and involve our institutions, rather than the individuals, without sacrificing our previous neutrality as critics of society.

We cannot afford as an institution to politicize ourselves—to become protagonists for a specific cause. If we do, we diminish our role as hostels for persons with a variety of views and opinions.

Fourth, there is the demand that we become and remain black institutions with a commitment to serve black students. This demand grows out of the fear that integration may engulf us, destroy our identities and thus diminish our service.

It is true that we live in a multi-racial and pluralistic society. Our educational institutions must reflect this reality. I for one will passionately resist the misuse of the slogan or aim of integration to eliminate or reduce our institutions.

I have seen the decline of black high school administrators in the South—black principals, more qualified than their white counterparts, reduced to the demeaning status of assistant principals in charge of buses.

I have seen the elimination of black schools and their absorption by the white ones with the discarding of the symbols of black pride.

I have witnessed resegregation in the midst of desegregation, with accompanying humiliation and dehumanization of black children, and with the dominant culture more in complete command.

I recall the black high school students in a western North Carolina city who, one morning, suddenly discovered they no longer had a school song and a trophy case—symbols of deep emotional meaning for them.

This is the dilemma of integration. Promote it we must, but not at our educational and psychological detriment.

When HEW insists that many of our colleges must lose their racial identification, we must understand what this really means. I must rise to protest.

A Different Form of Racial Identification

Black colleges will lose their identities as black colleges and simply become predominantly white with a minority black enrollment. We fail to see that racial identification has not ceased to be. It has simply changed its form. What we have then are all predominantly white colleges. The racial identity is still there, except that it is white.

But we are told the real concern is not the label or identity of the college, but the increasing of educational opportunity for black youth. The issue, we are told, is minority access to higher education.

This is more illusory than real. The dominant and genuine concern is not so much with minority access to higher education as it is with minority success in higher education.

This is where the black colleges have made their case—have proven their competency.

So long as our society is infected with any vestige of racism and disregard for human dignity, there will always be a need for black colleges to answer the needs of our black student populations.

We will remain symbols of pride for our people. We still belong to them. They have emotional investment and stake in our present and in our future. We cannot forsake this cause.

Let us build upon the legacies of our black and beautiful past—careful never to distort the realities and never to ignore our blunders and shortcomings—forever tolerant of dissent among ourselves and keeping our strong commitment to high levels of scholarship and service.

If we do, we will overcome the handicaps of our past and insure the future of our race.[12]

The Ford Foundation *Letter* for July 15, 1971 announced that it had given grants of $1,750,000 each to two black universities, Atlanta and Howard, "to sustain their efforts to become graduate centers of excellence in the social sciences." The *Letter* stated that these two are the only predominantly black universities among the estimated 250 American institutions that grant the doctorate. It was stated that Atlanta's student body is approximately eight percent white and its faculty thirty percent white, while Howard's percentages are fifteen percent and forty-eight percent respectively. In each case the administration and general image are characteristically black. It is fairly safe to predict that both institutions will still be predominantly black in the year 2000. It is also safe to predict that during the intervening years no other black institution will be accorded the right to offer a Ph.D. degree recognized by the academic establishment. It is the expressed hope of the Ford Foundation that Howard's and Atlanta's "bid for eminence in the social sciences is not only to stimulate a growing black intellectual life but to offer fresh insights for white and non-white students and scholars alike." It is further suggested that "perhaps a more humanistic and socially relevant study of man will emerge under black leadership as scholars at Howard and Atlanta examine traditional social science perceptions."

But in the immediate future the major effort and achievement in black-oriented education will be in the predominantly black undergraduate colleges where the majority of the administrators, faculty, and students is black. It will be in the hundred or more black colleges that Jencks and Riesman condemned as "academic disaster areas," as well as the eight they cited as meeting the current general standards for American higher education. What prediction can we make for their survival and their transformation into more racially oriented institutions than they have been? First, it is only fair to observe that the two white "authorities" whose judgments were made with such godlike omniscience and finality admit that their conclusions were based on very brief visits to a few black colleges with no general acquaintance over the years with the problems to be assessed, that their final judgments were formed on the basis of testimony of a few hostile blacks who had attended black colleges as undergraduates and had gone on to work in white universities and a few others who had merely spent a few years in white graduate schools and then became Negro college teachers. The caliber of informants they sought when they did visit black campuses was the kind that dealt in such gossipy items as incidents of "petty blackmail and fraud, ranging from such relatively subtle things as college officials' profiteering on textbooks to more egregious incidents like a president's 'borrowing' money from a new, untenured faculty member and not repaying it ... of grades being used to blackmail students into mowing lawns, sweeping offices, or even providing sexual favors [they admit that this sexual thing could happen on a white campus, but on a white campus the professor pretends interest in the exploited girl for herself since the white girl is more reluctant than her black counterpart to admit her willingness to use her sexuality for extrinsic purposes]."[13]

The black college of the future has two possible directions open to it. It can become a *revolutionary* institution with major emphasis on ideology and training for the overthrow of the current political and economic system of the United States as the only means of black liberation, or it can develop a curriculum that will devote minor attention to ideology and black philosophical identity and major attention to cultural, historical, political, and economic studies and disciplines designed to enhance the success of the black graduate in competing for and winning places of influence and power in the established political and economic fabric of the nation and thus help to change the establishment into a truly democratic and egalitarian system. All signs point to the latter prospect.

Since 1968 there has been much controversial talk among blacks concerning future directions for the black college. Under the rubric "The Black University," *Negro Digest* (now *Black World*) devoted the major portion of three issues between March, 1968, and March, 1970 to the subject. On November 13, 1968, a conference attended by nearly 2,000 students, faculty members, and nonacademicians was convened on the campus of Howard University for the announced purpose of discussing the issues involved in the concept of a truly black college or university. The invitations contained the following statement: "The concept of a black university is revolutionary. It emerges out of the frustrations of black students, educators, activists and community leaders who recognize that the present institutions of higher learning have no relevance to the total black community and who realize the contradictions of allowing themselves to be accultured into a society which debilitates black people . . . our responsibility as conference participants is to define the structure and mechanics of that university." [14]

The official roster included the names of such well-known blacks as Amiri Baraka (LeRoi Jones), Ossie Davis, Stokely Carmichael, Maulana Ron Karenga, Harold Cruse, and Dr. Alvin Poussaint, but reports indicate that the major plans and crucial decisions were made by the student leaders, a trend which was first established in the organization of Black Studies programs at white institutions. In fact, the conference was conceived, sponsored, and financed by the Howard University Student Association. Numerous workshops discussed the major problems that would be encountered in any attempt to establish and operate a black college or university designed as a revolutionary instrument for black liberation, but no viable guidelines were agreed upon.

The fact that no black leaders from the established black colleges appeared on the guest list of participants at the Howard University conference indicates that all currently solvent black colleges are primarily interested in the *evolutionary* rather than the *revolutionary* route to black.liberation and that their future development will move in the direction of the second alternative previously mentioned. There are signs that the strongest and most progressive colleges in this category will get financial assistance from some philanthropic foundations and from the federal government as they seek to implement black-oriented academic and community programs.

The Ford Foundation announced October 9, 1971, a six-year program of $100 million for minority education. Although approximately half of the total will be awarded to blacks, Mexican-Americans, Puerto Ricans, and American Indians to attend the colleges and universities of their choice, the other half will be given to a limited number of private colleges, not more than twenty, over the next six years to be used at their discretion for student financial aid, curriculum and instructional changes, faculty salaries, professorial chairs, endowment, and special projects. The main focus will be aimed at improvements on the undergraduate level in accordance with the priorities designated by the colleges themselves.

McGeorge Bundy, president of the Ford Foundation, emphasized in his announcement that this heightened commitment to black colleges "should in no way be interpreted as support of segregated education," since these colleges do not bar students of any race. "The central point," he declared, "is that it is important for American society that institutions under black leadership and with a tradition of service to black students have an opportunity to thrive and share fully in our national efforts in higher education."

In his initial announcement Bundy listed the first four black colleges selected for participation in the program as Benedict College, Columbia, South Carolina, and Fisk University, Nashville, Tennessee, both liberal-arts-oriented with a strong black focus, with the latter having the largest number of courses in black life and culture. The other two selectees are Hampton Institute, Hampton, Virginia, and Tuskegee Institute, Tuskegee, Alabama, both of which have developed high-quality academic programs on earlier foundations of agricultural and technical education generally associated with the name of Booker T. Washington. A brief statement of the philosophy of the two presidents of Fisk and Benedict, both of which were always oriented towards the liberal arts and toward the white genteel conception of education, might give some hint of the future directions of black colleges associated with the Ford Foundation concept, especially since President Benjamin Payton of Benedict has taken a leave of absence from his institution to accept the task of supervising the Foundation's $100 million project.

James R. Lawson, president of Fisk, in response to a request by *Black World* to react to previous articles in the magazine concerning the concept of the black university, said:

> Essentially, then, the education of black Americans must encompass at least three objectives—i.e. (1) an increased awareness and knowledge of their heritage and of the contributions they have made throughout history; (2) a motivation and ability to render much-needed assistance and services, of various kinds, to the total black community; and (3) the development of knowledge and skills necessary for gainful employment and satisfactory living in the larger ever-changing society. In terms of what is necessary for sustained upward economic and social mobility of black Americans, I think it meaningless, if not dangerous, to attempt to assign priorities as between these three objectives. They are all necessary. Moreover, they constitute the basis for the continuing validity and relevance of predominantly or traditionally black institutions of higher education."[15]

He admits that the realization of the three objectives will require "rather basic modifications in the curricula of our colleges and universities, modifications which involve new directions, new and different courses, and innovatively different techniques and method-ologies of instruction."

One indication of the thinking of Benedict's President Payton can be seen in his insistence when he assumed the presidency that a three-hour course in The Black Experience be included in the Liberal Core of 57 semester hours as a requirement for graduation. Benedict thus became the first and only accredited American college to require every student to earn as a prerequisite for graduation three semester hours in a course dealing exclusively with black life and culture. In his answer to the question concerning the concept of the Black University posed by *Black World* he expresses strong dis-agreement with those who maintain that the curriculum of the black college should accede priority to the humanistic disciplines such as "the social sciences, literature, art and the like." He regards such a contention as "a narrow conception of black identity which, if actually pursued, would isolate the black university even further than some of these same authors say it is today from the black community." He believes:

> A functional Black University will strive to engage in the kind of teaching and research and public service which provides people with the disciplines of thought and action by which they can mature as persons and help shape the world into a more human place of habitation. The irremediable blackness of Afro-Americans would be accepted both as a fact of life and as a positive value. But, it would not restrict the experience of black identity to the immediacies of skin-associated cultural values. The black experience is one crucible in which we work our way to a vision of and a connection with the human potential in all men. . . . A functional Black University will see the need for instruction in the disciplines of personal moral responsibility as well as the techniques of social action. Asserting and achieving one's humanity means that black people are not exempted from the universal idiom as well as a group style. Black people, too, need the art of transforming and transcending even the materials and patterns of black culture. In the words of the spiritual: "You got to walk this lonesome valley by yourself."[16]

It is clear that both President Lawson of Fisk and President Payton of Benedict, who are perceptive representatives of the established black colleges most likely to survive in modified forms into the twenty-first century, are acutely conscious of the need for new objectives and new emphases as they face the future. Both are committed to the enhancement of the black image in a cultural and utilitarian sense. Both are concerned that the curriculum and the application of the curriculum contribute to this enhancement. Both also reject the separatism of the advocates of the revolutionary concept of the black college by emphasizing the necessity for the black-college-trained products to compete with their white counterparts for places of preferment and power within the system. It appears that they are reconciled to the prospect of integrated faculties for the future, as well as the present. But certain troublesome questions arise at this juncture which must complicate even their liberated views of the situation: (1) In order to maintain the identity of the black college is it imperative for the majority of the faculty to be black? (2) Should there be a maximum percentage level set for white faculty members in order to maintain the black identity of the college? (3) Even with no more than twenty-five percent of the faculty white, what guarantee can there be that the nonblack members will or can conscientiously support proper emphases on black values? (4) Should any one individual or any one group of individuals at a black college be permitted to choose or prescribe the values to which the college community must subscribe? (5) Should black faculty members at a black college be expected to surrender their individualities for the sake of group solidarity? (6) Should the black faculty of a black college consist of representatives of all major shades of opinion in the black community? Although these questions may be troublesome, they must be wisely answered by or for the administration, faculty, and students of every black college that expects to face the future honestly.

At present some of the most distinguished black colleges have one or more departments with more white than black teachers. In a recent survey of 37 English departments in representative black colleges I discovered that twelve, approximately 32 percent, have white majorities on their faculties, and only two have no white members. Of a total of 475 teachers in the 37 departments, 254 are black and 221 are white. These statistics indicate that if departmental policies concerning the number and nature of courses in black literature to be offered had to be determined by faculty vote there would be almost an even chance that white members would have as much decision-making power as black members. This revelation indicates that forty-six percent of the English teachers in black colleges that enroll approximately 75,000 black students are not black. However, it is significant that eighty-six percent of the black department chairmen testified that they believe, without reservation, that white teachers are "capable of teaching courses dealing with the black experience if they are willing to make reasonable preparation by study and research."

On the other hand, my survey of 120 English departments in representative white colleges and universities revealed that of 4,815 faculty members only 106 (2.2%) are black. One-half of all white departments surveyed has no black faculty members, approximately one-third has one black teacher each, and the remainder has from two to five blacks. Ninety-six percent of white chairmen believe, without reservations, that white faculty members are capable of satisfactorily teaching courses dealing with the black experience if only black students would give them a fair chance, but most indicate that they prefer black or a combination of black and white instructors for such courses. Since on the basis of these statistics it is difficult, if not completely impossible, to imagine a department in a white institution with a majority of black teachers, should black colleges accept as satisfactory departments with white majorities?

Frank A. DeCosta, dean of the Graduate School at Morgan State College, and Frank Bowles, academic vice-president of Haile Selassie I University, Addis Ababa, say in their book *Between Two Worlds*:

> After all has been said and written about changing patterns, educational needs, emerging opportunities, community development, and all other ideas and phrases that are part of the social upheaval of our time, the fact remains that the role of the historically Negro colleges will be determined by their own definition of their responsibility. They face a simple choice. Either they accept the responsibility for the planning and direction of Negro education or they do not. If they do not, no one else will.
>
> The question of whether they enroll the majority of Negro students in higher education is not relevant to this point. The point is that the historically Negro colleges were created by Negroes for the education of Negroes. They have been responsible for the formation, the development, and the present condition of education for Negroes. They are in a position to understand the problems, to make decisions, to supply leadership, and, above all, to speak for the Negro in American education. If they fail to do so, they fail in their ultimate mission.[17]

Although I highly regard the important contributions that DeCosta and Bowles have made in their book to an understanding and appreciation of the historical role of the Negro college in American education, in the foregoing quotation I think they have overstated the power black college administrators have had in determining the general direction in which Negro higher education has moved in the past and will move in the future. I am convinced that the power structure of American society, represented by individual white philanthropists, the national leadership of religious denominations, philanthropic foundations, and U.S. government agencies, has set the rules and the limits for black colleges, even those that are under the auspices of black religious denominations. In my opinion black college educators do not face a simple choice of deciding the direction in which higher education for blacks will go in the future. Their only choice is to decide whether they will make their plans within the limits the white power structure can be pressured to accept, or to surrender the outward trappings of power and retire completely from the field.

The private black college has already seen the handwriting on the wall. In the spring of 1972 several of these most progressive institutions have experienced financial crises so severe that they could not meet their monthly payrolls. In two instances fantastic cuts in teaching and nonteaching personnel were announced for the following year. Among these hard-pressed colleges were two of the four that the Ford Foundation had recently selected as the most promising of the private group with the understanding that each will be given annually more than a million dollars for the next six years. There can be no doubt that "He who pays the piper exercises the right to call the tune."

The fate of black public colleges and universities is now being decided in the state legislatures. In West Virginia and Missouri the traditionally black institutions have already lost their racial identity. In Arkansas the A. M. and N. college at Pine Bluff, the only black public institution of higher education in the state, will become a branch of the University of Arkansas next fall by legislative decree. In Tennessee the white president of the new University of Tennessee at Nashville has pronounced black sixty year-old Tennessee A. and I. University a "dying institution" that must be annexed to or merged with his two-year-old fledgling in order to preserve the state's capital investment.

In North Carolina more than 500 black college students from all sections of the state met in Raleigh, November, 1971, to protest a proposed plan of white political and educational leaders to "reorganize" the state system of higher education. The law, if passed in its original form, would create a thirty-two-member Board of Regents with absolute authority over programs and budgets of all individual institutions. The students, consisting of representatives not only from the five black universities that would lose their semiautonomy but black students from practically every other black and white institution of higher education in the state, were aroused because there was general agreement among them, as well as among their elders, that "Such a plan would result in the phasing out of the predominantly Black institutions that are state supported, just at a time when students at these universities are developing widespread Black consciousness."[18] Although the students were well aware of the overwhelming white power arrayed against them, they felt that some faint hope could be kept alive if they could persuade the establishment to assign thirty percent of the places on the proposed state-wide governing board to black members, since blacks constitute that percentage of the population. Even if such a "generous" arrangement could result, the black minority could not be expected to have the deciding voice in charting the direction of black colleges under the board's jurisdiction.

In the light of the variety of limitations imposed on the black college because of its peculiar nature and the paucity of genuine opportunities for the control of its own destiny, what are the most promising future directions within the bounds of white toleration that might yield desirable results? One answer is in the reorganization of the entire curriculum of the college so that each course will reflect the realization of the black experience as a legitimate part of the American experience.

Such a realization will require that teachers incorporate in all social science and humanities courses unbiased information and interpretation of all significant aspects of black life and culture, as well as other ethnic minorities, which have been previously ignored by textbooks and instructional syllabi. This means that every course in literature (American and world), history (American and world), geography, anthropology, government, sociology, economics, psychology, philosophy, journalism, and so on, will include the black and other ethnic dimensions, as well as the white. In mathematics and the natural sciences, materials for illustrations and experiments will be concerned with black as well as white experiences. Problems in mathematics will include ghetto situations as well as stock market manipulations.

If these kinds of emphases were enforced, there would be no need for a Black Studies department in a black college, as there is no need now for a White Studies department in a white college. Under this kind of reorganization every graduate of the black college, white as well as black (it is understood that enrollment will be open to all qualified applicants regardless of race or ethnic origins), would be thoroughly familiar with the significant aspects of black life and culture and, therefore, prepared to accept the responsibilities of living in a multi-ethnic society. Of course, there would be opportunity for "concentration" in Black Studies on an interdisciplinary basis, as is the case now in most colleges that have Black Studies programs, but, as is also the case in most colleges that have such programs, the student would be required to have a major in an established department. Some black colleges have already begun to achieve this kind of projection. Fisk University and Morgan State College are two examples.

Another answer might be found in some of the recommendations of a task force appointed in 1969 by Robert H. Finch, then Secretary of Health, Education, and Welfare, headed by Frank Newman, associate director of university relations in Stanford University. The report, which was released in March, 1971, suggests that the college could consider adapting to the student instead of trying to adapt the student to the college. Additional specific recommendations include: (a) providing a diversified faculty that includes members whose experiences range beyond that gained in the traditional departments; (b) accepting experience as a legitimate part of education; (c) organizing the curriculum around the professional skills to be learned, including work experience and learning geared to community service; (d) organizing "courses" as responses to needs developed by the students as they progress; (e) considering the academic process essentially as a means to ascertain truth as against falsity, to gain knowledge as against ignorance, and to improve intellectual excellence as against shoddiness.

Finally, since the future of the black college is greatly dependent upon social change in the larger community, the black college could profit by the experiences of white Antioch College, whose Institute for the Solution of Social Problems has been in operation since the spring of 1970. The proposal for the establishment of the institute contains the following rationale: "In any complex activity or profession, training is necessary to insure that persons involved participate, not simply on the basis of abstract ideas or intuition but with understanding and skill. This is as true for the agent of social change as it is for the research chemist. To develop and carry out strategy and tactics for social change, a person must act as a social scientist. . . . This means that he or she needs training in social sciences but not in an ad hoc or value-free fashion. . . . As part of its training of agents of social change then ISSP courses cross the bounds of the traditional academic areas. . . . The result is a curriculum which, for the first time at Antioch and perhaps at any established college or university in the U.S., insures that the theoretical and practical education required for the training of agents of social change can be obtained." [19]

V

CONCLUSION

13
Thought Provoking Answers
to Challenging Questions

As we come to the end of this study, my inclination is to resist the temptation to announce a formidable list of omniscient conclusions that my research has "conclusively" proven. To those who consider such an inclination an irresponsible cop-out, I respond that I have tried to present my findings in such a manner that the reader has sufficient information to form his own conclusions. As a compromise, however, I have decided to answer twelve significant questions on the basis of my personal interpretation of the facts I have learned, the experiences I have encountered, and the opinions I have gathered during the two-year study, with the understanding that other knowledgeable and reasonable observers and/or interpreters have the right to honestly disagree.

(1) *What are the underlying facts concerning my involvement in this evaluative study of Black Studies in American higher education?* The answer to this question is important, for more than one chairman of a Black Studies department at my first contact hesitated to supply the information I requested for fear I might be gathering materials to be used by a governmental agency or racist organization to the detriment of the Black Studies movement. However, I succeeded in allaying the fears of at least ninety-nine percent of the doubters by explaining that the idea was mine alone, generated by the unfavorable reactions concerning the subject from black scholars whom I respected for their race pride and their broad scholarship and impelled by the determination to honestly determine for myself the validity or invalidity of their misgivings. A casual, unorganized search for reliable evidence proved so unsatisfactory that I decided to seek the opportunity and means to make a more organized and extended

attempt to satisfy my curiosity, believing that there might be others who also would like to be supplied sufficient evidence concerning the pros and cons of the subject to justify a conclusion. At first I thought a year's sabbatical leave from my teaching duties as professor of English at Morgan State College would be sufficient to help me achieve my goal. But after preliminary investigation of the possible means to be employed and the amount of time a thorough investigation would require, I decided to seek a grant from the National Endowment for the Humanities to provide travel funds to visit college and university campuses for first-hand experiences. My application was approved by NEH for a one-year grant. By the end of the year I had become so engrossed in the project that I knew I had to continue. At my request Morgan State College extended additional leave from full-time teaching duties for another year and NEH renewed its grant for 1971–72. I have explained in the Preface the origin and development of my interest in the subject and the procedures employed in the study, but I wish to add here that at no time has anyone even remotely connected with the National Endowment for the Humanities or any other organization (racist or pro-black) approached me with any suggestion as to how I should proceed, what I should look for, what my standards or rationale should be, or what the effect of my disclosures might be. I have been under no pressure from anyone to skew my findings in a particular direction. Neither have I at any time asked advice from anyone concerning my interpretation or evaluation of what I have observed. My quarterly reports to NEH have consisted entirely of information in the following categories: (1) Name of Grantee: (2) Grant Number; (3) Grant Period; (4) Amount of Grant; (5) Expenditures: (a) Salaries and Wages, (b) Travel, (c) Supplies, (d) Equipment, (e) Indirect Costs, (f) Other; (g) Payment Requested. I have attempted to make my final report, which is the basis for this book, as objective as is humanly possible considering my educational background and my racial experience. I must admit that the two-year experience changed my understanding of the nature and possibilities (pro and con) of Black Studies and the role they must play in American higher education. I trust that I have been able to convey a reasonable amount of the insight I have gained.

(2) *What is the origin of Black Studies?* Unlike the unhistorical assertions of many of the young partisans of Black Studies, from my personal experience and historical studies documented in Chapters 3 and 4, I am certain that Black Studies, under the caption "Negro"

and with a great concern for scholarship, were born on the campuses of more than one black college more than fifty years ago. In fact, during the academic year of 1921–22 there were an aggregate of eighteen courses dealing exclusively with black life and culture in the following nine Negro institutions: Fisk University, Lincoln University (Missouri), Howard University, Hampton Institute, Tuskegee Institute, Virginia State College, West Virginia State College, South Carolina State College, and Kentucky State College. The parents of this disadvantaged child, which was not to be properly christened until 1968, were such illustrious black scholars as W.E.D. DuBois, Carter G. Woodson, Charles S. Johnson, E. Franklin Frazier, Benjamin G. Brawley, and Alain Locke. It is unfortunate that the new militant champions of this evolutionary phenomenon which we now call Black Studies have sought to discredit and denigrate its origin and early development rather than to study its past to learn how its present might be enhanced and its future assured.

(3) *Is the concept of Black Studies valid and viable?* At least eighty-five percent of the educators (including important administrators of prestigious colleges and universities) I have interviewed, as well as a similar percentage of written comments I have read, emphatically agree that the concept is absolutely as valid and viable as that of American Studies, Russian Studies, Chinese Studies, Jewish Studies, Irish Studies, or International Studies. The description of an American Studies program in a reputable liberal arts college with an enrollment of 1,000 reads as follows: "The major in American Studies is designed for students who want to acquaint themselves with the life and institutions of the United States both past and present. . . . This major is of interest not only to Americans who wish to live a richer cultural life but also to those who plan definitely to prepare for careers in such fields as teaching, politics, journalism, or diplomacy." With the change of the word "American" to "Black" the above description could be properly used for a general description of the nature and purpose of a Black Studies major. The 1971 Bulletin of the Liberal Arts College of the University of Mississippi, which offers a minor in Black Studies, lists eighteen upper level courses in Black Studies offered by the university and suggests, in a description of objectives for the upper division, only two specific objectives: "(a) for special equipment for efficiency in professional, civic, economic, and social service; (b) for the attainment of the groundwork of a culture that may enrich his intellectual and spiritual character and provide him with resources for living a

large and useful life." It is clear that these objectives apply to all upper level courses, including those in Black Studies, and it is equally as clear that these objectives plus course listings provide evidence that at least this university located in a state with a history of indifference to public education for blacks has accepted Black Studies as a valid and viable concept.

The most vocal objections to Black Studies now seem to be coming from black scholars with tenure in the higher ranks of white universities and from civil rights leaders not connected with educational institutions who fear that these studies will only lead down dead-end paths. But in reality the criticism is based not on the lack of validity of the concept itself but on the fear that the concept might be abused. However, their fears have been so widely and effectively publicized that the public generally considers them in the camp of the enemy. This situation results from the fact that the critics of Black Studies never admit that there are good programs; they never cite a good program as a model which they approve, thus giving the impression that there is none.

(4) *What can a student do with a major in Black Studies?* He can do anything that one with a major in philosophy can do except teach philosophy. Yet I have never heard the major in philosophy questioned because of its lack of focus on immediate job requirements. In addition to being qualified to teach Black Studies in secondary schools, a student with a Black Studies major can qualify to enter professional schools of law, medicine, and social work, as well as various fields of graduate study leading to higher degrees, as is the case of any other undergraduate major with sufficient concentrated electives or required minors or second majors (most generally required in Black Studies). For example, a 1971 graduate of Yale University with a Black Studies major was admitted the following fall to the law schools of both Yale and Harvard—he entered Harvard. A 1972 graduate of Yale with a Black Studies major was recently chosen as a Rhodes Scholar for graduate study at Oxford University.

One black faculty member from a midwestern university offered this explanation: "We know that Black Studies, by themselves, won't get jobs. We know we need doctors, lawyers, and other professionals in the black community. But we hope that by the aid of the perspectives of Black Studies programs black professionals won't be as concerned with making $30,000 a year as they are with giving effective service to the black community."

(5) *Should all colleges and universities in the United States have*

organized programs in Black Studies? The answer is no. An institution should establish such a program only if it is willing to commit necessary funds to guarantee a program equal in quality to all other programs on the campus. This requirement means that the administration and faculty must have positive attitudes and the atmosphere on the campus must not be hostile. But failure to qualify for an organized program does not exempt the institution from establishment of a reasonable number of course offerings in Black Studies in the areas of the humanities and the social sciences. It is difficult to imagine an accredited college or university so steeped in racism that not a single teacher in the humanities or the social sciences would be willing to qualify to teach one such course in his area of specialization. If there is an institution unable to qualify in this respect, it is obligated to find immediately at least one such teacher for each of the two designated areas, preferably a black teacher even at a salary above the normal scale. In this age of enlightenment any college or university which refuses to include a proper emphasis on the black experience honestly and fairly presented is guilty of miseducation and should be censured by accrediting agencies.

(6) *What should be the objectives of an acceptable Black Studies program?* Chapter 5 discusses seven categories of objectives that represent more than 200 statements now being used as guidelines by current programs. There is no need to restate the information here. However, it is important, to warn, as some Black Studies directors have discovered by bitter experience, that objectives which are highly political and propagandistic will destroy all possibility of an effective program that can win meaningful support from faculties and administrations of reputable institutions. Furthermore, objectives that encourage racial separation in class assignment policies should be avoided. Students who wish to avoid mixing with other ethnic groups in classrooms and various academic experiences need not expect their narrow perspectives to be subsidized by college and university budgets. Objectives that confuse academic activities with community field work should be clarified to assign each its legitimate place in the curriculum. Community service must be included among objectives, but there should be provisions to require proper training and expert faculty guidance for students engaging in such activities for college credit, as well as exemptions for those who choose additional academic course work instead of community involvement. Complete

absorption in academic research pertaining to black life and culture can be a valuable alternative to community service.

(7) *What type of administrative organization is best?* The answer is that each institution should adopt the organizational pattern that fits best its educational philosophy and administrative style. A pattern which may prove satisfactory for one institution may be completely unsuitable for another. Evidence has shown, however, that the majority of colleges and universities with interdisciplinary patterns have encountered fewer problems administratively, pedagogically, and philosophically. Interdisciplinary programs profit by less tension and more genuine cooperation between faculty and students of the program and those unaffiliated with the program. Furthermore, the interdisciplinary approach enables the director of Black Studies to be a mediator between the members of the college community who are committed to the value and desirability of the program and the members who are uncommitted, rather than a bête noire to those who are still unconvinced. It is an undeniable fact that an adequate budget alone can never guarantee a respectable, effective Black Studies program. Continual tension and confrontation between the college administration and the Black Studies program will only end in a lessening of interest among black students, as well as white faculty and administrators, and thus lead to suicidal death of the undertaking. I know of programs with inadequate budgets but interest and good will among the general faculty and administration that are greatly superior to other programs with much more adequate financial support. An interdisciplinary program, which by its very nature requires that a successful director must develop the art of making friends and influencing other department heads and their faculties to cooperate in the development and expansion of his program, is more likely to become an effective, scholarly, prestigious operational venture than one that is completely autonomous or independent.

(8) *What kinds of courses should be offered?* In Chapter 7 I have listed the types of courses now being offered and the popularity of same. I pointed out that approximately two-thirds of the courses are in the area of the social sciences and that the three most popular courses in the order of their popularity are history, sociology, and literature. Of course, before the Black Studies movement began in 1968 there were more sociology courses with considerable emphasis on black life and culture than any others. It is a fact, however, that since 1968 such courses taught by white professors

have been forced to change their perspectives and major emphases in accordance with the new wave of black consciousness. Likewise, even in black colleges, social science offerings such as history, anthropology, psychology, economics, and geography have yielded to the demands of the black perspective either by creating separate courses or by modifying the coverage and point of view of standard offerings.

Since the humanities courses by their very nature have always professed an overwhelming interest in the *human* condition characterized by tenderness and compassion for the oppressed and the downtrodden, it is strange that humane disciplines such as literature, art, and music have lagged behind history and sociology in their efforts to reflect an honest presentation and interpretation of the black experience. There can be no excuse for any accredited college or university to fail to offer at least one course each in black history and black literature, or to incorporate a reasonable amount of basic materials prepared by black scholars or distinguished black writers into the subject matter of regular courses. Unless English teachers are willing to lead their students into meaningful encounters with the subject matter of black literature, they will miss the best opportunity they will ever have to understand some of the deepest, most complex social problems of this generation. Alfred Kazin, a very perceptive teacher and critic of literature, uttered a profound truth when he said in his essay on "The Function of Criticism Today" that the "essence of the modern movement is that it represents a permanent revolution of consciousness, an unending adventure into freedom. In the deepest sense, we can never *study* modern literature or art; we can only *be part of it.*" Certainly black literature is in the vanguard of this "modern movement" to which Kazin alludes.

(9) *What should be a student's qualifications for admission to a Black Studies program?* First, he must be a high school graduate, if that is a requirement for entrance by the college of his choice. Second, he must have demonstrated by his high school record, by special examination, or by interviews with admissions officers that he has a reasonable chance of succeeding in respect to the academic requirements of the particular institution. It must be understood that once he is admitted the college is obligated to provide any remedial aid necessary for him to achieve satisfactorily according to the scholarship standards of the institution. Any institution of higher learning is performing a disservice if it admits a black student (or any student) who has been certified by the act of admission as capable of

succeeding and then fails to provide remedial help if the student finds himself in academic trouble. It is more honorable and honest for an institution to deny admission to a student who is considered marginal by admissions officers if it does not intend to give supplementary aid to overcome that marginality.

Third, black students should not be chosen for admission on the basis of ideology (separatism, integration, assimilation, etc.) in matters pertaining to race. My two years of campus visitations have convinced me that the great majority of students in Black Studies programs in white institutions profess a belief in separatism (or black nationalism) as the only honorable choice open to blacks. The fact that this attitude is as prevalent among freshmen as it is among upperclassmen indicates that recruitment policies favor students who accept this point of view. However, a recent survey of 54,000 black students who were graduated from high school in 1971 and were hoping to enter college the following fall showed that sixty-six percent considered integration "good," six percent said it was "bad," and twenty-three percent expressed neutrality. The National Scholarship Service and Scholarship Fund for Negro Students, an organization that provides guidance services without cost to black students who want to attend college, conducted the survey which is believed to be the most comprehensive sampling ever undertaken of black students' characteristics and attitudes. The students surveyed represented more than 7,000 of the approximately 26,000 high schools in the nation. Incidentally, twenty-five percent of the students favored the concept of "militancy," although the term was not defined.

(10) *What should be the major qualifications for a director of a Black Studies program?* I am convinced that the chief component in the success or failure of a Black Studies program with reasonably adequate financial support is the director. I am further convinced that the most discouraging fact concerning the chances for significant improvement in current programs is the shortage of qualified directors with the potential for successful leadership. Since 1968 the rapid turn-over in tenure of directors has been fantastic, exceeding by far the situation in any other college or university program.

The following list of specific qualifications will not absolutely guarantee a director's success, but they are very necessary requirements for accomplishment: (a) The director must be black—especially for the present and the immediate future. (b) The director must have the appropriate academic credentials, including degrees and experience, expected of all other administrative officers of similar programs at the particular institution. (c) In philosophy and action the director must not be dominated by racial extremism in either direction. He or she must recognize at all times the right of blacks and whites to choose their own life-styles without harassment or overt indoctrination, provided that such life-styles do not jeopardize the rights and privileges of others. The director must accept the proposition that whites as well as blacks have to know the facts and proper interpretations of the history and culture of blacks as a necessary basis for true education. (d) The person chosen to lead a Black Studies program must have the administrative ability to organize and administer academic and community programs, the capacity to mediate differences between, among, and within faculty, administrative, and student groups, and the willingness to work with the college or university president as a cooperative partner rather than an uncompromising adversary. (e) The director must be innovative, flexible, and capable of accepting with equanimity criticism by blacks as well as by whites. (f) He or she should have some experience in black-related teaching and a willingness to challenge outmoded educational patterns and structures with the necessary imagination to project new, viable alternatives. (g) The director should have demonstrated interest, insight, and capability in the area of Black Studies by some acceptable research and/or publication in the field.

(11) *Should Black Studies be organized as a component of an Ethnic Studies program?* In the light of my observations the answer is *no*. I have heard only one indisputable advantage claimed for such a program—the arrangement would facilitate effective budget operations by combining similar offerings and activities in a single unit. But in reality how similar is Black Studies to other ethnic varieties? For instance, what specific courses do Puerto Rican, Mexican-American, Asian-American, Native American, and/or Black Studies have in common? Not even one common course can be justifiably prescribed as suitable for all of these ethnic minorities. Although no one has seriously suggested, according to the information I have been able to gather, that Jewish Studies should be grouped into such a pattern, a course in biblical traditions could be prescribed as a common course for a program of Black and Jewish Studies with a greater sense of fitness than any course for any two of the other ethnic groups mentioned above. The Bible with its references to the Jewish experience of slavery in Egypt as well as its influence on the

religious experiences of millions of blacks is quite relevant to black American culture.

It is believed by many affected observers that the tendency of some colleges and universities to choose the pattern of grouping two or more ethnic studies programs into a single operational unit is an unconscious or unacknowledged expression of the marginality of such programs.

The following arguments against ethnic grouping seem to be reasonably relevant: (a) Constant friction is generated among the minorities so grouped, thus discouraging effective unified action to tackle organizational and instructional problems that can be solved successfully only when attacked by participants dedicated to a common cause in which the personal stakes are high and unmistakably recognized. (b) Often great tension is stirred among the minorities when a director is chosen from one minority rather than another. The minorities denied this honor are continually seeking reasons to discredit the director in the hope of a replacement from their group. (c) Generally when financial support for a program of one minority is increased because of a compelling need not applicable to the others, the denied minorities charge discrimination with the usual increase of tension. (d) The college or university develops a false sense of financial support for minority interests by considering the one budget for all minorities as an adequate contribution to a single institutional unit, whereas if each minority program were given a separate budget the truth of inadequate support would be apparent. (e) It is unrealistic to expect a director with an ethnic background to administer a program for another ethnic group with an equal degree of understanding and sympathy that he has for his own.

(12) *Are Black Studies a threat or a challenge to American education?* Badly conceived and improperly administered Black Studies are a threat to effective, meaningful, mind-stretching, truth-seeking education. Badly conceived and improperly administered, and every fair-minded observer must admit that such versions are definitely in the minority, Black Studies can become a galling sore, a virulent cancer poisoning the bloodstream with more hate, more prejudice, and more racism of one kind or another than already exist on the college campus and in the surrounding community. Likewise, *thoughtfully and honestly conceived, and effectively and wisely administered Black Studies are also a threat.* They are a threat to blatant ignorance of well-meaning people who are supposed to

know the truth about the entire history and culture of their country and its people. They are a threat to prejudice and bigotry nourished by fear of the half-truths and unadulterated lies that miseducation has produced. They are a threat to apathy and inertia in vital matters that require action now. They are a threat to false and distorted scholarship that has flourished without condemnation or shame in the most prestigious bastions of higher education in this nation.

But, whether or not they are properly conceived and administered, they are nevertheless a powerful challenge to the national educational establishment to "straighten up and fly right," to examine as never before moribund concepts and outmoded methods that have not been seriously and meaningfully challenged during this century. Their challenge has led to the current trend of shared authority among administration, faculty, and students, a concept that was almost unthinkable before the black student revolt in 1967—68. Their challenge has forced accredited and even highly prestigious institutions to modify their elitist admissions policies to some form of open admissions. Their challenge has turned the spotlight on relevance as a legitimate concern which ivory tower scholars have scorned too long. Their challenge has forced colleges and universities to admit obligations to the surrounding community, obligations previously emphatically denied. *Are Black Studies a threat or a challenge?* The answer is BOTH.

APPENDIX A

Partial List of Colleges and Universities with Organized Black Studies Programs

Adelphi University, N.Y.
University of Akron, Ohio
Allan Hancock College (Jr.), Cal.
American River College (Jr.),
    Cal.
Antelope Valley College (Jr.),
    Cal.
University of Arizona, Tucson
University of Arkansas,
    Fayetteville
Atlanta University, Ga.
Bakersfield College, Cal.
Ball State University, Ind.
Barstow College, Cal.
Bates College, Maine
Benedict College, S.C.
Boston College, Mass.
Boston University, Mass.
Bowdoin College, Maine
Bowling Green State University,
    Ohio
Bradley University, Ill.

Brandeis University, Mass.
University of Bridgeport, Conn.
Brooklyn College, N.Y.
Brown University, R.I.
Butte College (Jr.), Cal.
Cabrillo College, Cal.
California College of Arts and
    Crafts, Oakland
California Concordia College
    (Jr.), Oakland
California State College,
    Dominguez Hills
California State College,
    Hayward
California State College, Long
    Beach
California State Polytechnic
    College, Pomona
California State College, San
    Bernardino
University of California,
    Riverside

University of California, Irvine
University of California, Los
  Angeles
University of California, San
  Diego
University of California, Santa
  Barbara
Canada College (Jr.), Cal.
Case-Western Reserve University,
  Ohio
Catholic University of America,
  Washington, D.C.
Center for Urban-Black Studies,
  Cal.
Central State University, Ohio
Chaffey College, Cal.
Chicago State College, Ill.
Chico State College, Cal.
City College of the City
  University of New York, N.Y.
City College of San Francisco,
  Cal.
Claremont College, Cal.
Cleveland State University, Ohio
College of Holy Names, Cal.
College of Marin (Jr.), Cal.
College of San Mateo (Jr.), Cal.
College of the Redwoods, Cal.
University of Colorado, Boulder
Colgate University, N.Y.
University of Connecticut,
  Storrs
Contra Costa College, Cal.
Cornell University, N.Y.
Dartmouth College, N.H.
University of Dayton, Ohio
De Anza College, Cal.
Denison University, Ohio
Depauw University, Ind.
University of Detroit, Mich.
Diablo Valley College (Jr.), Cal.

University of Dubuque, Iowa
Duke University, N.C.
Duquesne University, Pa.
Eastern Illinois University,
  Charleston
East Los Angeles College, Cal.
Elizabeth City State University,
  N.C.
University of Florida, Gainesville
Florida Memorial College, Miami
Florida A & M University,
  Tallahassee
Foothill College, Cal.
Fordham University, N.Y.
Fort Valley State College, Ga.
Fresno City College, Cal.
Fuller Theological Seminary, Cal.
University of Georgia, Athens
Grambling College, La.
Grinnell College, Iowa
Harvard University, Mass.
Howard University, Washington,
  D.C.
Hunter College, N.Y.
University of Houston, Texas
University of Illinois, Urbana
Indiana University, Bloomington
Indiana University-Northwest,
  Gary
Iowa State University, Ames
University of Iowa, Iowa City
Jackson State College, Miss.
Kansas State University,
  Manhattan
Kent State University, Ohio
Kentucky State, Frankfort
Laney College, Cal.
Lassen College, Cal.
Lehigh University, Penn.
La Verne College, Cal.
Lincoln University, Mo.

Lincoln University, Penn.
Los Angeles City College, Cal.
Los Angeles Harbor College, Cal.
Los Angeles Trade-Technical
   College, Cal.
Los Angeles Valley Junior
   College, Cal.
University of Louisville, Ky.
Loyola University, Cal.
University of Maine, Orono
Manhattan Community College,
   N.Y.
Marquette University, Wis.
Marshall University, W. Va.
University of Maryland, College
   Park
University of Maryland,
   Baltimore County
University of Massachusetts,
   Amherst
Merced College, Cal.
Merritt College, Cal.
University of Miami, Coral
   Gables
University of Michigan, Ann
   Arbor
Mills College, Cal.
University of Minnesota,
   Minneapolis
University of Mississippi,
   University
University of Montana, Missoula
Monterey Peninsula College, Cal.
Moorhead State College, Minn.
Moorpark College, Cal.
Morgan State College, Md.
Mount San Jacinto College, Cal.
Newark State College, N.J.
University of New Mexico,
   Albuquerque
State University of New York,

Brockport
State University of New York,
   New Paltz
State University of New York,
   Albany
State University of New York,
   Binghamton
State University of New York,
   Buffalo
State University of New York,
   Stony Brook
State University College of
   New York, Buffalo
State University of New York,
   Geneseo
State University of New York,
   Oneonta
New York University, New York
   City
Norfolk State College, Virginia
North Carolina Central
   University, Durham
University of North Carolina,
   Charlotte
Northeastern Illinois State
   College, Chicago
Northern Illinois University,
   DeKalb
Ohio State University,
   Columbus
Ohio University, Athens
Oklahoma State University,
   Stillwater
University of the Pacific, Cal.
Pasadena City College, Cal.
University of Pennsylvania,
   Philadelphia
Pepperdine College, Cal.
University of Pittsburgh, Penn.
Princeton University, N.J.
Randolph-Macon Woman's

College, Va.
Regis College, Colo.
Riverside City College, Cal.
University of Rhode Island,
  Kingston
University of Rochester, N.Y.
Rutgers University, N.J.
St. Augustine's College, N.C.
St. Mary's College, Cal.
St. Patrick's College, Cal.
San Bernardino Valley College
  (Jr.), Cal.
San Diego Mesa Community
  College, Cal.
San Diego State College, Cal.
St. John's University, N.Y.
San Fernando Valley State
  College, Cal.
San Francisco Art Institute, Cal.
San Francisco State College, Cal.
San Joaquin Delta College, Cal.
San Jose City College (Jr.), Cal.
Santa Rosa Junior College, Cal.
Shasta College, Cal.
Shaw University, N.C.
Solano College, Cal.
Sonoma State College, Cal.
University of South Carolina,
  Columbia
South Carolina State College,
  Orangeburg
University of Southern California,
  Los Angeles
Southern Illinois University,
  Carbondale
Southern Methodist University,
  Texas
Southwestern College, Cal.
Stanford University, Cal.
Stanislaus State College, Cal.
Staten Island Community

College, N.Y.
Syracuse University, N.Y.
Temple University,
  Philadelphia
University of Tennessee,
  Knoxville
University of Texas, Austin
Texas Christian University,
  Fort Worth
Tougaloo College, Miss.
Trenton State College, N.J.
Tulane University, La.
University of California,
  Berkeley
University of Redlands, Cal.
University of San Francisco, Cal.
University of Santa Clara, Cal.
University of Southern
  California, Los Angeles
University of the Pacific, Cal.
Upsala College, N.J.
University of Utah, Salt Lake
  City
University of Virginia,
  Charlottesville
University of Washington,
  Seattle
Washington State University,
  Pullman
Washington University, Mo.
Wayne County Community
  College, Detroit
Wellesley College, Mass.
West Valley College (Jr.), Cal.
Winston-Salem State University,
  N.C.
Western Illinois University,
  Macomb
Western Michigan University,
  Kalamazoo
West Virginia University,

Morgantown

University of Wisconsin,
    Madison

University of Wisconsin,
    Milwaukee

Wisconsin State University, Eau

Claire

Yale University, Conn.

Yeshiva University, N.Y.

Youngstown State University,
    Ohio

Yuba College, Cal.

APPENDIX B

International Dimensions of Black Studies

Although this study is primarily concerned with Black Studies in colleges and universities within the national boundaries of the United States, I have been tempted to take a brief glance at what is being done about the subject in other parts of the world, such as neighboring island territories, Africa, Brazil (with a larger black population percentagewise than the United States), and France (a former colonial power in Africa). In an address "An African's View of Black Studies," presented at an annual convention of the College Language Association, John J. Akar, the Sierra Leonean Ambassador to the United States, after expressing disapproval of several trends in Black Studies, offered the following advice:

> What have I been saying so far in my talk to you, Ladies and Gentlemen? I have been saying that Black Studies and African Studies are one and the same thing; that we must get the conservative academic fringe that insists upon separation, to understand that we know that this is yet another manifestation of the "divide and rule" policy which was the cornerstone of Colonial Strategy in Africa, particularly in the nineteenth century.
>
> I am saying that we must plan ahead and look beyond our immediate noses. And our planning must be phased. The first phase we have almost achieved, namely, allowing the teaching of Black Studies in the curricula of many American colleges. We now see this going on in varying degrees of professionalism and over-all competence. Our next step is to structure the curricula that they would stand any academic scrutinizing, whatever criteria are postulated. We should make Black Studies open to all and taught by all bearing in mind that although preference should and must be given to the Black man, the overriding consideration should be academic competence,

qualifications, experience and excellence. That Black Studies should research ways and means of bringing black people in America together into a potent domestic political force and then seek alliances with other ethnic minorities to broaden their base and solidify their indestructibility. That Black Studies should look beyond social problems and embrace all problems; look beyond America and embrace Africa and other parts of the world with people of African extraction.

In short, I am saying that it is now up to the Black Intelligentsia to pioneer a nation-wide movement to put dignity and humanity back into brotherhood and peace. Then we shall all see the dawning of a new day on earth. And when that dawn comes for all of us—White, Brown, Red, Yellow, and Black—and emancipates all of us from the "fear of bondage and the bondage of fear," then mankind will not look back with hate and anger, or look around with fear and trembling, but will look ahead with understanding and love.[1]

Africa

University of Liberia, Monrovia, West Africa

The University of Liberia is the major center of higher education within the Republic of Liberia, a nation of 43,000 square miles and a population of 1.5 million. The student enrollment for 1971–72 was 1,154, with 10 percent non-Liberian. The faculty includes 140 full-time members, approximately one-half Liberians and the others expatriates or visitors from seventeen nations. The university is organized into six colleges under a central administration headed by the president.[2]

The program of African Studies has been developed through the Institute of African Studies, an autonomous division within the university structure having the equivalent status with the colleges. The institute is concerned primarily with research activities in the total cultural patterns of the indigenous peoples of Liberia. Dr. Wolor Topor, the director of the institute, also serves as editor of the institute's journal, *The University of Liberia Journal*. Dr. Topor sees the institute's role as evaluating and preserving the cultural heritage of Liberia, a heritage that has been neglected far too long. Under his directorship the institute will seek to "reevaluate and reappraise what we have as a culture, and through understanding, try to assimilate knowledge and culture of other African and non-African peoples." The institute maintains close ties with other programs of African Studies in the United States and Europe.

Administrative support for the institute is strong. President
Advertus A. Hoff in 1962, when he was dean of administration,
strongly criticized the educational program in Liberia, saying, "An
outstanding flaw in the foundations of the Liberian educational
system is the subordination of native Liberian culture to the inroads
of foreign culture since the founding of the country. Customs, the
products of generations, have been condemned as inferior."[3] In his
induction address as the second Liberian president of the university
on March 24, 1972, President Hoff was more explicit in the direction
of his leadership. He observed, "This University must lead the way in
defining and transmitting the richness of our Liberian and African
culture, while placing this in the full and valuable perspective of all
human philosophy and artistic striving." He delineated the purposes
and goals of the Institute of African Studies, which, he said,

> . . .shall be responsible for promoting and conducting research in such fields
> as indigenous Liberian prehistory and history, ethnography and social
> anthropology, linguistics, musicology and dance, traditional and modern arts
> and crafts, and religion and other belief systems of Africa. It shall seek to
> develop resources for the preservation and appreciation of Liberia's rich
> traditional heritage, as we:l as for the promotion and enrichment of new and
> distinctly national cultural expressions and outlets.

Since the institute at the university is a research-oriented program,
since no college or department is designated African Studies, and
since no degree is offered in African Studies, the course offerings in
the area are integrated into the various colleges as a part of the
general curriculum. Dr. C. E. Zamba Liberty, dean of the College of
Liberal and Fine Arts and an African history specialist, describes the
integrated program as meeting both the manpower limitations of the
university and the societal needs of Liberian life at the present time.
He explains:

> African Studies is not, per se, a discipline but an amalgamation of Disciplines;
> it is not a singular area of study but a combination of many areas of study,
> demanding an interdisciplinary approach. The research center of the Institute
> will encourage a multi-discipline, team approach in which both the theoretical
> and practical sides of the study of African and Liberian tradition, culture, and
> life are brought together.

The following courses offered by the various colleges of the
university have their total or major emphasis on Liberian or African
culture and life.

College of Liberal and Fine Arts

Arts and Crafts—This is an advanced course which is devoted solely to African designing, weaving, and basketry, enameling (including jewelry), pottery and other small crafts. (two semesters)

Geography—This course is devoted to the regional study of the physical, human, and economic features of selected areas of the world. The focus is mainly African which is compared with the European continent.

Geography: Regional Geography of Africa—This course is designed to study the physical features, the land-forms, the climatic conditions, the human elements, and the economic development of the African continent.

Geography: Regional Geography of Liberia—The more advanced student is given a chance to increase his knowledge of the rather delicate Liberian environment.

Cultures of Liberia—Discussion of the various cultures of Liberia, including kinship and marriage, religion, the Poro, Sande and other secret societies.

Ethnography and Ethnology of Africa—Comparative survey of the principal African ethnographic and ethnic groups.

Acculturation and Applied Anthropology—The dynamics of cultural and social change due to contact and Westernization upon aboriginal cultures.

African Civilization—This course intends to survey the origin, structure, function and the social mechanisms for collapse or adaption and change of various African civilizations.

Studies in Population—Theory, composition and growth of world populations and their implications for agricultural, industrial and urban growth—Africa in general and Liberia in particular.

Social Change—Theories of social, cultural and institutional change; implication of change for social behavior, for personality development and for rural and urban industrial activities; emphasis on such changes in Africa.

Culture and Personality—An examination of the social and cultural development of the person. The formation of the self, role involvement; theories of sociology of personality and their implications in the African context.

Rurar Sociology—The structure and function of rural societies; institutional mechanisms of *Ruṛal* societies, role behavior and rural personality growth; emphasis will be on African and particularly

Liberian rural societies including their social, religious, economic and legal functions and functioning.

Urban & Industrial Sociology—An analysis of the urban process involving city growth up to the present; the preconditions for urban growth and the inter-relationships between urban and industrial societies; major processes for industrialization and their implications for Africa and particularly for Liberia.

Sociology of Law—Variations and variability of law; as an institution and its relation to other institutions; the structure and function of law in society with emphasis on social and normative control and as a means of social change; the implications of customary, statutory and common law to African societies.

English-African Literature—This course is a critical study of the contributions made by African writers and writers of African descent. (Two semesters)

African History—This course covers the history of Africa from prehistoric times in Africa to the present.

African History Seminar—A discussion course in which the historical development of African institutions, culture, languages, political systems, and recent developments in Africa will be highlighted.

History: West Africa—A survey of West African societies from the dawn of history through 1960.

History: East Africa—The world of the East African Coast (Swahili Coast) and that of the East African Interior comprise the two geographical divisions of this course.

History: 19th Century Liberia—An analysis of the Liberian past from the sixteenth century through the presidency of Arthur Barclay.

History: State-Building in Precolonial Africa—This course introduces the student to phenomena of centralized societies as they surfaced in the historical world of Africa before intrusion of the European.

History: Modern African Thought—A review and analysis of those African social, literary, and political thinkers of the past hundred years whose writings have exerted some impact upon the intellectual course of post-1945 Africa.

Liberian Government (Structural Approach)—An introduction to the Government of Liberia with emphasis on its historical development, political socialization of the masses, institutional structures, as well as a study of recent interior (hinterland) administration.

Liberian Government (Functional Approach)—A study of the functional (operational) aspect of the Government of Liberia.

Public Personnel Administration—A study of the philosophy of public personnel management relating to aspects of Liberian civil service.

College of Business and Public Administration

Economic History—A survey of the transformations in the principal ways in which man has made a living by combining new technological knowledge with an expanding human and material resource base; sketch of the impact of the forces of economic change on resource exploitation and the organization of economic life in Africa.

Industrial Relations and Trade Unionism—In this course an attempt will be made to study the philosophy, development, aims, structure and function of trade unions. Analysis will be made of trade union organizations in Britain, the United States, and at least two African countries including Liberia.

Traditional African Economic Thought and Practice—African ideas on property and economic organization, work and achievement, money and trade, traditional markets, trade routes and market centers division of labor and traditional cooperatives.

International Business—This course is devoted to a study of the problems that face the firm engaging in international business with particular emphasis on Africa and Liberia.

The Louis Arthur Grimes School of Law

Comparative Law—A study of the Civil Law System of Francophonic Africa. Principles of private International Law.

Domestic Relations—The family unit; laws of marriage, divorce and annulments; legitimation and adoption. The Matrimonial Causes Act of 1936 is discussed at length.

African Law—A comparative study of African social and legal institutions, with emphasis on customary law.

Labor Law—This course is designed to acquaint the student with several phases of the employment relationship in the Liberian setting.

The William V. S. Tubman Teachers College

Education: Seminar on Liberian Education—A foundations course

in which the development of western education in Liberia is related
to historical, cultural, and social factors. Cognizance will be taken of
the influence of the unique indigenous system of education–the
"bush" schools–in the Liberian setting.

Education: Special Workshop in Adolescent Psychology–The
workshop concerns itself with identification of the developmental
tasks of the adolescent in Liberian society.

Education: Special Workshop in Early Childhood Education–The
workshop concerns itself with the psychology of early childhood and
the application of psychological principles to an understanding of the
young child in Liberian society.

The College of Agriculture and Forestry

Because both agriculture and forestry are taught in the context of
Liberian and African life, nearly all courses within this college
emphasize local culture and environment. Besides the typical courses
of such a college–the courses in Rural Sociology, Nature and
Properties of Soils, Dendrology, Forest Management–a few specialized courses such as Introduction to Natural Rubber Production and
Logging Methods are offered.

Makerere University, Kampala, Uganda

In reply to my inquiry concerning Black Studies at Makerere
University the chairman of the Joint Board of Graduate Studies
explained:

In reply to your letter asking for details of our African Studies Program, I
can supply some for you.

For some years after 1963, we had such a Program, with a full-time
Director, offering an M.A. in African Studies by Coursework and thesis, A.B.,
Phil. and a Ph.D. However, after a few years this folded up, for political
reasons partly: it was felt that a University in East Africa should be pursuing
"African Studies" in very many of its Departments, and that there was no
need for a separate Institute to handle this.

Therefore, in Arts and Social Science Faculties, a Joint Board of Graduate
Studies, of which I am Chairman, superseded the Institute, and it handles all
postgraduate studies in the two Faculties. I enclose our leaflet, which shows
the fields in which the M.A. or Ph.D. degrees are offered. The B.Phil. is no
longer offered. You will notice that the M.A. is either by thesis alone, or by
coursework and thesis. In fact not many Departments offer M.A. coursework,
we tend to follow the British pattern where research degrees are purely by
thesis.

There is no coursework for the Ph.D. degree; it consists of three years' research. We have over 100 postgraduate students under the Board's supervision now, drawn from a great many countries. Entry qualifications required are quite high.

The syllabus outlining the requirements for the B.A. degree in literature includes the following four courses: The Structure and Development of the Novel; American Literature; Two Authors; and Prose: Style and the Art of Persuasion. The subdivisions in the novel course are Structure and Development, The English and American Novel (including James Baldwin's *Another Country*); The European Novel in Translation; The African Novel. In American Literature the works of four black Americans are listed: Richard Wright's *Native Son,* Langston Hughes's *Selected Poems,* Ralph Ellison's *Invisible Man,* and LeRoi Jones's *System of Dante's Hell.* In the course Two Authors, James Baldwin and William Faulkner are the only American authors listed as acceptable choices. For the course Prose: Style and the Art of Persuasion, James Baldwin's *The Fire Next Time* and Eldridge Cleaver's *Soul on Ice* are the only American authors listed.

Caribbean Territory

College of the Virgin Islands, Charlotte Amalie, St. Thomas

This program attempts to provide a unified approach to the human experience, an orientation that builds upon the valuable aspects of the black experience, in the Virgin Islands and beyond its shores, and theoretical, methodological, and substantive material that is needed in order for Virgin Islanders to deal successfully with the problems of survival and self-realization in today's world.

It should be pointed out that the Black Studies program is far more than a mere program of studies. It is really a new kind of education, one that seeks to prepare black people for leadership and creativity at the highest levels. It is marked by a human orientation and a commitment to human values. Materialistic systems are not ignored, but are properly subordinated to human concerns. The program is interdisciplinary in scope because it is recognized that the knowledge and techniques necessary for the adequate approach to important human problems must be drawn from many fields. Its philosophy redefines man's roles. He is seen not as the conqueror of other men or even of the environment, but as a being who must attain a positive, mature and harmonious relationship with other men and the universe. In short, this program represents a different approach to life, an approach at once very old and very new, which taps the philosophical and psychological resources of ancient African civilizations as well as the technical resources of the Western world.

It is called Black Studies because it has been designed for black people who everywhere suffer the disabilities that the conventional European-oriented kinds of education inflicted upon them. It is valuable to other kinds of people who need to learn more about blacks, and hopefully to learn how to develop and maintain productive, mutually satisfying relationships with them.

Black Studies Major

Primary Field of Emphasis
Introduction to Black Studies
Methodology of Interdisciplinary Studies
Basic Techniques of Research in the Social Sciences
Seminar in Black Studies
Field Methods in Interdisciplinary Studies

Secondary Field of Emphasis
African Civilization I & II and
Black Experience I & II or
Caribbean Heritage I & II or
Cultural History of West Africa I & II

Three of the Five Following Areas
Pol. Sci. 1211–122 Introduction to Political and Social Thought
Pol. Sci. 340 Caribbean Govt. and Politics
Sociology 381 Contemporary Caribbean Society
African Political Systems

Psych. 221–222 Introductory Psychology
Soc. 345 Race and Ethnic Relations

Econ. 221–222 Introduction to Macro and Micro Economics
Comparative Economic Philosophies for Underdeveloped Countries

Eng. 401 Caribbean Literature
English 408 Black Literature
Structure of Virgin Island English Creole I & II

Soc. 121 Introduction to Sociology
Soc. 124 Social Problems
Studies in Values

The following courses are suggested electives:
Geography 122 Cultural Geography
History 341 Caribbean History
Economics 461 Caribbean Economic Problems

Black Studies Minor

A minor in Black Studies may be added to a major in any field by satisfying the following requirements:

A.   Black Studies 100   Introduction to Black Studies
     Black Studies 101   Methodology of Interdisciplinary Studies

B.   Twelve credit hours from among the following:

African Civilization   Anthropology 255–256
     History 255–256
     Sociology 255–256

The Black Experience   Anthropology 257–258
in the New World   History 257–258
     Sociology 257–258

Caribbean Heritage   History 171–172

The general education foreign language requirement is met by having the students accomplish four semesters of work in the structure of an African language.

The university has a total enrollment of 1,644 students.

University of Puerto Rico, Rio Piedras

There is no program in Black Studies at the University of Puerto Rico. However, the director of the Institute of Caribbean Studies at the university explains that there are courses in the institute which by their nature "deal primarily although not exclusively with the life, history, and culture of black people." One example is a course entitled the Historical Development of the Social, Economic and Political Institutions of the Caribbean. The emphasis is on the black Caribbean rather than the Spanish Caribbean. Other such courses are Cultures of Africa and the Politics and Governments of the Caribbean. The institute, which was established as a research center in 1958, endeavors to stimulate and coordinate Caribbean Studies throughout the university. The three main campuses have a total enrollment of 35,000 students.

Brazil

Brazil is most often compared with the United States in respect to its racial composition. Slavery was introduced into Brazil in 1538, eighty years earlier than in the United States, and was abolished twenty-four years after emancipation in the United States. But on the surface, at least, racial conflict is not a problem in the South American country, although racial prejudice does exist. Melvin Boozer, a black American who recently spent four years as a Peace Corps volunteer in Brazil, says, "When Brazilians refer to race at all, they are denominating obvious physical characteristics as a convenience of identification. They imply nothing about the intelligence or the personality of the individual concerned when they say he has dark skin, kinky hair or ample lips. . . . What is more important to Brazilians is a man's education, his profession and his wealth."[4]

Robert B. Toplin, assistant professor of history at Denison University, Granville, Ohio, after five years of study here and in Brazil, concludes that although an extraordinary number of persons of African descent enjoy all the rights and privileges of their middle-class status in Brazil, they tend to be light-skinned. The dark-skinned blacks, he says, "noticeably cluster in the economic ranks of marginal people such as day-laborers, cleaning women, landless tenant farmers, the inhabitants of rural shacks and urban shanty-towns".[5] He suggests that because the mulatto without compromise can identify himself with the white majority, there is no strong black-awareness sentiment as there is in the United States. This lack of interest in black identity is no doubt responsible for the decision of the University of Brazil to offer only one course dealing with people of African descent. According to information in a letter from the vice-president of the university, dated February 2, 1972, a graduate course entitled *O Negro no Brazil* (Negro in Brazil) will be offered the first term: March to July 1972, for twenty-one students who have indicated an interest in the course.

France

I am indebted to Michel Fabre, professor of American literature at the University of Paris and secretary of the French Association of American Studies, for information concerning the nature and extent of Black Studies programs in French institutions of higher learning. There are more than fifteen French colleges and universities that offer one or more courses in Black Studies as defined by the criteria underlying my study. I shall give a brief synopsis of some of the most important involvements. I shall omit those programs devoted entirely to African Studies, as I have done in respect to American universities.

There are several campuses of the University of Paris. At the University of Paris III, with which Professor Fabre is associated, the following courses are offered: 20th Century Black Literature, senior level, 45 students; Afro-American Writers and France, M.A. seminar, 25 students who write 100-page dissertations on different aspects of Afro-American studies; Afro-American Studies, Ph.D. seminar, 17 theses in progress in this field. These courses have resulted from student demands for studies directly connected with their political interest in current American problems. At the University of Paris I, there are M.A. and Ph.D. level seminars on Afro-American Studies and on the Black Woman in Latin America. At the University of Paris VII, the course Modern Afro-American Literature has an enrollment of 160 students in six sections. The University of Paris VIII (Vincennes) has a junior level course: The History of American Negroes, with 60 students.

The University of Tours has a course: Racial Problems in the United States, with M.A. theses being written on James Baldwin, Richard Wright, Martin Luther King, Malcolm X, The Black Panthers, and Black Songs. The University of Bordeaux III has a M.A. Seminar on Contemporary Literature with Baldwin, Wright, and Ellison the major authors. The two courses at the University of Toulouse are: Literature of Racial Minorities in the United States; and M.A. Seminar on the Contemporary American Negro Novel. The University of Poitiers has a course: Black America in Search of Its Identity, featuring Richard Wright, Malcolm X, Claude Brown, Eldridge Cleaver, and the Soledad Brothers. At the University of Lille 90 students are enrolled in a course: Socio-Economic Conditions of American Negroes. The University of Strasbourg II has a graduate seminar in Black Theatre and an undergraduate course in Black Literature, first offered in 1966, two years before the push for Black Studies began in the United States. At the University of Provence a freshman survey course: Racial Problems in the United States has an enrollment of 700.

Notes & References

Chapter 1

[1] *A. Philip Randolph Educational Fund,* September 1969, p. 1.
[2] *Journal of Black Studies,* I (September, 1970), p. 3.
[3] *Ibid.,* pp. 84–85.
[4] "Toward a Sociology of Black Studies," *Journal of Black Studies,* I (December, 1970), p. 132.
[5] *Ibid.,* pp. 135–136.
[6] "Nathan Hare on Black Studies," *Integrated Education,* VIII (November–December 1970), pp. 9–10.
[7] "Black History and White Americans," *Integrated Education,* VIII (November–December, 1970), p. 23.
[8] *Ibid.,* p. 6.
[9] *Baltimore Sun,* December 27, 1970, Section K, p. 2.
[10] *On the Record,* SFC Pamphlet 70-S (April 1, 1970), p. 1.
[11] *Integrated Education,* VIII (November–December, 1970), p. 9.
[12] *Journal of Black Studies,* I (December, 1970), pp. 169–170.

Chapter 2

[13] Floyd B. Barbour (ed.), *The Black Seventies* (Boston: Porter Sargent Publisher, 1970), pp. 266–268.
[14] *Ibid.,* pp. 286–287.
[15] *Shadow and Act* (New York: New American Library, 1964), p. xix.
[16] *The New York Times,* August 1, 1971, p. E3.
[17] *God's Trombones* (New York: The Viking Press, 1927), p. 6.

[18] *The Militant Black Writer* (Madison: The University of Wisconsin Press, 1969), pp. 124–125.

[19] *The Negro Mood* (New York: Ballantine Books, 1964), p. 89.

[20] *Ebony*, XXV (August, 1970), p. 35.

[21] *The Crisis of the Negro Intellectual* (New York: William Morrow, 1967), p. 9.

[22] *Ebony, op. cit.*, pp. 54–55.

[23] *The Black World*, XX (January, 1971), pp. 6–7.

[24] *Ibid.*, p. 76.

[25] *Ibid.*, pp. 8–9.

[26] Reported by Walter B. Gordon, Baltimore *Sun*, August 11, 1971, p. 1

[27] *Search for a Place* (Ann Arbor: The University of Michigan Press, 1969), p. 1.

[28] *Shadow and Act*, p. 258.

[29] *19 Necromancers From Now* (New York: Doubleday and Company, 1970), p. xiv.

[30] *The Crisis*, 78 (April–May), p. 78

[31] *Black World*, XX (June, 1971), pp. 4–16.

[32] "Dialectology *versus* Negro Dialect," *CLA Journal*, XIII (September, 1969), pp. 24–25.

Chapter 3

[1] *The Autobiography of W. E. B. DuBois* (New York: International Publishers, 1968), p. 148.

[2] *Saturday Review*, September 3, 1966.

[3] *The American Race Problem* (revised by Jitsuichi Masuoka) (New York: Thomas Y. Crowell Company, 1970), p. xviii.

Chapter 4

[4] The basic source for historical information in this section not otherwise documented is my careful study of Dwight O. W. Holmes, *The Evolution of the Negro College* (New York: Bureau of Publications, Teachers' College, Columbia University, 1934).

[5] Holmes, p. 45.

[6] Almost all of the early black institutions bearing the name *university* were in fact only colleges (and many only glorified high

schools). They adopted the name university as a prestige symbol. Likewise many of their classical courses were too sophisticated for their students to understand because of the lack of proper background knowledge.

[7] Holmes, p. 73.

[8] "The Promise of Equality," *Saturday Review* LI (July 20, 1968), p. 45.

[9] *Ibid.,* p. 46.

[10] Holmes, p. 173.

[11] *Saturday Review, op cit.,* p. 58.

[12] From 1953 to 1960 the number of courses dealing with black history and culture gradually declined from six to one at West Virginia State College. From 1961 to 1966 no such course was listed in the college catalog. This phenomenon was probably due to the change in the student body from predominantly black to predominantly white. Not until 1968–69 did courses reflecting the "black experience" re-appear in the college catalog, when the student confrontation forced the issue in predominantly white institutions.

Chapter 5

[1] *Rebellion or Revolution?* New York: William Morrow, 1968), p. 97.

[2] Frank Satterwhite, *The California Association for Afro-American Education,* January 21, 1971.

Chapter 7

[3] "Clio with Soul," *Black Studies,* A. Philip Randolph Educational Fund, September, 1969, p. 16.

[4] *Ibid.,* p. 26.

[5] *Language in Uniform,* Nick Aaron Ford (ed.) (New York: Odyssey Press, 1967), pp. 111–113.

[6] *Searching for America* (Urbana, Illinois: National Council of Teachers of English, 1972), p. xvii–xviii.

[7] "Movement in English," *ADE Bulletin* (September, 1969), p. 46.

[8] *Black Theatre,* XLI (Summer, 1966), p. 30.

Chapter 10

[9] Charles E. Moseley (ed.), *A Pan-African Reader* (Chicago: Black

Studies Program of Chicago State University, 1971), pp. 21–22.

Chapter 11

[1] See page 31
[2] G. Kerry Smith (ed.), *The Troubled Campus* (San Francisco: Jossey-Bass, 1970), p. 43.
[3] Ford Foundation, Office of Reports, 320 E. 43rd Street, New York.
[4] "A Black Professor Says," *The New York Times Magazine,* December 13, 1970, pp. 46, 49.
[5] Smith, p. 98.
[6] "What Is a University For?" *Spectator,* October, 1970, p. 1.
[7] Nick Aaron Ford, *Instructor's Manual for Black Insights* (Lexington, Massachusetts: Ginn and Company/Xerox College. Publishing, 1971), pp. 10–11.

Chapter 12

[8] *Chronicle of Higher Education,* October 12, 1971, p. 7.
[9] February 7, 1972, p. 7.
[10] *The Academic Revolution* (New York: Doubleday and Company, 1969), p. 478.
[11] *Ibid.,* p. 433.
[12] "Black Students, Black Studies, Black Colleges," *The Chronicle of Higher Education,* November 22, 1971, p. 8.
[13] Jencks and Riesman, p. 427.
[14] George Davis, "The Howard University Conference," Howard University, *Negro Digest,* March, 1969, p. 46.
[15] *Black World,* March, 1969, p. 68.
[16] *Ibid.,* pp. 97–98.
[17] *Between Two Worlds* (New York: McGraw Hill Book Company, 1971), p. 250.
[18] Jim Grant and Milton R. Coleman, "Save Black Colleges in North Carolina," *Integrated Education,* March–April, 1972, p. 36. (In the fall of 1972 the state of North Carolina began the operation of its system of higher education in accordance with the pattern condemned by the black protesters, with Dr. Harold Delaney, a black educator, as one of the six Vice Chancellors.)
[19] "Proposal for the Establishment of ISSP," Antioch College, p. 1.

Appendix B

[1] CLA *Journal*, September, 1970, pp. 16–17.
[2] Information concerning the University of Liberia was supplied by Robert A. Cotner, Fulbright Professor, University of Liberia, 1971-72.
[3] "The Aims of Higher Education in Liberia," *The University of Liberia Journal*, II (July, 1962), p. 8.
[4] "Developing Human Communities: A Brazilian Experience," *The Crisis*, November, 1971, p. 296.
[5] "NEH Grant Profiles," *Humanities*, Fall, 1971, p. 3.

Bibliography

Periodicals

Black World. A monthly publication devoted to critical and creative writing by blacks, as well as monthly reports on current events relating to blacks. 1820 S. Michigan Avenue, Chicago, Illinois 60616.

CLA Journal. Official quarterly publication of the College Language Association consisting primarily of teachers of English and modern languages in black colleges. Morgan State College, Baltimore, Maryland 21239.

The Crisis. Official organ of the National Association for the Advancement of Colored People. 1790 Broadway, New York, New York 10019.

The Chronicle of Higher Education A weekly publication of news and reports concerning higher education. 1717 Massachusetts Avenue, N.W., Washington, D.C. 20036.

Ebony. A pictorial monthly publication of Negro life and culture. 1820 S. Michgan Avenue, Chicago, Illinois 60616.

Journal of Black Studies. 275 S. Beverly Drive, Beverly Hills, California 90212.

Negro History Bulletin. Published by the Association for the Study of Negro Life and History. 1538 Ninth Street, N.W., Washington, D.C. 20001.

Phylon. Quarterly review of race and culture. Atlanta, Georgia 30314.

Books

Barber, Floyd B. (ed.) *The Black Seventies*. Boston: Porter Sargent Publisher, 1970.

Blassingame, John W. (ed.). *New Perspectives on Black Studies*. Urbana: University of Illinois Press, 1971.

Bowles, Frank and Frank DeCosta. *Between Two Worlds*. New York: McGraw-Hill Book Company, 1971.

Cook, Will Mercer and Stephen E. Henderson. *The Militant Black Writer*. Madison: University of Wisconsin Press. 1969.

Cruse, Harold. *Crisis of the Negro Intellectual*. New York: William Morrow, 1967.

Rebellion or Revolution? New York: William Morrow, 1968.

Ellison, Ralph. *Shadow and Act*. New York: Random House, 1964.

Fisher, Walter. *Ideas for Black Studies*. Baltimore: Morgan State College Press, 1971.

Ford, Nick Aaron (ed.). *Black Insights: Significant Literature by Black Americans—1760 to the Present*. Lexington, Mass.: Ginn and Company, 1971.

Holmes, Dwight, O.W. *The Evolution of the Negro College*. New York: Bureau of Publications, Teachers' College, Columbia University, 1934.

Gayle, Jr., Addison (ed.). *The Black Aesthetic*. New York: Doubleday and Company, 1971.

Jencks, Christopher and David Riesman. *The Academic Revolution*. Doubleday and Company, 1968.

Kelly, Ernece (ed.). *Searching for America*. Urbana, Illinois: National Council of Teachers, 1972.

Rustin, Bayard (ed.). *Black Studies: Myths and Realities*. New York: A. Philip Randolph Educational Fund, 1969.

Smith, G. Kerry. *The Troubled Campus*. San Francisco: Jossey-Bass, Inc., 1970.

Index